PORT-AU-MIAMI

PORT-AU-MIAMI:

HAITIAN BOATS

(PART 1)

ALI "ZOE" ADAM

This book may be purchased on Amazon.com. For more information, mail-n orders, and bulk orders address BOATS Publishing, P.O. Box 63, Bergenfield NJ 07621

ISBN 978-1-7346443-1-9

Address at Zoe Pound inc

PO BOX 63

Bergenfield, NJ 07621

Website:zoepoundpublishing.com

Email: admin@zoepoundpublishing.com

Facebook: Port-au-Miami: Haitian Boats

CONTENTS

SYNOPSIS

Port-au-Prince, Haiti. April 4, 1983.

It's a regular hot and humid day at the neighborhood park. Playing soccer with my brothers Pierre and Joe, and my seven uncles. We had no idea my mom and dad planned for an exile to America, while my three sisters stayed home with my three aunts, cooking and selling all the pigs, goats, cows, and chicken. The 17 members of my family were in ahhhh listening to Dad and Captain Baptiste explain our exile on a boat America called the "Freedom Boat."

On the second day at sea with four hours to reach the U.S.A., a windy storm with thunder and lightning caused the "Freedom Boat" to jump a massive swell, killing my seven uncles, two aunts, my brother Joe, my Dad, and my three sisters includ- ing my twin sister (Jane).My Mom, me (Jean), and brother (Pierre) went through a lot at Miami, Dade County Krome Immigration Center, mostly like in the famous movie Scarface, even Jean and Pierre killing Captain Baptiste at 13 years old for having part into losing 14 members of Adam's family.

Having total respect for moms dream of being a lawyer and pilot one day, we remain morally humble through hard times dealing with cynical kids at Carol City High School verbally punishing us, saying we came to U.S.A. on the Banana Boat, we ate cat, we stink, we need a horse brush to comb our nappy hair, etc.

The money on the trees, thoughts of what America had were lies to Jean and Pierre. So then Jean and Pierre became rebels to mom's moderate thoughts. Hooking up with Ricardo (who is Cuban, but tells everyone he's Haitian) who saw the young rebels kill at the immigration center, plus Syco rides the school bus with Jean and Pierre and helps them fight all seven Americans, all instantly become family along with two Haitian friends (Gerald and Crip). They formulated a young crew known as (Haitian Posse).

Growing in the life of crime, they start by snatching unsus- pecting

1

victim's purses and eventually graduate to cynical crimes. So enjoy the takeover of Port-Au-Miami by Jean and the rest of the Haitian Posse......

(PART 1)

CHAPTER ONE

Port-au-Prince, Haiti. April 4, 1983.

It's a regular hot and humid day at the neighborhood park. I'm playing soccer with my brothers Pierre and Joe, my seven uncles, and a few friends. We are on a field filled with rocks, mini hills, and orange dirt, which came from the mountain mudslides. It was eighteen of us playing with no sneakers or shirts, with only tight pamper-like shorts on. My brother would play with only a shirt and no shorts. After cutting through people, he was making his way down the left side of the field towards the goal. I was racing down the right side towards the middle as he yelled my name.

"Jean!"

I prepared myself for his 15-yard kick to the middle of the field to me. Two of my uncles were on my trail. Pierre kicked the ball to me and I timed it just right. I head-butted the ball to the left top-corner and scored.

"GOAL! GOAL! GOOOOAL!" yelled my Haitian warriors and myself, winning the game 2-1.

We took a short walk after the game to a corner where a stream was running water from a mountaintop. All of us bathed and drank water. Then we engaged into a dispute about our president Jean-Claude "Baby Doc" Duvalier. He had person- ally killed eight journalists for his misrepresenting funds of

1.2 billion dollars. It was aide money from a devastating 6.4

earthquake that shocked the island capital city of Port-au- Prince. It caused endless tragedy. The journalists reported that they saw no new artful crafty new beginnings in the Baby Doc Administration. Just the same no lights for weeks, if not, months, airport with no air conditioning, hospital begging for medical supplies, and lack of food for the people. Also, getting caught after 9 p.m. on the streets, you were a rebel, and was now a target practice for Baby Doc's army of men. But our main topic was still on the first goal scored in our soccer game and claiming that Pierre's dick was a distraction. This brought laughter from the crowd of Haitians.

My brother Joe said to me, "Jean, what are you over there thinking about? You always pondering about something."

Besides putting on the sweaty shorts after bathing, I was wondering why Mom and Dad been acting strange for the last eight months. Why my three sisters, two brothers, and myself, had not been to school throughout the year. The sixteen pigs, twenty-seven goats, fifteen cows, and over fifty chickens, kept me and my brothers home since we had to gut them ourselves. The pigs were my favorite to gut. When I cut both of it's ears, the pig would shout a piercing scream, which brought me joy and kept me riding it like a bull. A good strong juicy pig gave me a twelve to fifteen-minute ride out of this world. I beat the ass out of the pig with the side of my knife, wearing my special

N.Y. Yankee's hat.

The pig would yell, "OINK! OIIIINK! OIIIINK! Then slowly the yelling subsided to a minimum. The pig's speed slowed down and it would drop dead. The pulse on its neck would jump, with its eyes just staring at me. I would say to the pig. "I'm going to gut you for the next five hours to pieces."

Pierre liked to cut the chickens' heads off and watch as they went crazy speed-walking and flying as high as three feet in the air. Without it's head, sometimes we could still hear a gurgled scream from the chicken. Everyone knew he enjoyed the chick- ens' heads and that he would go to the woods to cook all the chickens he could hide from mom and dad. My father often argued about the chickens' heads being money to my mother, but mom would always win. She snuck the chicken heads to Pierre.

Gutting the goats and cows were boring, but all six of us chipped in and helped gut them. Dad was the one to boil the water using coals to heat it to about 120 degrees. He dipped the pigs, chickens, and cows in the boiling water. Even before we gutted the animals, their flesh was smelling tasteful.

Dad said, "Jean, make sure you get everything out of the pigs because they're the number one selling meat during the summer."

"Yes, Dad," I replied, dragging the pig by it's back-feet to my favorite area, which was under the cherry-tree where there weren't many flies to bother me.

I stuck my knife from the asshole through the belly, and up to the nose. From there I took the good ole insides out of the pig and separated them. I put certain parts in certain bags which had been marked by Dad. Filling up every bag and asking for extra ones made my dad smile and say, "yes, Jean, get it all out."

The chickens and goats were easy also, but the cows had to be cut out in certain sections, which my older brother Joe handled with Dad. We'd be gutting and cooking while Mom and my aunts went selling at flea markets, factories, and restaurants.

I put on my smelly shorts. Walking towards home, my broth- ers and uncles would try to hitch a ride on a bus. They were usually going about thirty-five miles an hour. Knowing we had about four miles to walk, we stopped around at a mountain- top called "Pentroville" to relax before continuing on. Pierre had his string of five chicken heads around his neck like the rapper Run from Run DMC. I had a pair of glasses I found on the street with no lenses, walking pimpish, side by side with Pierre. A light-skinned Haitian named Walker lived along the path of our trip home. He often snuck us food, drinks, and Doritos when we were in Pentroville. His house was big; it had about nine rooms, a tennis court, and four cars. He had two pretty sisters that we couldn't dream of being with.

At Walker's house, we watched a T.V. station called M.T.V., on which Michael Jackson songs came on all the time. My uncles and them thought they were Michael, spinning around, kick- ing their feet in the air, and holding their crotch. Walker once threw a look-alike of Michael Jackson's glove into a group of about ten of us. We fought each other all

6

the way home that evening, which Uncle Mike won. He had to fight each of us for the glove. On this trip, Walker threw out six pieces of clothes, as he usually did on every trip, and we all fought again, There was a matching shirt to the N.Y. Yankee's hat Walker once threw. After fighting for so long, I went to biting. Everybody retreated from that shirt and it was mine. At times Pierre cheated by drawing his knife. We all knew he would use it because of his short temper. Uncle Mike was the only one to challenge the knife fight. My brother Joe and Uncle Nick ended up having nothing. We laughed all the way home around 7 p.m., to where we knew we all would find a nice small dinner for each of us.

Staying in a three-bedroom house with nineteen other peo- ple, there was no privacy at all. My mom and dad shared one room with six kids, seven uncles in another room, and three aunts with a set of one-year-old twins in the other. We had to walk to the woods to get peace and quiet, plus it's where we all took a shit. Due to lack of sewer pipelines in Haiti, burying the waste in dirt was all we knew.

Mom and Dad had been acting real strange. They said we all going to church, which we never had much time for. Dad always thought we were missing out on money.

"Something funny's going on." I told Pierre. "What is it, Jean?"

"I don't know, but something funny's going on."

Sunday morning we woke up early and Mom cooked us oatmeal for the millionth time. It tasted great. We all got a banana and headed back to church. In church, Mom and Dad were alone with the pastor for about three hours just pray- ing. My sister Stacy slept on my lap while Tasha slept on her back. The two-inch bugs were getting to me along with the steam-room that the church was. My aunts and uncles all were huddled talking back and forth a distance away, acting real enthusiastic with smiles while jumping around happily with each other. I sensed something passionate was about to happen, but the last passionate thing to happen that brought joy to me was catching a N.Y. Yankee's hat at Walker's house.

We walked outside the church, finally, and had to take a taxi because

7

dad had sold his Isuzu jeep one month ago. He told us he was trying to get another jeep, but we never questioned Dad when he spoke. He was the house-leader who everyone in the house looked up to as a dad, even my uncles and aunts. He raised half of them also.

A taxi pulled up, F-150 style, with long wooden stools to the left and right of the truck's bed. There were four built-in poles to hold on to through the heavy bumps and deep potholes in the streets of Port-au-Prince, Haiti. My uncles had to jump on the top of the homemade metal shelter on the back of the truck. Four people were in front. The mob of twenty was still not enough for the taxi driver to brag about amongst his colleagues. Before all of us were in the truck, Pastor walked out to mumbo jumbo with the driver. He wanted to be given five minutes.

Pastor looked at Dad and asked, "may I talk to all the kids alone?"

"Please do, Pastor," Dad responded.

All six kids were grouped around the corner-stoop outside the church, I was holding one of the twins, and Marie was holding the other.

The pastor was dripping in sweat with a washcloth in his right hand. He stood positioned at a 180-degree angle to us all. He looked each of us in the eyes and said, "in the beginning was the word, and the word was with God, and the word was God. Jesus died for our sins in the midst of trials n' tribulations. Pray to Jesus to save your souls. Never question God's view on life, remembering there is life after death." Looking at Jean, he continued, "starting with Psalms twenty-third, the Lord is my shepherd."

Expressionlessly, I watched between Mom and Dad. I said the powerful prayer while the other kids joined me.

Calmly, Pastor said, "Marie, start Matthew six, Our Father which art in heaven."

Marie actively smiled and started the prayer. The rest of us joined in with her as well.

Pastor said, "absorb doze prayers in time of trouble." Then he jokingly concluded, "now, you guys jump in that pick-up." "Thank you, Pastor," Dad said, as we filed into the truck.

Pastor answered, "yes, and don't worry about Jean-Claude Duvalier."

My uncle Mike said, "the teeth of the sharks are sweeter than Duvalier's hell."

Mom swiped Uncle Mike with a tap on his arm saying, "the kids!"

Between the prayer by the pastor, Dad selling the jeep, the animals, and the remark that Uncle Mike said out loud, all I could think of was "Run DMC." For some reason, thought of N.Y. Yankee's, The Cosby Show, and Michael Jackson dances raced through my mind rapidly. I watched the other kids for suspect signs, seeing nothing unusual from them.

The one traffic light in the capital of Haiti, the bumps, the potholes, set off a partisan debate between my uncles about President Baby Doc. During his twenty-five years in office he has done nothing fundamentally to build sectors of industry in Haiti. The political debate gave sleep to other kids during the forty-five-minute drive.

I stayed up listening to the intriguing topic about my country. Injecting a comment of my own, I said, "Aunty Marie, Baby Doc have the power to turn on our lights?"

She replied, "yeah, but soon you could have enough lights to waste." My other aunts all laughed at this as if it was a personal inside joke. The taxi pulled to the bottom steep of the moun- tain where it could go no more. Dad paid the cabby and we all jumped out. Leading the way to a straight-up three-mile mountain climb, Dad turned and addressed us. Tonight I have to talk to everybody at 8 p.m. in my room. Don't nobody be late."

Pierre looked at me. "You think dad know Mom been sneak- ing me all the chicken heads?" He asked.

"No, stupid, that's not it," I answered. "Dad knows Mom gives the chicken heads to you. This must be about the some- thing strange that's been going on."

Pierre looked pitiful. "I hope you right, Jean." "I know I'm right, Pierre. I know I'm right."

My aunts and uncles had an anxious hop in their step as they passed Dad going up the hill, acting touchy-feely towards each other. It was weird like to all the kids' eyes. Marie noticed something on the ground. "Uncle Mike would you please put me on your neck? My legs hurt."

Uncle Mike said, "sure, Janet Jackson!!"

Mom smirked with stiff eyes at Mike. She then started some church songs and everyone joined in. The moment was joyful, filled with the unity of one big Adam family. It gave all of us smiles, like the country was not depressing to live in.

We walked in the house around 6 p.m. My mom and aunts had prepared a well-cooked three-course meal of rice, maca- roni, and chicken that we all shared together as a family. We drank water to wash down the food. After 7 O'clock, mom gave out carrot cake for dessert.

I said out loud, "whose birthday is it?", to get a cunning description of what 8 p.m. would bring to the Adam family with everybody's belly full, which was also an unusual aspect.

When 7:50 came around, my aunts and uncles were all headed to my parents' room. Pierre uneasily went on in with Joe and my three sisters plus I. There were mumbles between every- body when dad walked in with a serious look on his face.

"Everybody please give me your full undivided attention to what I'm about to say," Dad spoke.

Everyone just anxiously stopped talking, giving dad all awareness of the quiet room. Dad sat on the bed with Mom, who was rocking back and forth full of anxiety of a possible letdown response from the family crowd.

"As you know," Dad continued. The Adam Family is extremely poor. I worked hard in my life without finding any true growth in my work process. I love my family and it hurts to see me argue about too much rice on a plate to my family. Watching my four-year-old baby girl put a water-pot on her head every morning kills me inside. Telling everyone to drink tea when you get a headache is not what I truly want to say. Last year,

September, I told all the kids at the last meeting that you will not be able to go to school this year. I was sad and full of rage inside of me. All my brothers and sisters in the room that I wake up to at 5 a.m. every morning, telling you to go look for a job where I know there's no job out there to go sign for. I want you to know, I do it out of hope. Haiti is our country. Where we were all born at, the blood in our veins, the cheekbones in our face, the nappy hair you all got from your mom, which brought a smile to mom's face saying, "that's right, I love my nappy hair." Dad looked back at his family crowd saying, "what I'm about to speak, you have a choice to it."

For the first time, Dad chose to give his kids a choice. Usually dad dictated what we were going to do, act, say, walk, even eat.

Dad said, "today is April 15th, 1983, and the Adam family, we are going to the United States of America."

We all shouted out, "yeahhh!! YESS!!! YESS! I love you Dad- dy!!! Yeahhh!" We jumped around together chanting, "U.S.A.!! U.S.A.!! U.S.A.!!U.S.A.!!" I don't know how we didn't cause another earthquake.

Uncle Mike turned into Michael Jackson in the middle of the circle. I took next with Pierre doing a side-to-side dance. Everyone took a dance and the circle screaming to Dad to go in the middle and dance. We all yelled, "go Dad! Go! Go!"

He finally got in the middle doing a funky James Brown- like dance, which was hilarious. He funked for five minutes straight. I never knew Dad had those kinds of steps.

Mom said, "get away from my superstar," as she came in the middle of the circle, her afro-puff-like Diana Ross saying, "born in the U.S.A., I was born in the U.S.A."

The chants restarted. "U.S.A!! U.S.A.!! U.S.A.!! OOOEEE, I love

11

you God!! U.S.A.!!U.S.A.!!"

The twins went to crying and Mom said, "okay, okay, okay, you guys are scaring babies. Let's wind it down. Plus we have a lot of praying to do before we go on our expedition."

My aunt Marie, who was very dramatic, just fainted. We caught her before she reached the ground.

"Jean, Jean," Mom said. "Go get some water for your aunty."

I rushed and got some water out of the bucket we kept in the kitchen. We instantly got Aunty Marie back on her feet.

"You okay, Marie?" Dad asked.

Aunt Marie, who loved attention and occasionally practiced voodoo with people's spirits said, "I'm sorry. Go ahead on with what you were saying."

From the statement my dad got back to leadership mode with a poker face saying, "I have a lot more to say besides we going to the U.S.A. The trip will be life-threatening but with prayers our destiny is with God. And, to my knowledge, Aunt Vicky and Aunt Marie, with the twins, will be staying in Haiti. I will ask this once, who else is staying with Aunt Marie in Haiti?"

Everyone looked at each other saying nothing but shaking their heads side-to-side as if to say, I'm not staying in this hellhole of life in Haiti.

Dad said, "okay we will be leaving a week from now at 3 a.m. We have a lot more things to accomplish before we leave, but it's nothing drastic to the point where we won't be leaving a week from now." Everyone was exhaling with smiles. "Nobody should know we're leaving. Is that understood?"

"Yes," everyone said.

"Is there any questions?"

As there were none, Dad concluded saying, "now get some sleep," with a concerned smile.

Sleep was out of the question. My uncles and aunts went one way. Us six went another towards the woods to talk. As we huddled, we just held each other doing the Indian dance.

Pierre said, "when I get to the U.S.A. and find my personal money tree, I'm going to buy Dad a Benz, get me a big gold- rope chain while eating steak, lobster, and shrimp all day long."

There was a theory in Haiti that money literally grew on trees, which we all believed.

I quipped, "when I find my money tree, I'm going back to Haiti to be President. I'm going to buy a soccer team to chal- lenge the world in the Olympic games. I'm going to get a Benz to put a big Haitian flag in the place of the antenna."

Everyone laughed.

Joe said to me, "the girls mostly talk about the American boys spoiling them."

The night was unusual due to the full moon that stood high in the sky. It was gleaming a light over us as if we were the chosen kids of change in Haiti. Laughter was engaged through the whole night, laughing was desirable to the soul.

Sleeping was limited to five to six hours max. We went in about 5 a.m., woke up around 10 a.m.

Mom looked at the girls. "Ladies don't wake up at 10 a.m. no matter what the previous occasion is. In fact, I'm going to need you pretty little ladies today with me to go sell some meat to some factories."

The girls cherished the idea of helping with the process to go selling to factories.

I looked at my brothers. "Let's go to Walker's house, Tom & Jerry about to come on at twelve.

"Okay," they replied.

Walking down the hill to Walker's house, we kicked a soccer ball between the three of us all the way. When we reached Walker's house, he met us at the door as if he had been waiting for us.

"You on time. Tom & Jerry about to come on." He threw us a box of something called Little Debbie with three fruit juices. His sister Cathy was by the window along with him. Cathy was so pretty with long hair to her back and green eyes. Her

skin complexion was light. She always laughs with us. "Jean," she spoke. "I see you got Pierre wearing shorts today." I said, "yeah, I told him we were coming over here to watch

T.V., so put on some shorts."

She smiled. For a moment I swam in that smile dreaming of her in my passenger seat of my Benz with four kids in the back seat calling us Mommy and Daddy.

"Jean, Jean, Jean!" Cathy was saying. "Huh?" I'm sorry Cathy."

"Where your mind at? Do you want some M&M's or some chocolate chip cookies?"

"Um, um, um, it don't matter." Pierre said, "both."

"No," I said. "Just the M&M's would be fine." I hit Pierre across the head for his remark.

Joe was locked in Watching Tom & Jerry. I still was thinking of how gorgeous Cathy was. I wished she would just blow me a kiss, so I could blow her back a thousand kisses.

Walker sensed my outlook. "There's a new show called 'The Cosby Show' that you guys have to check out. It comes back on next week."

"Next week," Joe said, "we won't be here."

Pierre kicked him right in the ass. Cathy and Walker paid Joe's remark no mind. But I asked both of them, how was it like in the U.S.A. They both went to a place called Miami during the summer.

"I like it, but Haiti is better to me," Cathy was saying.

Walker said, "I want to stay in Miami. I get to play basketball with my friends, get the new video games that come out, ride my bike to the park. It's so much to do in the states that I can talk for hours.

In all three of our minds we were saying, 'soon we will be saying that.'

Cathy uttered, "Haiti has a better beach than The States."

I went swimming in Cathy's words of me on the beach while my baby Cathy had on her G-string yelling, "baby, baby, baby, bring me my towel."

Cathy said, "Jean, you hear?" snapping me out of my fantasy. She laughed, watching me blush at her. "You losing it, Jean."

CHAPTER TWO

I was thinking of how slow that week was going by. I did the normal things with my family, but most of all, I hung out on five branches up the cherry tree in the back yard. *I really want to leave Haiti?* I thought. I mean, it's where I was born. The food was never enough, hot showers were unheard of, and not going to school was educationally bad for all of us. The joy of being around my family was complete love that I didn't want to lose. Though, I did hear the U.S.A. had a harsh racial tension in the air, Haiti had its own problems in other areas. Haiti was either rich or poor, and 75 percent was poor with no way of getting rich. None of us spoke English, but I thought we could

learn it. We knew the main words to get by.

I was tired of being crammed up in a bedroom house with twenty people while sometimes visitors came from out of town pushing the number of people in the little house up to thirty. There was no A.C. *Why Duvalier tomorrow don't just go buy all the poor families houses, giving the poor each 100 thousand dollars to start businesses in the community? Why don't U.S.A. come to Haiti offering help? Why God made Haiti the poorest country on Earth?*

I thought about Uncle Mike's comment outside the church, "The teeth of the sharks are sweeter then Duvalier's hell."

It sounded like we might swim to the U.S.A. Hopeful- ly we could catch a plane on American Airlines, which we saw on the T.V. commercials. *We are really leaving Haiti like this,* I thought. *I think I'm going to stay with Auntie Marie.*

I held those thoughts as I stripped the cherry tree naked before I made my final decision. "What are you thinking about, Jean? We going to the U.S.A., U.S.A., U.S.A." I climbed the cherry tree from limb-to-limb more accurate than a monkey. Feeling fortunate, I was happy about a chance for success in the U.S.A., U.S.A., U.S.A.

"Jean! Jean!" Mom yelled. "Jean, Jean!" "Yes, Mom."

"Is everything okay? I've been looking at you from the kitchen window.

You look a little depressed. Is everything okay J.J?

"Everything fine, Mom. Can I help with anything?"

"No, just get ready for tomorrow night. This will be an expe- dition overseen by God only, so just pray in the mean-time of unanswered questions, okay?"

"Yes, Mommy."

Leaving the room, Mom patty-tapped Marie on the shoulder.

Marie was coming towards my way.

"Jean," my sister said. "You almost finished all the cherries on the tree."

"I know. What you want, Marie?

"Dad is in the cow-barn talking to this man. I think it's about going to the U.S.A."

I jumped down from 15 feet on my two legs with no prob- lem saying, "let's go to the stinky pig-barn where we can hear everything being said in the cow-barn." I grabbed Marie's hand, trickery hip-hopping towards the stinky bar. "Marie, how you know they are there?"

"They were in the house, but Dad kept saying, 'give me five minutes for we can go to the cow-barn to talk.' The strange man said, 'No problem.' Dad told me to get him some lemonade, so I did. Then I walked over here to where you were."

Before opening the stinky barn, Marie and I took one last big breath of air, and then went inside the barn's roof. We could hear Dad talking to some strange man, calling him Captain Baptiste. The man looked about 49 or 50 years old but could go for 42. He was dirty with a scarf around his head, tattoos and scars, along with an eye-guard.

Chewing tobacco, he said, "you gave thirty-six thou- sand. I want my other four thousand."

Dad retorted, "I have the four thousand in my pocket. I just want you to assure me that I would have enough life guards for all the women and kids."

17

"Look, Jean, I've been on the sea for over thirty years. Truly they don't need no lifeguards, but I will make it a priority on my list of agenda. Now pass me the four thousand dollars."

"Wait, I hear there's four boats going out. I'm not going on your son's or friends' boat, captain."

My son's been on these trips for ten years and doze friends are guys I started piracy with, transporting my Haitian people to a better life in the U.S.A." He spit out some tobacco juice.

Dad said, "how long you said it would take?"

"It's a six hundred-mile journey to Miami, two days maxi- mum. Plus the weather is going to be great on the seas, so I might just break the two days down."

"What about American Coast Guards and Haitian Coast Guards?"

"Well, that's why I need my four thousand dollars for, I can pay the right people what I promise them. Jean, I have places to go, people to see, I'm turning down people with more money to bring you to Miami."

Dad nodded his head. "How many will be on your boat?" Captain Batiste said, "About forty to forty-five max."

"I don't know, Captain."

Baptiste yelled in a high-pitched voice, "Jean, what the hell are you going to do? Now, I'll give you back your money."

"I done sent suitcases with my stuff with your people already." Captain said, "Jean!!"

Dad pulled four thousand dollars out of his pocket saying, "your Haitian people, huh? But you want your money in U.S. currency."

Captain Baptiste quickly grabbed the money from Dad's hand. "Thank you for the payment. Make sure you jump on the 'Freedom Boat.'"

Dad looked puzzled. "That's the name? "Yep, the great 'Freedom Boat.'"

My dad walked Captain Baptiste out the cow-barn and through

the field opening the back-house door.

Marie looked at me, "I'm scared Jean, to jump on the boat with that crazy droopy-looking man."

"You have to trust Dad's decision, Marie. Now let's get the hell out of this stinky barn before we consume so much pig-sloth smell that we turn into a pig."

She smiled, "Daddy's rich, you see all that American money he handed that Captain? It looked like a million dollars."

Grabbing some clothes that were already on the outside clothesline, I said, "Let's go take a shower at the fountain head mountain peer before Dad puts two and two together."

That night the Pastor came to the house. He was one of the only people, outside of Captain Baptiste and crew, knowing we were going to make our exile out of Haiti to the U.S.A. Grouping amongst all the family, Pastor took a stand in Dad's room, giving us confidence in the journey we were taking in less than seven hours. He insisted that we not question God's puppeteer choice on our life. Cries came around the room knowing we were really leaving Haiti. Holding one another and recanting life in Haiti was mostly the superficial display of the room's sadness. Polarized by the words of the Pastor saying, "by tomorrow night, God willing, you will be half way to the U.S.A." the room was just in disarray of sadness. Dad's previous speech asking who wants to stay in Haiti never came out of no one's mouth.

While Pastor was preaching over the sorrow and cries, he mentioned, "strong affection, devotion, and hope is what I'm looking for out of the Adam family."

With that, everybody got a feeling of strength and loyalty from each other. Dad interjected, "let's execute our mission to the United States of America." Everyone smiled at that. "Let's go, yes, I'm going to get ready."

Mom said, "Jean, Pierre, come help me in the kitchen!" She had fixed about a hundred peanut butter and jelly sand-

wiches with sprinklers of green leaves in the middle of them. They were each wrapped in zip-loc bags. Mom wanted us to strap the sandwiches all around her using a body-stocking over them to stick them against her body. Besides that, Dad made it mandatory for everyone to carry a galloon of water and a blanket. The little clothes, shoes and miscellaneous things were already packed in two suitcases in the hands of Captain Baptiste's mule.

The Pastor stayed to drop us off at the ocean port where our pursuit of happiness roots would start.

Aunt Marie went ballistic again screaming and hollering. "Don't leave me!!! Don't leave me!!! Make sure you send for me to come to the U.S.A.! I want to see Miami too." It started crazy but she put some laughter in it as Dad convinced her that she would be sent for. Aunt Vicky and the twins were also told not to worry, to keep themselves up with the little they had in

Haiti. Dad had left them two pigs, two cows, and three goats with little expenses for them to get around with until they could figure out how to get Aunt Marie to Miami.

Dad screamed, "let's start our journey to America!"

We walked down the mountain jogging with happiness reach- ing the truck the pastor had to drop us off at the port. At Duva- lier Ocean Port, there were at least three hundred fifty people in sight on the port. I surely was thinking at that moment, *Baby Doc is going to come over here and make an example of us.*

Pastor didn't get out the car for too much commotion, along with political reasons. We jumped out the jeep watching Pastor reverse as he waved to us.

Dad said to us all, "what you waiting on? Follow me."

When we reached the port, Dad gave a mule some kind of papers. We all jumped on the Freedom Boat and found a nice little corner, just enough to condense our little crowd of sixteen in the back right of the boat. It looked nothing like the "Love Boat" we saw on T.V. at Walker's house. These boats looked hand-made to me, with all-metal through four boats. They were shaped like Peter Pan's hat. The Captain's steering wheel in the middle of the boat was narrow but deep, inside of at least sixty inches of space. It looked suitable to me.

Dad was walking behind Captain Baptiste who had gadgets around his waist and a map in his hand. The captain constantly looked up at the clouds in the sky as he was being followed by a mob of at least nine people. Dad was among them.

"I paid you for life jackets for all the kids and women," Dad spoke. "What you mean you have only one life jacket?"

Captain yelled to the mule, "we leaving in twenty min- utes! I want you to balance everybody, right now, so the boat won't tilt!"

Dad, who was livid, put his hand on the Captain's shoulder.

"Where the fuck is doze life jackets?!"

"There is no more, Jean. Now let's go, I'm about to be off-schedule."

Dad looked at him. "Remember you owe me, Baptiste. Remember you owe me!" The mules on each boat were bal- ancing the crowds. Mom whispered to Dad, "It look like more than forty to forty-five people on this boat."

"You right, it must be every bit of ninety people on these boats."

Marie said, "Mom I'm hungry."

Mom reached between her breasts, pulling out one of the peanut butter and jelly sandwiches. She gave it to Marie.

The captain announced through his bullhorn, "We off to the U.S.A.!" The Freedom Boat crowd roared at the sound of this outburst.

Dad strapped the one life jacket around Mom as we drifted further across the water. We all were shaking to the point of feeling a real anxiety attack. People on both sides of the boat started getting seasick throwing up right and left, regurgitating weeks of food. The mule went to passing out some kind of pill for those vomiting. None of us Adam's

21

needed the pill.

Twenty to forty-five minutes into the ride we calmed down. About sixteen hours into the trip it was as if there were ghosts making noise in the air of the sea. It must have been why the Freedom Boat passengers went to singing some good ole church songs with each other. The chanting of The Lord's songs kept a peaceful atmosphere throughout the boat.

When you've been blessed it's like heaven- heaven. When you've been blessed pass it on- pass it on.

Mom prayed for about four hours straight, around the twen- ty-sixth hour of this grueling trip. Fear was read inside every set of eyes. It had to be about fifteen degrees, all wind with a view of nothing in sight. Those that attempted to look over the ship saw fins of twenty to thirty sharks.

When the sharks would jump at the birds that hovered close to the boat, at times the sharks would head-butt the Free- dom Boat.

When I say, "nothing in sight," I mean *nothing in sight.*

There were only sharks, three trailing boats behind us, and the blue ocean.

The morning sun came back out, which I was glad about. I had prayed not to see another night like the last one. If I say I didn't see glares of ghosts the night before, I will be lying.

Our respiration seemed to dry up quickly and caused gagging all around the boat. Breathing just wasn't comfortable.

Mom must have reached inside her back, body, and stom- ach all through the first thirty hours for peanut butter and jelly sandwiches. The only strength was found in watching Captain Baptiste steer the boat in complete calmness. He often whispered to the mule who occasionally walked around with the many gadgets giving hand signs to the other three boats that steered behind the Freedom Boat. We overheard "sixteen more hours". But it felt more like months if not years went by.

Then the inevitable happened. Rain.

Rain.

Rain.

It poured, and poured, and poured wildly. It poured violently. My mom rocked back and forth keeping two of my sisters on her chest. My Dad had me and Joe in his arms. Pierre and Marie were together in the blanket of Uncle Mike. My other uncles and aunt eased into a group together. The back of the boat where we were at, started to flood with water. All the back passengers moved around. The mule navigated everyone in the back to new spots on the boat.

Then the wind got violent, adding lightning with harsh thunderstorms that sent screams throughout the boat. It was pathetic how the Freedom Boat jumped waves in the storm. Someone rolled, bumping me to the front of the boat where I lost awareness of my family.

As I stood up looking to my right, a shark rode a wave jump- ing higher than I seen yet. While I was looking for some of my family in the wild mayhem, the boat jumped what appeared to be twelve feet in the air, causing a mob of people to rush to the back, squashing me. Seeing my two sisters, Marie and Tasha, I reached for them as lightening struck giving quick bursts of daylight.

While the harsh winds twirled the Freedom Boat, screams cried out, "God save us! Help! Help! Help!"

I lost track of my two sisters. The biggest wave ever held the boat five seconds in the air. Nine or ten people got thrown over the side into the shark-infested waters. "Jesus! Jesus! Jesus!!" Someone begged.

Flashes of my past life started to go in front of my eyes. Grandma Adam always said if life flashed in front of me, I should yell out the word "rebuke."

"Rebuke!!!" I shouted. "Mom! Mom! Mom!"

I just wanted the thundering to stop, but it did not. "BLAC- CKKAAA! BLACKKKKKAAA!" It cracked repeatedly.

The roaring, shout, and raging wind wouldn't stop. The boat did a three-wheel motion on a wave. At least forty people fell off the boat. "Helllp! Helllllp!" They yelled.

I held the right-corner metal with my index finger, using all my force possible.

Pierre screamed, "Mom! Mom!"

There were no more than fifteen people on the boat. Hearing my brother's voice, I slid in his direction. He pointed to the ocean. I looked at Mom with urgent eyes. "Help!" I said.

Pierre held my feet, watching a shark eating some- one. I reached for my mom. "Hold on to my arms, Mom! Don't let go. Don't let go, Mom!

A mob of people went to helping Pierre pull me, with my mom at the end of my hands. The thunder stopped with force- ful winds. Rain still poured heavily as the boat shifted from side to side. The living Captain maintained, wheeling the boat to a moveable pace. Mom had me on her left side and Pierre on her right. We were eye hunting for the others.

"Do you see anyone else? Do you see anyone else?" Mom desperately wailed. "Where's my babies?! My babies! Aaaaah- hhh! My husband! My babies!" She had me and Pierre in a headlock position, not able to come out of it. "Where's my sister Lord? Where's my brothers Lord? Where's my babies Lord?"

My seven uncles are dead, I thought in sorrow. *My brother Joe is dead. My twin sister Marie is dead along with my other two sisters. My aunt gone too. Why? Why? Why?*

In silence I cried with Pierre and Mom. My mom started again, rambling in misery. "My babies. My babies. Nooooo!! Tell me it's a dream."

It was oblivious to think our missing loved ones were safe on this crew of fifteen. *My Dad is dead,* I thought. *How could this happen? Why?*

A man went crazy, striking the captain in the face. A crowd of five of the passengers restrained the attacker. "Listen, let this man get us to land before you kill him."

"How much longer?" Someone asked the Captain.

"Less than two hours."

The Captain resumed, controlling the boat with the crowd of five holding the angry man. Under Mom's headlock, I looked at Pierre with a look that I never did before. I communicated with my eyes that I wanted my brother to pay attention to Captain Baptiste. I blinked my eyes for four seconds. Pierre looked back blinking his eyes for four seconds. We already knew what we had to do.

Captain Baptiste was steering the boat and engaging in argu- ment with the angry fella. "I lost my right-hand man! Look behind us, my other boats are gone! You think I could of pre- dicted this?"

For a moment, I felt sorry for him too. *But he belongs with the sharks,* I thought. I took my mind through a three-minute

daydream, thinking about the sharks eating my dad, brother, sister, aunt, and uncles. Shaking my head I looked at my mom. She let go of her tight grip around me, still praying. Pierre looked disoriented. I wondered if the two of them had their minds in the same place as mine. I wondered if we would ever really talk about what just happened?

Thirty minutes later a helicopter with the American flag painted on the bottom of it came our way with six speedboats. *The Americans are here to save us,* I thought.

A man on one of the boats held a bullhorn up to his face. "Turn around!! Turn around!!" The men on the other boats pulled out as many as nine machine guns. "Turn around!!"

The Captain said, "They going to kill us, let's turn around!"

Almost all the passengers on the Freedom Boat crawled towards him. "Get us the fuck to land or we kill you by pieces!!" Someone threatened.

"Turn around!!" The man on the first American boat contin- ued to order.

We saw buildings at a distance. "Captain, take us all the way to land," the same passenger said.

Captain pleaded, "don't tell the Americans you guys paid me money, okay?"

"Get this damn boat to land old man!!"

Upon reaching land, men with guns and blankets came rush- ing in our direction. They came off land and onto the boat. "Is everything alright?" One of them asked.

"Don't worry, everything is going to be alright."

Mom begged, "go get my family, they fell of the boat."

The officer looked Mom very sternly in the eyes. "Lady, those sharks killed your family. It's time to move on."

"Noooo!" Mom cried. "Send us back there with my family, please!"

The officer turned to one of his colleagues. "Get this lady some water with some hot chocolate right now." He then gazed back at Mom. "It's okay lady, it's okay, you're in the United States of America."

My mother cried and cried. Pierre and I held her tight. It was just the three of us now. Just the three of us.

Just the three of us.

CHAPTER THREE

Dade County's Krome Avenue North Detention Center had been our new home for the past eight months. There were Immigration and Naturalization Service (INS) officials all around the compound.

The living arrangements were not arguable to me. In fact, we were living in "paradise" to me, having different breakfast choices like eggs, bacon, cereal, and grits. I stayed away from the oatmeal, but I did love the apple juice every morning. At twelve noon, a three-course hot meal was served. At 5 p.m. there was another hot meal with a soda fountain that poured out Coke all day. It was unbelievable.

The officials gave us all new clothes, socks, t-shirts, drawers, which I had extra due to Pierre hating to wear underwear. They even had hot water and we got to shower in it. My skin started looking American.

The facility was pumping A.C. all day, which I don't like too much, except when I was under the thick blanket that had been given to me by the officials. I watched T.V. all day long while attending a three-hour English-speaking class that was mandatory.

A group called The Red Cross periodically came through over the months with different medical supplies to attend the people living in the facility. Every time they came, I ran to my room. They had a needle the size of Pierre's dick, wanting to stick it in our arms. It gave me horrible pain, so I ran

The facility was very tolerable to me. I was having a great time there. The one thing that bothered me, and there were not many, was the bigness of the chicken breasts and legs that were on our evening plates. I couldn't pinpoint how they got chicken to get so damn big. But I ate it like a caveman.

The mishap that happened on the ocean was not really talked about among us three. We spoke about the good times in Haiti. During the first month in the INS facility my mom and some others from the Freedom Boat were offered to go look at a heap of bodies. They had floated on shore weeks after our arrival.

27

Mom went for our family because kids were not allowed. She came back saying out all the bodies, she only saw Dad.

We went to a funeral that gave Dad a personal gravesite. All three of us, plus others, attended. Mom had to be dragged away from the grave.

Being in the prayer-hall and helping in the kitchen is all Mom really did at the INS facility. One evening, she told me that I was a brave man. "Thank you for saving my life," she said, hugging me. "When you was born, we chose another name for you, but seeing the struggle you gave my pregnant stomach, your dad said, 'give him my junior.' Thank you Jean, thank you, baby. You the oldest, so watching over Pierre is some- thing I want you to pursue, as your dad would've cared for him."

"Alright, Mom," I said, tearing up. "I love you."

"Thank you, Jean. I love you, and Pierre. I live for you two. Thank God for you two." The INS facility held over eight hundred people. About two hundred were Haitian, the others were Cuban. All of us had exiled from countries to America.

There were a lot of rumors that I had learned from a kid the same age as me. His name was Ricardo and he was 13 years old. Ricardo, who showed me and Pierre around, told us about Cuba, that President Castro was feuding behind a political move that happened at the United Nations embassy in Cuba. Thousands of Cubans stormed inside the embassy demanding to leave Cuba. Castro told the embassy to release the people to him for they had to go to prison for killing a Cuban officer in front of the embassy. The United Nations heard through reports that Raul, President Castro's brother, was setting out to kill many of the Cubans that begged the United Nations embassy for exile to America. America was willing to accept all the exiles, asking for boats to bring them to the U.S.A. Ricardo said that's when Castro counteracted with a reply of, "no problem. I will flush my toilets." He then fired his hardcore criminals, mentally ill, political dissidents, disease-carrying prostitutes, and delin- quents. Some of them got off the boat still wearing hospital wristbands and gowns.

Through my mom, I heard the United States might deport us back to Haiti. When I brought this up to Ricardo, he said, "don't worry, my dad was sentenced to life in prison in Cuba. He's not going back there. We will tear this facility down taking the Haitians with us."

I said, "Ricardo, I'm not going back to Haiti either."

My brother, who just turned 12 years old, the day before, February 17, 1985, was hyped about tomorrow's soccer game. Haitians against the Cubans.

Ricardo was good on the soccer field, but not like me and Pierre. We thought he had no chance.

"We will see this weekend," our friend laughed.

We spent the whole day with Ricardo them, and went to take a shower. That night I told my brother we were going to Ricardo's room. When we approached the room, we smelled an unusual scent. I knocked on the door.

Ricardo's dad opened the door and told us to come in.

Watching him pass a weed joint to Ricardo was unethi- cal, I thought. He offered me and Pierre some, but we declined, making it known that our mom would kill us.

"This is a big weekend coming," the father said. "Especially Monday." I thought he was talking about the weekend soccer game until he continued. "Monday, Florida governor Bob Graham has a decision to make about the rest of us that await visa cards to get out of this INS building to the streets of Miami. If the governor say 'no!', we're going to tear this place upside down. Besides, it's good timing because out there in Miami, there is a decision that has to be made." He stopped to puff the joint, blowing it towards us. "It's about an all-white jury that might acquit several officers in the beating death of a black Marine Corps veteran. Doze minority neighborhoods out there like Hialeah, Liberty City, Little Haiti, and Overtown are going to erupt if the jury come back not guilty. If you ask me, these racist motherfuckers don't like to see the minorities get their money up. We got lighters in here, stacks of books and newspa- pers to burn up, and knives to cut whatever they got standing."

"You got knives?" I asked. He pulled out nine knives?

"Can I get two of them?" I requested. I looked at my brother blinking my eyes for four seconds. Pierre looked back at me nodding his head up and down. I took two knives and thanked my friend's father for them.

"Nice picks," he said.

I told Ricardo that Pierre and I had to go back to our bedrooms to our room to talk about something.

"Handle your business," was his reply.

Once outside, I let my brother see the serious in my face. "Let's go take another shower before we get to our room."

Taking a nice hot shower with the two knives close by, my mind went to Captain Baptiste. I had been mad inside of me watching Baptiste brag about his many journeys on the sea. It was rumored that he might get indicted to criminal deten- tion in federal court but nobody on the Freedom Boat told the authorities that we gave him money so he stayed in the facility with no consequences.

So he thought.

Coming out the shower, I waited for Pierre. I talked to him about a plan, concluding by letting him know not to think about it. "Let's just play some good soccer games tomorrow."

"Cool."

We went to put on some deodorant, baby, lotion, and brush- ing our teeth. My mom said, "My handsome boys come go to sleep."

Saturday morning, February 18, 1985, we woke up and did the usual shower, teeth-brushing, and putting on deodor- ant. After having a nice breakfast we headed to the T.V. room to watch some Tom & Jerry. It gave us laughter to ease the tension about the five-team tournament going on in a couple of hours. I asked Mom if she was coming to watch the games.

"I promised I would help wash some pots and pans in the kitchen," she told me. "If I finish early, I'll be over to the field. Plus we got to cook lunch and dinner, so don't be on the lookout for me, just have fun."

The field the officials put together looked great. It wasn't exact length or width, but it would do.

Two teams were Haitians, three teams were Cubans. We played the first group of Cubans where we won 4-1 with Pierre making two goals. The age group went from 10-35. It didn't matter if we were kids or not, we were getting treated like men on the field.

I watched Ricardo and was impressed with his play. They beat the other Haitian team 3-1 with Ricardo scoring two goals as well in the win. Since we scored four points, Ricardo's team had to play the other Cuban team which they beat 3-0.

Playing head to head against Ricardo's team wasn't as easy as I thought it would be. Two hours had passed by with no one scoring. We were both sluggish from the previous games, especially Ricardo, which later on would be his excuse. I saw fatigue in the Cuban man that contested me. Showboating for the crowd, I kicked the ball from right foot to the left foot, spinning it around the Cuban to a stand-still. He got dizzy and the crowd roared with laughter. I kicked the ball from my right towards the goal. The goalie slapped it with his hand in front of Pierre who booted the ball into the back of the net. The crowd ran onto the field yelling, "GOOOAAALLL!!! Goooaaallll!!! Goooaaalll!!!

All the Haitians came running to lift Pierre in the air. They put clown smiles on their faces chanting, "Haiti!! Haiti!! Haiti!!"

Ricardo came over. "You lucky I was tired."

"I don't want to hear that bullshit," I grinned. "We won."

The winning team players all got hundred-minute calling cards to use anywhere in the world. Pierre and I gave ours to our Mom. She smiled at that. "I need these cards bad."

Being broke and not having funds to buy calling cards, Mom would have to stand in a line of hundreds waiting on a fif- teen-minute free phone. And the lazy counselor usually didn't offer it for weeks at times.

Talking to Aunt Vicky and Aunt Marie sent a different kind of peaceful feeling to Mom.

There was tension in the air from the Haitian's winning, but I think because everyone had bigger problems at hand, the game was just a game, like it was supposed to be. To be care- ful, I told Pierre who, throwing his smile right and left taunted,

"I'm the Michael Jordan of soccer!," to keep on his shoes in case it goes down.

The weekend wore on and Monday hit me with life without dictatorship. The verdicts on the seven white police officers who beat the black Marine Corps veteran all came back as "NOT GUILTY!!!"

The streets of Miami were tired of America's views on minorities. The people took to the streets with explosive anger, throwing fire to white businesses and blocking the highway. Some also threw pictures of Martin Luther King reading: *You killed King. You killed Kennedy. But you won't kill our kids anymore.* It was shocking to see the events of rage the people created to

express their feeling to the government. The sight of the seven cops walking out of the courthouse smiling made me wonder, *Where have I lost my family to?*

As everyone was watching the news on all twelve T.V.'s, an exiled man by the name of Dr. Greg Curtis barged in the middle of the hall in eye view of everyone. "Governor Bob Graham had denied anymore visas for the rest of the exiles from Cuba and Haiti!!"

The rage erupted among us all in the facility.

The T.V.'s immediately came off the wall. The glass that stood up, chairs went straight through them. Fire was soon to come. People went to cutting off the alarm system, which eventually stopped blaring. The scene looked like the famous beginning of a movie called "Scarface."

Pierre and I ran to the room to check on Mom. She was terrified. "Don't go out there you two, stay put right here."

"Mom," I said, looking around. "We need water in case the fire comes here."

"What, Jean?! Why we need water? Don't leave me here!" I said, "Pierre, stay here with Mom."

With fire in his eyes, Pierre did something he never did before, cursing in front of Mom. "Fuck you!! I'm coming with you. Mom will be okay right here with the door shut."

I went and grabbed the lady next door, telling her to go in the room with my mom.

Pierre and I then jetted off looking for our man. Running around the place, we looked up and down, but the fire was spreading in view of everyone. Then I saw the good ole captain in a corner looking right to left about to flee to somewhere, taking a wide run. Pierre knowingly took the other wide run towards Mr. Captain, leading him straight to me. At 13 years old, I looked Captain in the eye the same as I did the pigs, sticking my 10-inch knife in his gut. He was choking me with two hands but I felt nothing. Pierre went wild, stabbing his back.

Slash! Slash! Slash!!!

I could feel my knife inching up to Baptiste's belly button wanting to reach his nose. He let go of my neck. I dug deeper with my knife. "You thought you can get away fucking with the Adam Family, motherfucker?!!"

Pierre kept slashing. "Let my brother go, motherfucker. Let my brother go!"

Ricardo happened to turn the corner. I looked at him, pulling my knife from the dead man's stomach. "Pierre, let's go yo!!" Ricardo took little steps backwards, looking in silence. We gave our backs to him, running to clean ourselves. We put on the clothes we hid in a game room and destroyed our bloody clothes by throwing them into a blazing fire that was right

on time.

As soon as we ran into Mom's room, she immediately took a sandal off her foot, beating me in the head, back, and arms. My brother caught some whips too. Mom kept screaming, "Where the hell you been at? Don't you know we going through enough? Huh? Huh? Huh?!" She was livid. "Where you was at, Jean?"

I averted her piercing gaze. "The Cubans took the bucket of water from me."

She did not believe one word of that, even after Pierre repeated the samething.

The inner riot kept on. The sprinkler system calmed most of the fire. People ran to the field jeering at the cops who were geared up in front of the 20-foot gate. Nobody challenged to go across it. Some went up but eventually came back down. While we three Adams were outside taking it all in, Mom said, "I feel tension. Let's ask Jesus forgiveness in case events take the rest of us." So she prayed.

I eyed my brother sympathetically. All the people inside were getting pushed outside by an army of force that shot tear gas inside the facility.

Mom looked up at us. "I can't believe after all this, those people about to deport us all."

The crowd went from rage to reality. It was possible that deportation back to President Castro and President Duvalier's administration would be dreadful.

The hours seemed so long that, after becoming exhausted, most of the crowd sat on the field in different huddles.

The eight loud speakers went to making some irritating squealing noise as a voice said, "I have news for everyone in this Krome Detention Center. I've just been informed that Governor Bob Graham has overturned his veto signature that he made before the Florida Congressional Committee. The result of this grants everyone already in the United States amnesty to stay under the political Asylum Act that was just proposed two hours ago by the governor. This means in the coming weeks everyone in this yard will be getting seven-year visas that must be renewed every seven years."

The crowd of angry rioters suddenly became enthused, roar- ing, "Yeahh!! Yes! Yes! Yes! Castro, go to hell! Baby Doc, go to hell!!!"

The happiness among crying mothers, as well as grown men, caused strangers to hug and embrace each other. It felt so electrical.

My mom and a group of at least forty ladies went to the guards asking if they could go clean up inside. The one in charge allowed them in. The others in the field wanted to give a helping hand.

We came to find out that during the eight hours we were on the field, homicide detectives had raced through the half- hearted investigation before making the announcement on the loud speaker and leaving the facility.

I walked into Ricardo's room. He quickly handed me a small piece of paper. "Here goes the number to my dad's sister in Miami. When we get out of here let's hook up, alright? My dad likes you two."

I tried to hand him back the paper. "We don't need your number Ricardo, we have our own dreams and in it consists of bringing Haiti to the forefront."

"Alright, you two be easy. Hope to see you guys around."

Pierre said, "We not leaving yet. Let's hook up through the week to play that Pac-Man machine 'cause nobody has beat my score yet in here."

Ricardo responded, "alright."

Through the week, Mom wondered if everything was okay, seeing us in the room most of the days. We eased her worries by letting her know everything was fine.

The detective that kept interviewing people walked around the facility inspecting the T.V. room, game room, and observ- ing all of our body language. I was sweating nervously at the authorities, not the murder I caused. Pierre kept asking me a million stupid questions.

Mom asked, "Did you hear about the Captain? He got stabbed over twelve times."

"Must have been that angry man on the Freedom Boat." "Yeah, it could be." Brushing off to more important things,

she said, "I got to file a whole bunch of papers tomorrow about getting a place to stay, visas for all three of us, what area of Miami are we going to stay in, just all kind of papers. Make sure you be around in case they ask me to take pictures of you two."

Ricardo walked in the room when Mom left. "I'm scared of your Mom, she be looking mean sometimes. But what Pierre told me about how you guys lost your whole family, I'm surprised she still have will power to move on. She a strong lady, but she is a mean lady to me."

I laughed at that. "She don't got no problem back-slapping us in front of a hundred thousand people. She's real stern, but it's all out of love."

I asked to step out to the room for one second. He did. Closing the door, I looked at Ricardo in the eye. "Listen, you didn't see nothing you hear me?"

Ricardo looked back at me fiercely. "Jean, who the fuck you think you stepping to like that? I'm no rat."

"Under the crazy circumstances, I have to look at you in the eyes to tell you what's on my mind."

My friend took two steps in my face with both his fists clenched. "Go find someone else to check like that. I'm not the one, buddy."

"No disrespect, Ricardo, okay?"

He opened the door asking Pierre if they were still going to play Pac-Man. Pierre was all for it, asking why Ricardo was turning all red on him. I got nothing to do with what you and Jean talked about, so let's go."

I'm happy they both gone, I said in my head.

CHAPTER FOUR

The weeks in which we were supposed to be set free with visas, turned into months. Mom complained that the case managers were taking forever with their caseloads.

My dad had wrapped all our Haitian government papers such as birth certificates, marriage licenses, school information and all kinds of well-needed information around his body. They were still strapped on him upon the authorities finding him on shore, but were badly destroyed.

Mom continued saying how financially we were helpless in all aspects. Her status was getting updated with new informa- tion every other day, but not having any family member in the

U.S.A. to co-sign for us, caused some difficulties.

Then one day, Mom said, "I did get an address to where we going to stay."

We moved with anxiety, "where Mom?! Where!"

"A neighborhood called 'Little Haiti' at an apartment complex called 'Salbam Palm' projects, number 217."

"Yeah, Mom?!" Pierre was excited.

"Yeah, but I'm in the process of getting you in school with a bunch of Haitians. I didn't even want to live around a bunch of Haitians."

Pierre was confused. "But Mom, doze are our people. Plus, we can get along better with our own."

She said sternly, "You go to school where I say you go at. Don't

question nothing I do, boy. Plus, before we leave here, I got to have a heart to heart talk with the both of you. I didn't come all the way here, losing all my family for you two to embarrass me. Those are my people?!! You don't have no people here but me and God." She was getting angrier by the second. "Don't leave this room today. And did you finish those books I put on the shelf?"

"Mom," I said. "There's eight books I left there."

"What's so important that you can't start to educate yourself? Don't leave this room, and when I come back, I will ask you some questions on the books."

We both said, "Yes Mom."

She left with a strong look on her face. I looked at Pierre. "Uh oh, here she go."

"I know. Why would she try to put us in a school way out, when doze people think we should be around our own people?"

"I don't know."

Ricardo strolled into the room. "I leave tomorrow homies. Let's go kick the ball around a little."

Pierre answered with sorrow, "We can't go anywhere." "Your mom, huh?"

"Yeah."

Ricardo laughed. "Let me get out of here before she come back."

We were in the room talking when Pierre noticed Mom was coming back. We stuck our noses in a book that we weren't reading. She came by, stuck her head in the room, and left. We looked at each other once she was gone again.

"Drama queen, drama queen," I spoke to Pierre. "She going to start being hard on us like Dad was, even harder, I think. I see it coming right now, but at least we going to be in Little Haiti, little bro. Did you hear, apartment 217? Sounds like we going to be in a big building with three hundred floors. I hope we have a water-view with a two-car garage."

"What about the girls?" Pierre asked.

"I don't know, Pierre, I don't know. But they are going to give us a lot of things knowing that we are dead broke."

From the months after Mom knew we were going to be staying in Miami. She got to acting tough on us. Waking us up early in the morning for six days straight, Mom took us in the kitchen to help wash pots, mop floors, and help with painting the hallways. We would be so tired walking in the room that we went straight to sleep.

Most of our friends, plus Ricardo, had already left to the outside world. The facility still was all we knew. Mom gave speeches from the morning till night. She wouldn't even give us updates on what was going on with the current circumstances. All we could do was anticipate that soon we would be in

Little Haiti, Miami.

January 6, 1987, after Pierre and I waxed our room. Mom walked in with a smile. "The floor is pretty. Did you do the three ladies' rooms down the hall also?"

"Yes, Mom."

Screaming in enthusiasm, Mom said, "I got good news! I got really good news!! I just got a bus to a great school called 'Carol City High School,' and we are leaving this place tomorrow!"

We boys jumped up and down, going off. "Yeahhh!!!" "I'm so happy," Mom said.

We were even happier.

Mom continued. "Listen, I'm going to treat you like men, but you're my boys. We lost a lot, but we have to move on in life not staying depressed. Life is determined by what you think and how you act. I want you at your best behavior at all times. I went through a lot to get this school. Jean, I had problems getting you in the 10th grade, so they're putting both of you in the 9th. You boys can earn extra credit by going to night school, as well as day school. I've gotten seven thousand dollars from the government to help start off. I will also be looking for a car to get us around. Oh, and before I forget, they got a special bus that will come pick you two up from Little Haiti. I tried hard not to move in the area, but if that's where we have to start, so be it, for we will grow, as your father would want us to grow. So let's get some sleep 'cause tomorrow will be a new day in life for us, and we will take advantage of the situation. I hope you still want to be pilot, Pierre, and put that stupid soccer ball down. I hope you still want to be a lawyer, Jean, because I know you can do it. You are an Adam. "She grabbed us into a tight hug, kissing us. "I love you. I love you." And she cried.

We were full of her speech, getting nonchalant hugging her back. We loved our mom and letting her down was something we knew would seriously destroy her. We all sat up chitchatting for another hour or two before falling asleep. Mom couldn't stop humming church songs throughout the room.

The next morning, around 9 a.m., we heard on the P.A. system in the hallway, "Mrs. Adam, Jean Adam, Pierre Adam, please pack your belongings and come to Gate 1."

I stretched. "Here we go, Pierre." Pierre said, "I'm scared."

"Me too, but we been waiting on this for a while now." Mom came storming in. "Let's go boys."

We smiled heavily, carrying the little belongings we had, walking to Gate 1. The staff and the limited people that were there loved my mom's helping spirit. Some cried, some held her tight, even hugging us.

"Take care of your mom, she's a great loving lady."

The head kitchen official said, "You got my number call me. I will miss you dearly."

Mom said, "As soon as I get a phone, I will be calling you." Coming up on Gate 1 we took some fingerprints, took some pictures and my mom signed a bunch of papers. She put them all in a stack of folders she had acquired through the paperwork

process of this day coming.

The lady helping Mom said, "There will be a van to take you to three stops of your choice."

We got outside through a gate that slid open real slow. It was like deja vu. We were now looking at all of what America had to offer. Wow, was what the eyes were saying. "Wow," Pierre muttered. "Look how tall that building is,"

Mom looked around ready to tear up saying, "thank you God. Thank you God."

A white van pulled up in front of us. Opening the door, the driver said, "Mrs. Adam?"

"Yes."

"Get in, I'll be taking you to any three spots before taking you home."

"I just want to reach a bank, get some cleaning supplies and go to my new home."

"No problem."

We put our stuff in the van. Pulling off from Downtown Miami, we were in awe sight-seeing through the clear windows. The buildings were all tall. As we drove, they were getting shorter. There were all kinds of cars.

"That's my car!" I called out, pointing at a black convertible. "That's my truck!" Pierre said, pointing at a red truck.

There were stop lights and no commotion-filled traffic jams in the streets. We were pointing at people and waving, but nobody really waved back except this one man with a shopping cart full of Coke and Pepsi cans. The streets were very clean. The people all had on clothes.

"Want to hear some music?" The driver asked, "Yes!" He put the dial on 99.1 Jamz.

"Oh, that's a nice song," we said.

Not having cable at the INS facility, we were limited to only constant Spanish music. Mom looked around at all the amaze- ment also. When the driver pulled up to the bank she told us to stay in the van. After spending about twenty miles in there she came out, thanked the driver, and made it known she wanted to go get some cleaning supplies.

We were seeing McDonald's, Burger King, Pizza Hut, and all kinds of other restaurants. We screamed out seeing any one of them hoping Mom would get the point. But arriving at the cleaning supply she let us jump out asking if she could take the offer on the third spot.

41

The nice Driver said, "No problem, Mrs. Adam."

Mom sounded real important to us. The supply store was big, full of things to buy. We got a mop, broom, and a lot of smell-good stuff, plus all kinds of things I couldn't even read. Pierre and I carried all the bags for Mom.

"My two strong boys." She said. "I love you."

When we got back in the van, the driver said, "I just got my next appointment canceled. If there's anywhere else you want to go after the supermarket, let me know."

Mom replied, "No, after the supermarket, please take us to the apartment."

"Yes, ma'am."

The driver was doing most of the talking about the local areas and how to get around, even stopping at a bus stop to get manual. We drove into the parking lot of the supermarket that read "Win-Dixie." It was so big I said, "Wooow, this is real amazing."

Mom agreed, "This is a true one-stop shop here."

We got a shopping cart just like the one man I had seen earlier was pushing. Our family streamed down the aisles of the super- market. Mom got us chicken legs, breasts, thighs, rice, maca- roni and cheese, donuts, oatmeal, and seasonings.

When we saw Dorito's, Pierre and I went crazy. "Dorito's! Dorito's! Mom you got to get us some of that!" She said, "Where you seen that before?"

"In Haiti."

"On the next trip. Right now, I got to get what we need until I get a job."

To appease us, she got a big can of Kool-Aide that gave us smiles. Next, we got peanut butter and jelly, fish, and end- less slices of ham, turkey, and cheese. Going up to the coun- ter, I looked at the register hoping it could be mine one day.

Pierre grabbed a magazine that had "Word Up" on the top with a picture of Run D.M.C. on the front. Opening it, Pierre showed me a big poster of the rappers inside.

I looked right at my mom. "Mom, you have to get this to put up in our room."

She looked at us as if we had lost our minds. "Those cra- zy-looking men are not coming anywhere in sight of our apartment."

Seeing the sadness in our faces after we loaded all our bags into the van, Mom asked the driver, "can we stop at Kentucky Fried Chicken?"

We marveled at that. The driver took us there and Mom even bought him some food.

After that, we were driven to the apartment complex where we were going to live. It didn't match what I thought at all. The buildings were only two stories high, looking like a good version of our barnyards in Haiti. There were people outside hanging out, and I could tell they were Haitians. We stopped at building 40, number 217.

"I got the key in an envelope somewhere," Mom said to the driver. "Please give me a minute, I'm sorry."

"Sure, no problem."

After Mom found the key, we picked a couple of bags up some stairs. We instantly found apartment number 47. Mom reached for the broken doorknob, seeing the door was already open. There were two men on cardboards sleeping in our apartment. The driver barked at them, "get the fuck up out of here! This place is now occupied, so don't let me catch you here no more, or I will call the police!"

The two men raced to pick up their unidentifiable objects, jetting out the door. The driver helped us bring our things from the van to the apartment. Opening the kitchen cabinets made me think the rats in our past pig-bar were small.

Our new place to live badly needed painting. The doors inside were off the hinges and the place was real stinky. It was all messed up. Mom sure didn't think so. "It's just a little prob- lem here and there. We will

43

have this place in order within three days."

She talked to the driver about a car and he agreed to take her to a friend the next day. She showed me and Pierre where our room was, which was in front. Hers was the same small size. The bathroom was really foul. That's where most of the awful smell came from. Pierre and I shook our head side to side like, what's going on here? The right words couldn't really be found to explain what we were going through right then. We simply knew this was nothing like the Cosby Show we watched at the INS facility.

We had been cleaning for over five hours. The Kentucky Fried Chicken we ordered was good, but the apartment's strong smell just overpowered our appetite. We still did the best that we could.

"Everything is perfect," Mom said. "This kind man will come tomorrow, and I wrote down everything we need. School don't start till six more days. We will have a phone, clothes, a home. Don't worry yourselves, we been through worse back in Haiti." We looked like; I guess she's right there. With all the sheets,

towels, and blankets mom got out the INS facility, she fixed a quick spot for the three of us to lay down. Seeing this, Pierre said, "I want to go back to the facility."

Mom backhand-slapped him. "Get your ass on the floor and lay down."

I dove to the floor quickly. Sleep was alright due to all the work we put in, including two hours of scrubbing the wall.

One thing she didn't tell us was that the driver would be coming around at 5 A.M. She was already up, rushing us to get up and put on the same clothes we had on yesterday. She put some oatmeal in boiling water and we were out the door eight minutes upon the driver's arrival.

He was driving a truck that sat two in the front, so he let us into the back where we sat for a bouncing ride. We couldn't see anything in the back. Our journey took us to somewhere that had a big sign reading: Opa-locka Swap Shop.

It looked like Downtown Haiti had moved to Opa-locka. Mom said, " I can get everything from here, can't I?

The driver nodded. "Yep. I come here early every week and get the good stuff that goes away fast."

Pierre and I looked like, all these Haitians and Cubans done brought their junk to Miami.

The first thing we got was a bedroom set with piss marks on the mattress which got me punched in the back for making a remark at what I saw. The sun was hot and it was very humid. My mom was having fun buying this junk, the used pots and pans, the sandals, hygiene products with no name on them.

The outsider fish market spread within the two-mile con- densed place. We got hungry so Mom bought some soup from a lady. All of us were sweating like crazy. The driver knew every person here, talking loud to all of them as they all talked loud back. It was not hard to tell that this was an every Saturday and Sunday event, where Pierre and I would face a Saturday 5 A.M. wake-up to the Swap Shop.

I showed Mom that the light lamp she wanted was already chipped, she said, "don't worry about that, we're buying it."

The toilet seat is the only thing I saw that was brand new. I had a massive headache and so did my brother. We went to sleep in the hotbox truck, waking to see Mom still having fun shop- ping. She handed me a bag of shrimp that looked awful. The cereal she bought came in a bag as tall as me. *Why did she buy*

shoeshine polish? I later found out. The used Bible and fifteen

books she purchased were supposed to put big smiles on our faces so we faked it.

Mom said, "I wasted money yesterday at that expensive Winn-Dixie supermarket. The ketchup, season, bread, cook- ies, cleaning supplies, I could have got all that right there at the Swap Shop."

It would be like a mini auction. For instance, when a seller would announce having an item for, say fifteen dollars, a buyer like Mom would speak up. "I got nine dollars!"

The seller might try to push that price up by saying some- thing like, "someone just offered me thirteen dollars, they will come back around to get it. You want something else?"

"No! I'll give you nine dollars and fifty cents right now." The seller would go off on a rant, *you this, you that, you think I stole this, blah, blah, blah, blah.* But it always ended the same. "Give me eleven fifty."

Sold to my Mom.

The crazy thing was that even for unnamed ketchup, this process went on and on. The black and white T.V. was a bidding that went on for twenty-five long minutes with Mom getting the T.V. for twenty dollars. The medicine looked outdated, but everything else was outdated and belonged in the garbage. We couldn't tell our mom that.

She found haven at the Opa-locka Swap Shop.

At 5 P.M., the driver rushed my mom to hurry before the car lot closed. Mom thought she had so many more things to buy but she also knew she needed to go shopping for a car that day. With no room to sit, us two in the front, we sat on Mom's lap. While we were stinking up the front, I asked why they were smiling at that Fred Sanford junk.

The old man claimed he knew cars well and that he was a mechanic. He proceeded to drive us into a used car lot. The look didn't really impress us but we got out running all around the lot playing with each other. Pretending like we were driving the cars was fun, until Mom chose a car. It was a 1981 four- door Toyota Corolla so filthy that a car wash couldn't wipe off the dirt on the blue car. It didn't take too long for them to get everything done like papers, tags, and insurance.

Mom drove with Pierre home, following the truck. The nice man stopped to buy oil, head gaskets, and whatever the car needed to get going.

Reaching home around 9 P.M., we were beat having to drag all the junk into the apartment. We ate a quick sandwich and went straight to bed.

Around five o'clock the next morning, mom tried to wake me and Pierre up.

"I'm not feeling good," I complained. "I will stay here and put all these things up."

Pierre joined in. "I don't feel good either, can I stay and help Jean?"

"Okay, but I'm going to buy clothes for you two today." "Yeah?"

"Yes. The Swap Shop clothing section was where I didn't get a chance to go. While I'm away, you boys don't go outside for nothing."

Waking up around a normal teenager time of 1 P.M., my brother and I sifted through the pile of junk. We grabbed the four-feet cereal bag with the powdered milk to fix us some- thing to eat.

Pierre asked, "did Mom say she's going to buy clothes for us?" "Yep, you didn't hear wrong. She went clothes-shopping, so

prepare to put a big smile on your face."

"Things are going to change for the better, right?" "We in America, Pierre, it has to."

"Look at all this stuff Mom bought. You think we ever gone get some McDonald's?"

"I don't know, but that cereal was good." "Yeah, It was."

Putting the bunkbed and Mom's bed up was the hardest part of everything we did, but it was nothing. The carpet was laid down in the living room and bedrooms. Mom had brought a video game to connect to the black and white T.V. The game was Tecmo Bowl, an American football game that looked pretty interesting. The way Pierre set up the books on the shelf in the room would make Mom proud. We always were in competition to impress Mom, so the pile that we structured to the best of our abilities was looking real beautiful to us.

We chilled around 5 P.M., popping some cans of ravioli in the microwave that Mom got for fifteen dollars. It made me say that Swap Shop had some good food, 'cause that tasted even better. We hoped Mom wouldn't be mad that we ate six cans between the two of us.

While going to put a garage bag in the trashcan, we heard a quick, "Bow! Bow! Bow!" It was shots from a gun.

Pierre and I ducked. Looking out the window we seen a car pull off.

Someone on the floor was shot, yelling, "Help! Help!"

Three ladies came out calling for help also. After thirty minutes an ambulance came to pick up the man that was shot. He was moving, so we said he's not dead.

"I see why Mom said to stay in the house," I said.

Finishing up the little rest of putting the house together like paintings, and fake black panther in the living room, we chilled trying to find a channel on the raggedy black and white T.V. Staring out the window at a crowd that looked to be gossiping, we saw Mom pull up. Running outside kissing Mom, we hauled endless bags back and forth."

Mom said, "I had needed you two, is everything alright?" "Yes, Mom."

When we got inside, she looked at the apartment with joy. We wanted some more of that. Her enthusiasm turned into showing off the clothes she had bought for us. She pulled out two suits saying, "this is what I want you to wear at school for the first day."

We complained, "Mooom."

She squinted her eyes. "I've been out there going through all kinds of clothes, don't you 'Mooom' me. This is two nice suits I bought. It will have all the kids looking up to you, watch and see."

For some reason we were mad, but believed what she said.

The shorts were just so tight on us. Mom told us they were perfect because she didn't want anything falling off of us. The shirts had fifteen colors on them. The jeans were the best thing; they had the name Wrangler on them. She pulled out four pairs of black Chinese shoes and four pairs of sneakers named MA 500's. We didn't like the Chinese shoes, but we figured the MA 500's were popular sneakers in the U.S.A. They were brand new with a tag saying '$7.99.' Pierre and I fought over the one Superman shirt mom bought. She ordered us to share it.

Mom pulled out some clippers. "I know how to cut hair, don't worry."

"No, Mom." I whined.

She looked for the brand new black and brown shiny belts to wrap around her fist. There was already one in case we mumbled any word of unappreciation. Our whining costed us one strike apiece.

She showed off two pairs of black dress shoes that she wanted us to wear on the first day of school. Then Mom asked if we had eaten, if the microwave gave us problems. We told her everything was okay. She passed us the hangers to put in our room. When Pierre grabbed the Superman shirt to put on a hanger, he brushed my arm. I punched him right in the mouth. He tried to scoop me up. I punched him with a two-piece. He bit me on my thigh. I hollered when he kicked me in the face.

Mom came in with the belt and finished us both off. Slash!

Slash! Back. Slash! Arms. Slash! Ass.

Slash!

Slash!

We were concerned, enduring the slashes. Crying out loud made it worse. We sat on the floor. Mom made us get on our knees in separate corners. Then she left.

"I'm going to beat your ass, Pierre," I threatened. "Fuck you, dummy."

"Don't try me."

He came towards me punching on the top of my head twice. Mom rushed in telling me to go in her room and kneel in a corner there.

We were on our knees for forty-five minutes or more. My knees were killing me. I suddenly smelled some good cooked food in the air. To my relief, Mom called us to come eat. We had rice and beans with some goat. It surely cheered me and Pierre up. The great Kool-Aide topped the meal off.

Mom sent us to our room for the night complaining about spending 2,100 dollars in two days. Her plan was to go look for a job that Monday morning. Walking up and down the hall- way she kept on saying, "I need a job. I can't believe I spent so much money and you two ungrateful boys didn't even see the big picture of what we're going through." She talked nonstop to herself in the kitchen, hallway, her room. "I knew I forgot something. I got to get that. Money being spent, I got to find you two a job. I don't have a T.V. I make sure you two get everything you want."

She slammed the door.

I woke up first the next day finding a note Mom left.

It read:

There are six hot dogs and some boiled eggs and biscuits left on the counter. Also paint the walls.

I ate four hot dogs since the punk made me mad last night.

He came walking in and cracked a boiled egg.

I said, "that's fucked up how you smacked me on the back of my head while I was on my knees."

"You lucky Mom came in and saved you." "What?!!"

Pierre tried to sling a kick to my chest. I fell back catching his second kick and hit him with a right fist. He fell back. I fol- lowed up with a left and r ight uppercut to the stomach, and then I pushed him with little power. When a glass fell and broke I looked at my brother like, *see what you did?*

He said, "Don't blame me, you did that. I'm going to let Mom know."

"Look," I said. "Don't say nothing. Let's throw it in the outside garbage."

"I'm not going out there," Pierre retorted. "Alright, I will, but don't say nothing."

"Okay, just let me wear the Superman shirt first." "Alright." I slipped outside saying in my head, *I hope Mom*

don't pull up, Jesus.

Finding a little corner, I threw the broken glass cup inside the dumpster. On the way back, I looked up thinking, I had just saw Ricardo with two other boys, but I said, "Nah, that's not him."

When I got back inside, Pierre and I made peace, and laughed at what Mom would have done had she caught me outside. Mom came home around seven o'clock telling us she didn't find a job.

My brother and I were five days away from going to Carol City High School. I couldn't wait. Through the little days in between, we stayed home playing Tecmo Bowl and watching

T.V. shows like W.W.F., Tom & Jerry, and The Cosby Show. talked about how fresh we were going to be, who would have the most girls, what days we should wear our shoes and sneak- ers, the 5 A.M. bus ride, and school.

CHAPTER FIVE

Monday morning we woke up at 4 A.M. real energetic about school. Mom said she was going to follow the bus to our school, and take us in the office to check us in.

She had perfectly ironed our suits. They hung neatly in the room. The haircuts we got, we later learned were called a 'super bowl' because they had no fade at all. The clippers were sharp, so Mom eased the pain by sliding some cooking oil on it. Mom took total charge of our morning even shining our shoes. Once we dressed, she told us we looked like lawyers, which I was glad to hear since becoming a lawyer was my goal to reach for myself and Mom.

The breakfast of sausage, eggs, and grits with biscuits tasted so good. When Mom gave us both one dollar and fifty cent, we felt real important putting our first pieces of American money in the wallets Mom got us. Her happiness was so energetic, we thought she was going to school also.

Around 5:30 A.M. the sixteen-passenger small yellow bus pulled up outside. Pierre and I walked out to jump on the bus. There were four people on the bus who all looked Haitian in my eyes.

The bus driver looked me and Pierre over. "You two boys look real nice. I wish my son would wear a suit."

Mom stayed in the doorway happily jumping up and down. Me and Pierre sat together as the bus pulled off. I tried to be friendly to a guy across from us by saying, "sak-pa-se. What's your name?"

He replied, "Syco." "You Haitian, Syco?"

His one word was, "yes."

"You got to Carol City High School?"

"Yes." He never looked at me to answer my questions.

Pierre and I talked to each other. Having Mom follow us felt confirming. The forty-five-minute ride gave us the best view yet of Miami. Kids were everywhere. The holidays were over. School started back and it looked like everyone was happy about going to school, except this guy, Syco, next to us.

The bus reached this wide building that had about nine more long yellow buses in the front of it. We pulled up in front of all of them. Pierre and I stood outside the bus, awaiting Mom. She took a while. A bell rang loudly making us jump.

Eight minutes later, an officer said, "where you two belong?" I said, "it's our first day, we waiting on our mom."

Mom strolled up saying, "can you show me the front office?" "Yes, ma'am." He took us to the front office.

We met the principal. He said. "I wish more kids' families would put a suit on them."

After signing all kinds of papers, we got a schedule. We were used to one class a day in Haiti. Here in the U.S.A., we had seven classes a day. Having to move around every hour was new. Mom was adamant on the administration about putting me in the 10th grade, but she failed, and 9th grade with my little brother was my reality. Overlooking the schedule, we noticed that we had no classes together. We promptly alerted Mom to this with sadness in our eyes.

"I know," she responded. "I changed it. You were in four classes together, but I want you two to be on your own."

Mom walked Pierre to his class, and I could have sworn everyone was clapping. But when I walked into my Social Stud- ies class, the whole class went to laughing out loud. I laughed with them, walking over to the teacher. They wouldn't stop laughing until the teacher, Mr. Brown, raised his voice. Some stopped till all was eventually silent. I didn't understand.

The teacher said, "Class, this is Jean Adam."

They went to singing a song called "The Adams Family."

I laughed, feeling so nervous in the classroom. There were about thirty kids in there including the kid, Syco, I'd seen on the bus. Ten minutes later, four kids sang the same song. "The Adams Family." Again, I laughed. The teacher called the singing kids to the front. I finally saw them. Mom had encouraged me to always sit in front listening to the teacher.

As the four walked backed, one kid said, "have you been to the Super Bowl!?" He pointed at my new haircut Mom had given me.

The class laughed harder than before. So did I. Going to change classes was hectic, but the security guard helped me. I was late to second period. When I walked in, again the whole class laughed.

Pierre and I had been learning English well, especially at the facility. We learned a lot there. Our accent was heavy; while heavy might be an understatement for our bad English. When we spoke, most people asked us to repeat it again.

When I saw Pierre at lunch, he said pretty much the same things that happened to me happened to him. For lunch, the school server said we could go back for seconds, thirds, or fourths. "Just eat till you get full."

They had pasta, which was so good, we wondered why the whole school wasn't in there to eat. We saved our dollar and fifty cent aiming to reach ten dollars to buy a video game called

Mike Tyson's Punch Out.

Mom wasn't home when we got there. Talking about the first day, we discussed how American kids loved to laugh.

The next coming months of school were dreadful. I walked into third period class, and saw the kid Syco was in there with me. We also had four other classes together. The kids were making fun of my brand new MA-500 sneakers. Teasing me, they sang a song:

Bo Bo's, they make your feet feel fine. Bo Bo's, they cost a dollar ninety- nine...

They sang it over and over again. I was the joke of the room. A kid asked me, "hey, Jean, what's for lunch?"

I knew the schedule from going in the lunchroom everyday for the past four months. My heavy accent delivered the answer. "Hamburger. You can eat as many as you want."

"Okay, tell me when they got cat-burger."

The class erupted with laughter as well as the teacher.

Even I laughed.

A girl asked me, "They got fruit?" "Yeah. They give apples a lot."

She said, "let me know when the banana boat comes."

Laughter went on with kids falling out their chairs, causing more laughter. I jumped up to help one guy who fell. He pushed my hands saying, "don't touch me."

The teacher focused on me. "Don't get up, Adam, remain in your seat, and everybody cut the nonsense. We have work to do."

Nobody listened to her. For laughing was all that went on. I saw Pierre at lunch. He had on his favorite Superman shirt. He told me the kids in his class were singing a song:

I believe I can fly. I believe I can touch the sky.

They sang all day in class and wouldn't stop. The old teacher just sat there. When I walked though a crowd of guys in the hallway, someone slapped me in the back of my head.

"Why you do that?! I said angrily. But nobody admitted to it. I was mad.

"Let's go, Jean," Pierre said, looking at the eleven guys.

On the bus the next morning, Syco spoke saying, "hey Jean, when everybody laugh in class, just look at whoever said the joke and say, 'your mama.' Okay?"

"Okay." I nodded. "Why you never talk to me?"

He said, "I went through what you going through. You have to beat someone up."

"Oh no, Mom would will kill me." "Well, you will be the joke of the class." "I don't care, I just want to be a lawyer."

Syco turned his face. I kept talking but got no response.

Pierre whispered, "he's crazy."

"I don't believe he's crazy," I disagreed."

In first period, one kid loudly asked another if he had seen some show on HBO.

"Yeah," the second kid grinned. "I saw the Haitian Body Odor." The class laughed with tears. Once the bell rang ending that class, the teacher asked me to stay, so I did. She thought I needed

to wear deodorant.

"Mom got me a good one from the Swap Shop called 'Burt,'" I informed her.

"I don't think that lasts long enough. You need a better one. I will buy you some speed-stick, okay?"

"Okay."

Pierre and I were playing our new video game when he asked me if we ate cat in Haiti. I told him not that I know of. The kids in school had kept saying taco-cat barbeque was for lunch. It was a lie because beef tacos were for lunch. I heard them laughing and looking at me. I looked back at them saying that taco-cat barbeque sounded nasty, but they always repeated what I said in a weird voice, mocking me.

"Don't worry about them," I told my brother all the time.

The last day of school was called "Cracker Day." For some reason, nobody picked on us. They instead, picked on the white kids, even beating them up with three or four people on the person. I recalled how in Haiti when I fought, it was one on one.

With the last day complete, we jumped on the yellow bus to go home. Mom was happy we had finished our first year of school in the U.S.A., but she was mad as well by us making B's and C's on our report cards. We passed to the 10th grade with ease.

The summer was spent at home, going to the Swap Shop, and attending church on the weekends. Mom found a job in the summer pushing lawnmowers around. The job she had was taking care of a 72-year-old white lady who adored us. She took us to our first McDonald's trip, where we ate two Big Macs each. She also took us to

Six Flags, which I enjoyed. The bumper car trips to Race-A-Runner made me think of changing my lifetime goal from becoming a lawyer to a racecar driver, which made Mom pinch me for just saying that. Behind the old white lady, the fields in Boca Raton, Fl., were long. We put in about sixteen hours throughout the week doing lawns. Mom kept money while a pair of Patrick Ewing sneakers is all we wanted. We started getting our haircut at the Swap Shop. Mom dropped us off at the Virginia Key Beach, leaving us with some Kentucky Fried Chicken. She told us she would be back at 3 P.M. The water felt so good as Pierre and I played soccer in the sand, showing off for the crowd that never really looked our way. We heard music so we went looking for it. We found it. We had never seen so many blacks in one spot. The DJ who kept yelling, "DJ Uncle Al!!!" had some speakers going up at least 20 feet high.

A rapper called "Uncle Luke Skywalker" was there with eight girls. The girls were on top of the speakers looking like they were going to take their clothes off. The rapper said, "don't stop! Pop that pussy! Let me see you Doo-Doo Brown!"

The girls bounced their asses up and down, some popping their pussy to the crowd. It was my first sexual experi- ence, I came in my shorts. A girl in the crowd said, "they fake! Them bitches fake!" And she started taking her top off.

Uncle Luke said, "take it off! Take it off!"

And the girls did, doing the Doo-Doo Brown to the crowd.

Men threw money at her.

The guys were wearing gold chains with Mercedes Benz gold pieces, gold rings as big as Oreo cookies. Their mouths had gold teeth in them.

The rapper said, "I want everybody to chant the answer with me. All hoes!"

The crowd responded, "Suck dick!" "All niggas!"

"Eat pussy!" "Bulldaggers!" "Suck pussy!" "All faggots!" "Drink dick!"

It seemed like everybody knew the words. The crowd bopped side to side looking drunk with 40-ounce bottles of Colt 45 malt liquor, smoking weed all around as if it were legal.

"If you believe in having sex, say 'hell yeah!'" "Hell yeah!"

"If you believe in having sex, say 'hell fuck yeah!'" "Hell fuck yeah!!"

A girl our age walked by looking at Pierre. "Boy, what kind of monster you got poppin' out them shorts?"

Pierre's eyes got big, smiling at the girl who winked her eye at him and walked away. He said, "You see that?"

"Yeah," I was still astounded by the whole glorious event. "This is what I'm talking about. We got to come here more often."

When I looked at the clock it was 5 P.M. We ran to where Mom was pacing right and left with a belt in her hand. She slashed me first as I tried to jump in the car with Pierre on my tall getting those backslashes.

Slash! Slash! Slash!

She went around, got in, and talked the whole way home. At times, she backhanded whoever was close to her as she drove. She hurt us saying, "you never going to the beach again!"

Pierre kept apologizing. "Sorry Mom. Sorry Mom."

I dreamed of all those girls that whole night. Pierre stayed up to watch the Sunday night Bruce Lee Karate Show that he would never miss. We both loved to watch karate. But I had to dream on the events that happened earlier.

Our first summer wasn't bad. School was starting the next day. We had earned us some Reeboks and Patrick Ewing's. We had learned the hard way that MA-500's were not cool at all, in the U.S.A.

The first couple of months at school brought us the same harsh jokes: we eat cat, Haitian Body Odor (HBO), comb your hair with a horse comb, and the stupid songs. One time, a Haitian on the bus named Nick, told us the best thing to do was say that we were Jamaican, that nobody messed with him because they thought he was Jamaican. He even knew how to speak Jamaican.

Pierre and I looked at each other. "We can't do that," I frowned.

We from Haiti."

Speaking in Creole, Nick said, "well please, don't tell nobody I'm Haitian. I was just trying to help you. At lunch, eating some good pizza, Pierre complained that when he walked in his class, a boy pointed at his socks and said, yesterday, he played for Green Bay, and today, he plays for the Raiders, that Pierre needed to make up his mind. The whole class laughed at him. Leaving lunch we saw the crazy-looking Haitian, Syco, coming down the hallway. A group of six that we were passing

said, "hey dirty Haitians."

We were walking by when one of them said, "what, you came off the Freedom Boat??"

Pierre's feet and my fists went to striking them. I hit the first who fell like a bitch. Then a two-piece knocked the other one down. Pierre aimed at faces with kicks and had blood shooting out somewhere. Some boy yelled, "hey, the Haitians acting stupid!"

Two more came to help the boys. Syco came in punching one in the face. We fought till the five security guards came in to separate us. We had little bruises but the guards were marveled at how we beat eight boys, as one of them was on the floor crying, "my two front teeth!," with blood dripping down his mouth.

Talking shit, Syco kept saying, "whatever, whatever."

We were taken to the office. Mom had to leave work to come and get us. We already knew this spelled slashes. The principal said we would be suspended for ten days. The guards wrote on the report that there were no guns, but they found five bullets on the floor. We didn't understand that at all. Mom asked the principal if she could sign the permission to beat us. He rejected the thought of that.

Mom said, "oh, yeah? Well I'm going to beat them right here myself."

They stopped her as she was unstrapping her belt from around her waist. *Thank God,* I thought. I knew Pierre must have been thinking the same thing.

Pulling both our ears, Mom escorted us to the car constantly pinching us. Seeing as some of the kids were watching, I was mumbling for Mom to stop and trying to resist.

"Oh," she said. "You fight back? Let's go fight at home."

Once home, Mom told me to jump in the shower and get myself ready to go straight to bed. She then came into the bath- room beating me with an electrical cord. I hollered for Haiti to hear me but got no help at all. She wildly went looking for Pierre who was hiding. She looked, looked, looked, and found him in her closet.

Slash! Slash! Slash!

Pierre and I went in our room and just cried, cried, cried, falling asleep. Mom came back while we slept, beating us with all her strength.

"I work two jobs for you two and you want to fight?! Let's fight! Let's fight!"

The whipping should have killed us. I don't know how we survived it. She unplugged the T.V. and games, put it in her room, and told us to come eat like nothing was wrong. While eating, she said, "I want you two inside the house reading books. I will cook in the morning for you. Eat it and go back to your room and read."

"Yes Mommy."

Going to the room, I looked at Pierre's back where endless welts looked like interstate 95 condensed and mapped out on his back. Besides a scratch from the fight earlier, a welt on my neck to my shoulder burned when Pierre touched it.

I said, "I thought she was aiming for my dick."

Pierre laughed. We started talking about the fight, feeling good about it. "Pierre, I'm about 5'7, weighing about 140. You about 5'6, weighing about 140, and we beat them down. They can't fight. You know we are used to fighting our uncles in Haiti one on one. I could kill any one of those dudes."

All that ripping animals apart with our bare hands had them calloused and bruised. We had gutted animals that looked like they had Freddy Kruger's face, giving us hands that were as tough as steel.

Around 11 A.M. someone knocked on the door. We woke up and I looked out the door seeing Syco.

"Pierre, it's Syco, should I open the door?" "I don't know."

Syco kept knocking. I said, "I'm going to open it, man, fuck that."

Syco walked in saying, "sak-pa-se." We answered, "nap-boule."

"I got ten days, what about y'all?" "Ten days too."

"I didn't know you two could go like that. We beat the shit out of doze American niggas. Doze dudes going to want get-back, so I think we should go to the Popeye's Chicken restaurant in front of the school and wait to see who wants some."

"We can't leave here," I said. "Mom tried to kill us last night, look at my neck. She going to kill us for sure if we leave the apartment."

Syco frowned. "You like when they messing with you? 'Cause they're going to really be on you two even harder in school, if you don't put a nip in the bud of doze dudes. You really think doze dudes done forgot about it?"

"They got what was coming to them. I don't think they want more," I replied.

"Well let's go find out before going back to school." Pierre said, "He's right."

I shook my head. "I know."

Syco was all business. "Come to my house at 11 A.M. tomor- row. We going to take the city bus number 27 to school and chill at Popeye's."

"Alright, Syco." He left.

Pierre said, "I hope I see them. I need to take this beating shit out on somebody."

"Yeah, me too."

CHAPTER SIX

Walking to Syco's house was the first time we walked any- where since moving to America. He lived on 54th, which was two blocks away from the projects we lived in. He opened the door saying, "sak-pase."

"Nap-boule." I said. "Why they call you Syco anyway?"

He answered, "My name is Ganeo Jablegoa. I was born in Haiti too. My dad is a pastor and a realtor on the side. My mom died coming to the U.S.A. I went to private school and got picked on worse than you. I stabbed a kid in the eye with a pencil and got kicked out of school. I went to Carol City Middle and now High School. People heard about what happened and started calling me Syco. I've been to juvenile detention a couple of times, plus programs. I hate these rude, think they bad, black Americans who belittle Haitians."

Damn he talks, I thought in my head. The way his eyes squinted and then popped up real wide, north to south with that hand language he used matched the name "Syco."

He continued, "I carry bullets in my pocket and throw it at people I hate."

I looked around. "Your dad's here."

"So, Dad don't care if I have eight people in here. I don't think he even know I'm alive sometimes; all he do is chase money. I know he got another house 'cause he spends three days a week away sometimes. He told me he's moving out when I turn 18."

"What did he do when you got suspended?"

"Nothing, really, I mean he said 'Stay out of trouble' before him and his friends went shooting at the gun range. He gave me fifteen dollars, so I got us, if you don't got no money."

"We got five dollars."

He said, "we got twenty dollars." "I like that, Syco, 'we.'"

Pierre said, "I believe you really are crazy." Syco didn't laugh, only we did.

With Syco's bad communication leadership, we went to one school called Edison High School and then to our destination. God bless Uncle Mike, who always said, "you can't buy alle- giance of loyalty." So we finally jumped on the number 27 bus and got off on 183rd Street. When we got to Popeye's Chicken, we ordered some food, which we ate like someone had us on a timer. We then went to the corner where we could see the school that was to let out in two minutes. Syco pulled out an El Producto cigar with a bag of weed asking us if we smoke. I said, "nah, I'm good."

Pierre concurred. "None for me either."

We check our shoes to make sure they were tied. At a short distance we saw four of the guys that Syco said hanged with the Ewing boys, who we had already fought. They saw us but kept their heads straight. When crazy man went into his pocket and threw a bullet on one of them, they said, "oh, you Haitians must think you're bad!"

We squared up with them and they went like bulls. Pierre did a karate kick that hit one in the face. Syco was punching wildly and yelling in Creole, "Colan giet ma moun kalanbe santy," while giving a dude one to the jaw and one to the eye. My man caught me in the ribs, but my knee technique was too much for him. We whipped them bad, had to even pull the crazy man off one dude. The Popeye's employees came outside in time to see us run off jumping on a jitney bus.

"Them dudes soft, acting tough." I laughed.

We got off three stops down. There was a big group hanging outside. I recognized one of the original Ewing Boys we had fought. He was standing with some girls. Pierre, hot in the pants, got there first with same kicking-shit, catching one dude in the chest so hard that he fell. The other ran as we kicked the hell out of their friend with six different feet right in front of the girls.

Laughing, Pierre said, "girls, you need a Haitian in your life."

One girl sucked her teeth. "I don't fuck with no dudes that take me out to a restaurant to eat cat."

The other girls didn't laugh. Syco went in his pocket and threw a bullet at the one with the smart mouth. She screamed. "Ahhh! God save me! God please get this voodoo off me. God, I don't believe in voodoo."

Everyone went to laughing at the asshole.

We went home after telling Syco we would come over to his house the next day. The whole day had been so much fun, Pierre and I couldn't wait to go back to Syco's.

We were a spectacle of Mom's thoughts when she came in around 8 P.M. to find our noses planted in books. "I'm going to think about giving your video game back next week if you keep up the good work."

Going back and forth throughout the week to Syco's three-bedroom house in Little Haiti was fun. Next door to him was a major weed hole called "Superfly" that kept a line of people trying to get served. Syco expressed once that he wanted to rob the dudes next door. He said they had a lot of money in that house. Half the things said I let go by my head.

We went to a school called Central High School to go looking at some girls. Somehow we got into a fight, 'cause of Syco of course.

I was mad at Pierre because he took nine puffs of Syco's weed joint. He hurt me whenever he said, "I'm not his daddy, but that's my little bro."

Syco always told us we had to change our dress clothes for some reason. After we arrived at his house he would give us long white T-shirts that we were able to cover the ridiculous brown leather nameplate on those Wrangler jeans.

"The cheap Reeboks can pass," he told us. "I wear Nikes only. But you have to stop with doze colorful shirts."

"They look to good to us," I reasoned.

"Please, I will bring two plain white T-shirts on the bus when school starts, and please just bring a folder, the bookbag with all the books makes no sense. The books are already in the class, those you carry are for home."

Pierre said, "We told Mom that. She insists on us carrying them, but we going to leave them."

Syco laughed and we had to laugh with him because he didn't laugh much.

Not seeing Syco for the weekend had Pierre and I understand how good a friend he was. The Swap Shop had a circus around that we watched. It was cool, but we wanted to go back to Virginia Key Beach. After church Mom stopped at McDonald's. We were surprised.

She said, "Please just do right in school. School is real impor- tant, an education can get you far. The reason I work hard is because I didnt' finish school. I had to work selling sodas at seven years old in the middle of the street. Please stay in school."

We said, "we will, Mom."

We spent pretty much the whole next week playing a game at Syco's house called Street Fighter. Me and Syco almost fought when he passed Pierre his joint.

"I do what I want to do," Pierre protested.

"Stop talking crazy man," I said. "I don't want that smell on you when we go home, for I don't get a beating."

"Alright then, I'm going to take my clothes off for the smell don't get on them."

I was pissed. "Do what the fuck you want to do, but if I get a whippin', I'm going to beat your ass."

"Yeah, whatever." Looking at Syco, Pierre said, "I'm good, I don't want none of that shit, yo."

The long two weeks had given us a brotherly vibe with Syco.

We saw him as family and he saw us the same way.

Monday morning, jumping around on the bus, we already had T-shirts under our so-called colorful shirts that we got at the Swap Shop. Syco told us to give him the shirts. He went to take the fake Jamaican-Haitian, Nick, on the bus. "Hold these shirts. And on our way home, you better have them, you hear me?"

65

The faker quickly said, "no problem! No problem! I don't want no trouble. The whole school been talking about you three crazy Haitians. They all scared of you. I will fold the shirts up, you see?" He demonstrated by folding the shirts right then and there. "I'll put them in my bag. When we get back, I'll remind you. We Haitians got to stick together!"

"Get the fuck out of here with that," I said in disbelief at Nick's nerve.

Syco, Pierre, and I got off the bus and entered the school. As we walked up the hallway, the students acted much differently towards us. They saw the three of us together with all our long white T-shirts on, Pierre and Syco with pencils behind their ear, and pimp in our step. We walked Pierre to his class to make sure everything was okay. He walked in the class not hearing any laughter of bullshit.

Having the first period together, Syco and I walked in the class and went to sit in the back. A dude waved at me saying, "sak-pase." I looked at him like he was stupid. The teacher just looked at us. Not one joke was said about us, not one joke. Not even a whisper. We shared some laughs with others, talking about a T.V. show called "In Living Color."

Going to lunch, we ate outside instead of inside. Syco helped buy the food. Pierre, who was full of enthusiasm, said, "a girl wrote me a letter. Look, look, look. She put it on my desk."

We read his letter, where the girl was asking Pierre if he had a girlfriend. It had little boxes for him to check his answer, yes, no, or maybe. She had written her phone number "call me" right next to it. Pierre was jumping up and down. "I don't got no phone number!"

Syco said, "give her mine. Just call her when you come to my house. I got my own line."

Walking past the pussies and laughing at them felt so cool. We heard that a couple of them went and got their big brothers. There were all kinds of rumors, like, they had guns. We weren't afraid. They would have to catch us slipping, which was out of the question. I had already told Syco to keep his bullets in his pocket. "You need to wear a glove doing that

66

bullshit anyway."

"Alright Jean," was his response.

For the next couple of months, we started skipping school, taking girls to Syco's house, and playing video games. When Syco's dad spent nights out, we took his car. The four-door Toyota Camry rode smoothly. We loved skipping out to other schools.

The last four months had opened Miami life up to me with a lot of different thoughts. Mom's one and a half hour drive to and from work at Grandma Julia's made it impossible for her to keep up with us. She said she would get a phone in the house, but the light pole in the apartment complex came down causing constant waits.

Mom gave us permission to walk to a pay phone to call her everyday at 7:30 P.M. plus for any emergency. Our knowing how to get past the school attendance didn't give Mom the heads-up on our skipping school.

One day, after Pierre and Syco got as high as they could get, we went to a local restaurant called Shaker's Restaurant. The guy at the register was talking to a customer, giving the customer the food he had ordered. "Here's your beef stew with rice and macaroni, one iced tea, and a red velvet cake."

The customer checked the food, looking onto the plate with a strange expression on his face.

The register boy said, "why you looking at the food like a bunch of Haitians cooked some stewed-cat for you?"

Syco and Pierre were jumping behind the counter beating on the worker, while I kept hitting buttons on the cash register trying to open it. I took the whole register saying, "let's go!"

We jumped in the green Camry, laughing and speeding off. "The bitch-ass nigga going to learn with them slick-ass

comments," Syco barked.

I counted the money, coming to find out there was four hundred and thirty dollars in there. We cheered loudly. I thought we were rich as I split the money between the three of us. I said, "they had some good food over there, too. We can't go back there for a while. In fact, there's another Shaker's in Liberty City. That's the one we go to from now on, okay?"

They both agreed. Pierre said, 'I'm still hungry, where we going to get something to eat at?"

I was quick. "Let's go to the restaurant, Fish City, in Carol City."

Fish City restaurant was a drive-thru soul food restaurant with several benches and tables outside. We ordered thirty-five dollars worth of food, drinks, and deserts that Pierre paid for. Everything sat, spreading all over the big round table.

As we were eating and talking about the previous incident, a four-door box Chevy Caprice with a 90' front and 90' back, along with some rims and tires called Hammers and lows, sparked our attention. We were looking at the bowling-ball paint job, which was three different colors of blue, royal blue, powder blue, and metallic blue. Through the clear windows, we could see all white-pillow insides.

Syco stood up recognizing the car. The passenger and the guy in the back-right seat jumped out with the guns pointed at Syco. "We been looking for you, motherfucker," the first one said. Pierre ran around the building with quickness. With my bad-sounding English, I said, "nooooo! That's my

friend." I jumped in front of Syco.

The driver then got out of the car saying, "Hold up! Hold up!" I was shocked. "Ricardo?!"

The first gunman, who we later came to find out, was named Crip, turned to Ricardo. "Where you know this Haitian from?"

Not seeing Pierre in sight, I said, "Ricardo, this my friend."

Ricardo addressed both gunmen. "I know this Haitian. His name is Jean. This a real ass Haitian here, he don't know what's up with Syco."

Syco started going off. "Ya really going to pull guns out on me?"

The Crip dude held his gun more steady. "Syco, you a disloyal nigga."

Pierre came running back around the restaurant's wall surprised to see our old friend, "Ricardo!" They hugged with Ricardo slightly lifting Pierre up.

Ricardo couldn't believe his eyes. "What the fuck you two doing here with this slimy dude?"

"That's our friend."

Crip frowned. "You a fucked up nigga, Syco."

Syco's eyes got wide. "How the fuck? Your family said you not fucking with me, even your dad act like he was going to call the police or get a gun when I came to your house the next day after you got shot!"

"Nigga you lying," the second gunman, Gerald, hissed, "I should kill you. Why you didn't come to my house or call me or Ricardo?"

"I never thought you two would pick sides like that. I thought when I ran, you were coming to my house the next day or even that day. One day turned into two, three, and now we are here."

Gerald sneered. "But you shot Crip!"

Syco suddenly looked sad. "I'm sorry. You my brother Crip. It was a mistake. I got love for you."

I noticed the guys respected Ricardo by not shooting yet. Looking at what I thought in my mind were two Haitian gunmen, I said, "someone tell me what's going on! Because if I don't know nothing about Syco, I know he's loyal. Someone put me up on what's going on."

Ricardo said, "These dudes came in Sable Palm projects trying to grab a pocketbook out of this car. We don't allow dudes to grab in the projects if you not from there or know someone there. So we pulled out guns on them."

I interrupted, "We stay there, too, Ricardo. And I think I seen what you talking about. Was it outside building 42?"

"Yeah. You stay there? Never mind that, like I was saying, Syco's dumb ass went to shooting at dudes and them, standing behind Crip. Almost paralyzed him from neck down when he shot him in the back.

69

Now my nigga got a supporter to help him lift up his right leg. He can walk but with a cool limp now. But seriously, we been looking for dude 'cause he just never came by."

Syco said, "can we talk please, Crip? Please, Ricardo? Y'all my brothers and you know that."

Ricardo spoke up. "Let's go to Gerald's house, he still stay in Scott projects, you know where he stay, Syco. In fact, Jean and Pierre ride with me. That's cool, Crip?"

Gerald and Crip went to jump into Syco's car. "Yeah, this my dude, he just be doing dumb shit that will get a nigga killed."

Syco's crazy eyes grew wide. He said nothing.

Still outside, Ricardo nodded towards me and my brother. "What school you two go to?"

"Carol City."

"That's how you know Syco?" "Yeah."

"Carol City got some bitches out there that's wife material. You got to hook me up, 'cause Syco don't know none of the bitches."

Crip said, "let's get out of here."

Jumping in the car Ricardo was driving, I remembered Pierre and I having to check in with Mom. "Ricardo, I need to go by and make a call at a certain pay phone."

Cool, you can call when we get to Scott projects in Liber- ty City."

"Nah!"

Ricardo grinned. "Something to do with your mom, huh?

Close the doorman. I got you."

I relaxed in the soft leather seats. "Whose fly ride?" "Mine." Ricardo took pride in his answer. He turned up the

booming car stereo system. It was playing a rap song.

Woke up quick at about noon, just thought that I had to be in Compton soon. Got to get up before the day begin. Before my moms start trippn'

70

about my friends.

"Who's that?" I asked, moving my head in rhythm with the song's heavy bass beat.

"Eazy-E."

With my hand, I motioned for him to turn the music down.

He did, saying, "ke saoui vle moche."

I was impressed. "Damn, you fluent in Creole, nigga?" "Yeah, I've been around nothing but Haitians since I left the

facility."

That's cool, we will talk about that later. Now, how do I get one of these fly rides and a beeper like you?"

"I got you, Jean." "Tell me now, bro."

Pierre scooted up to listen to Ricardo talk. Our friend said, "the tourists that come to visit South Beach come from a lot of different places around the world with a lot of money. Most of them rent cars from Budget, Hertz, Avis, and a couple of others. The cars they get say the word "Lease" on the bottom. Sometimes you can just have the eyes to know them after doing it one or two times. At times you catch them with an open map holding it high looking for directions. They usually love to ask for help." He laughed. "From 183rd Street in Carol City to 8th Street in Overtown, it's all open for goons to get them. A lot gets lost inside the streets of Miami. I hold three spark plugs around at all times. Right now I got two pieces under my tongue, look." He showed us three pieces in his hand. "The purses have trav- elers checks, cashiers checks, jewelry, cash, a lot of cash. The most I hit for is twelve thousand dollars with Gerald and Crip. Syco got broke-off and wasn't even on the trip."

I said, "my mom got twenty dollars in her purse. You caught a purse with twelve thousand in it?!"

"Yep.

"Damn, Ricardo, I need you to take me out bro."

He pulled to the pay phone. Pierre got out to call Mom. I said, "It's good to see you man."

He said, "You too, Jean. You know that I see you as family. I've been telling all kinds of people about you two, especially Gerald, that's my man. He knows all about you. I don't know how Syco didn't put two and two together."

"Syco don't know how to explain himself, but I understand him, plus loyalty is something that can't be bought."

"That's real Jean. You look good, but are those Wrangler jeans you got on?"

"Yeah, that's part of my problem."

Pierre got in the car telling us everything was good with Mom. "We can stay out till late. She chilling up North."

I said, "good."

We went out to the apartment complex that had a sign read- ing "Scott projects."

Seeing the dude, Crip, laughing, took off some tension.

Gerald said, "Ricardo been talking about you two that he met at Dade County Krome Detention Center. You two were going through a lot, family wise. Make sure none of these dudes don't creep on you to kill you. That will hurt your Mom. I stay with my aunt. My mom and dad are in Haiti. I came with my aunt and uncle. My uncle done got an American girl that took him out the house. Their little girl died on the boat coming here." I knew the feeling of losing loved ones. "Sorry to hear that."

He said, "it is what it is. Let's smoke."

"I don't smoke."

Pierre pulled out his little stack of money. "Where the weed at?"

Gerald replied, "them Dogg Pound dudes got some in the back project."

Crip interjected. "I heard about the little money y'all hit for earlier. I smoke, but only every once in a while, not twelve times a day.

Maybe one or two joints."

It was fine with me. "Yo, me and Crip going to stay here and chitchat. Y'all can go ahead."

The others went to the back-project to get Dogg Pound weed. I asked Crip how long people had been calling him by that name.

"My name is Mark. It's crazy how we just so happened to be talking about weed. When I do smoke the brown shit or green shit, I be searching for some purple haze, crip weed, and that's how I got my name too." He laughed. "I live with my mom and dad in Little Haiti. My mom sick, and my dad, who loves her to death, takes care of her and go to work. She been having kidney problems and can't pay for it. I heard they charging like over a hundred thousand dollars. At times, I feel like Dad sends me to go find money. I'm the only child, but it is what it is. My mom lay down mostly seventeen hours a day, she rarely goes anywhere, and when she does, it's on a wheelchair. And I don't know where me or my dad going to find a hundred thousand dollars at, but it is what it is."

"You got a car?"

"Nah, I told you, I give whatever loose money to my dad. Gerald looks out for his people too, but he got a Ford Taurus. Ricardo pretty much spoils himself."

The other four came around the corner laughing up a storm. We all chilled for another two hours together before it was time for me and Pierre to go home.

Ricardo said, 'I got you."

I stood up. "Let's hook up tomorrow to go grab some tourists' pocketbooks. And listen everyone, for no reason should you come to my apartment under no circumstances. My Haitian mom is crazy. All of you should understand. I be with her through the weekend."

"So what time should we look for y'all?" Gerald asked. "We will be at Syco's house at 11 A.M., that's cool?" Ricardo answered, yeah, for everybody.

Gerald laughed. "One thing I don't miss is the whippin' my mom used to give me in Little Haiti."

I said, "I still get that bullshit." They all laughed.

Me and Pierre stayed up talking on how we had to help Mom get money and stop wiping that old lady's ass for a job. We reflected on how we had thought there was a money tree in America for everyone. It hadn't turned out that way at all.

He said, "We could have stayed in Haiti with our family."

I said, "Yeah, but that Baby Doc crazy though. But, check it, what's your vibe on them other dudes, Gerald and Crip?"

Pierre said, "I didn't get to fill Crip out, but Gerald sound cool to me. He's your age, 16, and he sound like he was going to ride or die for Crip. Ricardo said he's like a big brother to him."

"Yeah, me and Crip talked. That's why I wanted me and him to chill while you left with the rest. He's 15 years old, with a lot of anger in his heart, but I like his outlook on life."

We talked about grabbing tourists' pocketbooks and went to sleep. I woke up early around 8 A.M. I planned for us to not even go to school to sign in and then leave. Sooner or later, Mom was going to find out.

Accustomed to cooking in Haiti, I cooked some eggs and sausage for me and Pierre. I knew what I might be doing that day and felt a little uneasy. There was some fear inside of me, but I knew the butterflies would go away. Pierre slept a lot; I woke him up at 10:30 to eat before we went to Syco's house. On our way walking to Syco's, a policeman stopped us asking why we weren't in school. Using the worst English possible, we told him we just came from Haiti. We finally reached Syco's

house. Ricardo and Crip were already there.

We greeted them. "Sak-pase."

"Nap boule," Ricardo said. "We waiting for Gerald to pull up."

When Gerald pulled up, we grouped into a huddle. Gerald was talking, saying his car had window tints, that Syco's car would be on the watch-out for any heroes that may try to get behind us. Crip would drive that car. Two would go in one car, three in another. I wanted to ride with Gerald, and so did Ricardo. It was agreed. All of us got some pieces of spark plug. "Alright y'all," Gerald said. "Let's drive around the rental

car place to see if someone is coming out of there." We said, "that."

We rode for about forty-five minutes. I kept saying that every song playing on the car stereo system was the rapper Scarface. "Yeah, Geto Boyz is the shit." Ricardo bobbed his head to

the beat.

The song said:

This year Halloween fell on the weekend. Me and Geto Boyz went trick or treatin.' Robbin' little kids for bags...

I said, "Look, look, Gerald, there go someone with a map on the dashboard."

He shook his head. "I'm going to funk this one for you Jean!"

We followed the Cadillac sedan. I looked back to see Crip driving a good distance behind us. We pulled up at a red light in the right turning lane. The Cadillac sat at our left. Gerald eased into the back seat where I already was, jumped out, and threw the spark plug, with his two hands following the spark plug's lure, right inside the car. The people just froze. His hands came out with a big Gucci bag. Our back door was already open. He jumped back in and we spun to the right on a different road. Crip pulled to the spot where we originally were at for the light to change. They watched and waited to see if the car we

just robbed would move. They didn't.

We were gone out of sight.

All the boys met back up at Syco's house, laughing. "I see the play," Pierre said. "You done spoiled me. We could do that on a bike. They stayed right there just looking stupid."

"Yeah, that's the book game," Gerald said.

Looking into the purse, we found twenty-five hundred dollars in crispy, fresh, hundred-dollar bills. I watched Gerald real close when he counted the money. He split the money six ways, even.

I said, "shit, let's get the car and go back out." He said, "nah, that car is hot."

Syco chipped in. "We can go put some tints on my dad's car."

Gerald moved his head from side to side. "We got another car, let's go."

Around 3 P.M. we were still driving around when, on a one- way, right by a project on our way home, we saw a rental car with 'Lease' on the bottom. Myself, Crip, and Syco were in Syco's dad's car.

"I got it," I said. I jumped out, hit through the window, showing off, snatched a pocketbook from inside the car, and walked back to the car.

"You crazy," Syco said, laughing.

Crip drove us away. The other three were chilling at Syco's house smoking when I walked in holding my first piece of loot. Inside the purse we saw three hundred and forty three dollars, and a bracelet that we later sold for six hundred dollars.

The next day we went to Foot Locker and went crazy in there, buying up expensive shoes. Ricardo wanted to go to Cross Colour's clothing store to get an outfit. We all got Cross Coloured down. I let Syco know that Pierre and I had to keep our stuff at his house.

"Oh, yeah!" Pierre said. "And I want to chill with all of you tomorrow, but I got to wear these outfits to school for the rest of the week. And Ricardo, come pick us up in that box Chevy homie."

"Cool."

Syco said, "I'm wearing nothing but some new black Dickie's.

We bought some of those Dickie's outfits too."

Ricardo let Syco hold his car. When he turned into the park- ing lot, everybody marveled with smiles looking at us. Pierre had told Crip to beep him every thirty minutes and I think Crip did it every ten minutes.

One girl got bold telling us she wanted a ride. Pierre told her we were going to his house. She had no problem with that. We took the girl to Syco's house, and she let all six of us fuck her. She was an animal. Pierre went for seconds and thirds.

The weekend came by and we chilled with Mom. She asked about when our report cards were going to come out. I told her it would be next month and that made her happy. Mom couldn't wait to see our report cards. Pierre and I didn't know how we were going to get out of that one.

That Sunday morning, we rode three hours away to Orlando. We were going to see a lady we called "Auntie Cheryl," who stayed a couple of miles away from us in Haiti. She sold cooked meat to factories back then and then she came to U.S.A. two years before us. She had two boys and girls who we truly didn't like back in the day. They didn't play soccer. They were in private school in Haiti and had gotten to the U.S.A. because of their grade point average in school. Mom, used to compare them to us, school wise, I hated that. They spoke French instead of Creole and loved to put on suits for no reason at all, sometimes. Taking the trip to Orlando in a rental car wasn't bad. We slept most of the way. When Pierre, who sat in front, tried to change the radio to a Hip-Hop station, Mom pinched him saying, "what is this? That's trash right there. Jean, you like this noise?"

"No Mom," I answered wisely. "What station is Marvin Gaye on?"

"Let me find it." She looked at me in the rear-view mirror. "I asked you to look over your brother. Have you been looking over him, right?"

"Yes, Mom."

We got to Auntie Cheryl's house with the brats outside to receive us. They stayed in a three-bedroom house. The dad came out asking Mom if everything was alright. He wanted to talk to us boys.

He told us stories about Dad, which was cool, but he wouldn't shut up. At times, he tried to speak French. I used to hear Dad say, "I don't like that dude."

The kids had a pool that was not built-in. We jumped in it roughly and broke it, playing too hard with the brats. They had all kinds of games to play with and already had four trophies from school. We were glad for them, but they didn't go through what we went through back in Haiti. They had their dad in politics in Haiti, which helped them a lot. Haiti is 95 percent politics, if not, a full 100 percent.

Mom said we were leaving and we were glad. Through the trip, she talked about how all of us would be in three years, financially and educationally.

We had school the next day, and Mom had to work, so when we got back home, we all went straight to sleep.

Pierre and I took the bus to school the next morning at Syco's bus stop. All three of us were dressed in black Dickies. Syco also had on a black glove. We had letters saying that we were in Orlando for eight days because of a family death. The little brats in Orlando had written a letter for us to bring to school, hooking one up for Syco too. I neatly put away my paperwork. Syco kept saying he didn't need it, but he put his letter in his pocket also.

When the bus pulled up, the driver asked us why we came to that bus stop and if our mom knew. I pulled out my paper just showing her the death catastrophe we had been through. "Yeah, I done heard it all," the driver waved. "Where's those

nice suits you used to wear?"

We walked onto the bus not paying her any attention. In school, showing every teacher the notes got us by. The whole time I was ready to leave and get with the rest of the boys. Not seeing them through the whole weekend, I was wondering what they were all up to.

After school, the bus dropped us off to Syco's house. Crip, Ricardo, and Gerald were posted up smoking weed.

The driver said, "I knew it wouldn't take long before you two started changing."

We looked at her saying nothing. Syco snapped, "bitch, why don't you shut your fat-ass mouth and just drive?! Old Bitch!"

I was pulling Syco to get him away.

The driver responded, "I'm going to write you up! Your mom is a bitch!"

While she was about to close the door, Syco threw a bullet at her. Ricardo them went to laughing. I looked at Syco mugging my face. The driver pulled off.

"Man, what do you get out of that dumb shit, yo!" I asked Syco. He looked back at me crazy.

Pierre said, "fuck that bitch. Sak-pase, homies!" Crip said, "let's go grabbing pocket bags."

"You can't go out everyday," Gerald said. "Why not?"

We went inside Syco's house playing some video games. Pierre, Gerald, and Ricardo went to grab books. All the rest just chilled, only getting up so I could call Mom at 7:30 at the pay phone.

Walking back from the pay phone, I entered Syco's house to see the others laughing, talking loudly and happily. They had grabbed three different pocket bags with three thousand five hundred dollars combined. We split it evenly. I shared my thought that we should save the money to get a truck. Every- one agreed.

The rest of the week, all we did was go grabbing books. On one occasion I rode a bike with Pierre on the handlebars to our projects. On our way back to Syco's house, a lost tourist was coming in the entrance trying to back out. Without hesitation, Pierre jumped off the bike and sparkplugged the passenger window with the little pieces we always kept for times like this. The driver tried to pull my hand and hold it. I put sixteen good teeth on his arm. He screamed and let me go. Pierre stuck the book in his pants and picked the bike up, riding it. I jumped on the handlebars.

We made it to Syco's and announced that we had caught one slipping. The big Fendi bag had sixty-seven hundred dollars in traveler's checks. We all went singing the Ice Cube song that was playing in the cassette player.

Once upon a time in the projects, yo. I damned near had to slap a hoe. I knocked on the door. Who is it? It's Ice Cube come to pay a little visit to you...

Crip, who was looking out the window, told us to stay inside, that the hood was hot. The rest of us turned to rappers celebrat- ing like we were corporate gangsters with the funny-looking traveler's checks in our hands.

Ricardo let us know we had three bitches coming over form the Pork-n-Bean projects in Liberty City. We heard those girls were always money hungry. The three of them Papaine, Lean- dra, and Janeka had a little name for messing with dudes who had money. They were the kind of girls to spread your name around town, either saying you real or you pussy. Being good boosters, they stayed with name-brand clothes on with fresh hairdo's, big bangle earrings, about six bracelets each.

Gerald looked at Leandra. "Can those booty shorts breathe?" "Yeah, don't worry about what's breathing in these shorts." "Alright, little mama."

Papaine, who took the lead to me, was black as coal. It was a pretty-black with three gold teeth in her mouth. She shook her hips side to side, going to sit on the dirty couch in the living room. They said they were sisters, but Janeka was not as black as the other two. Seeing Crip and Pierre come form the back into the living room, the girls asked how many Haitians were in the house.

Ricardo said, "ou pa bese coune tut by gue co sa."

Papaine said, "no, no we leaving," in a smiling way. "Even Ricardo speak that shit. Girl, where these Haitians come from?

Crip said, "Haiti."

Leandra asked us our names since they only knew Ricardo's. Pierre, who always changed his money in one-dollar bills, snapped on them. "What, you bitches think we some broke ass Haitians? We don't beg around here, plus, you hoes want to know too much. What you need?" His money came out of

80

all four pockets with hundred-dollar bills on top.

Gerald pulled out nothing but two big stacks of money.

Crip said, "bitch, we got green, hoe," throwing a chunk of money at them.

Papaine got up and chose Gerald. She looked at Pierre's dick and said, "I'm not fucking that dick there. That big pole not going inside me."

Ricardo went to barking out loud, "This what I'm talking about, roof, roof, roof, roof! We not begging, we paying, bitch- es. What, you thought my niggas was some pretty-ass niggas, Papaine?"

Leandra said, "Damn, all this bad English with cursing turn me on."

As I threw her the Fendi pocket bag. I said, "just make sure all the boys get some." I took her to Syco's dad's room and gave her the business.

Pierre had Janeka right where she sat at, on the couch, hitting her from the back while she sucked Crip up. I left Syco with Leandra and went looking for Papaine. Walking through the hallway, I saw Crip fucking Janeka from the back while Pierre got sucked up.

I slipped in the room with Gerald and Papaine. "Nigga, you still fucking?"

He said, "Nigga, put that dick in her mouth. I'll be here for a minute bro."

Syco, who only fucked one girl, Leandra said, "this nigga, Ricardo, trippin' man.

Pierre, with dick in Janeka's mouth said, "What happened nigga?"

He said, "that crazy motherfucker is fucking her in the ass crazy. That bitch in there yelling 'Papi,' like she like it too. I'm going to roll a joint and post up in the back. I done got off, I'm good."

I was good after Papaine's wet mouth. Pierre went to Lean- dra. "I heard you could take some dick. Your home-girl Janeka can't take it."

Leandra, butt-naked on the bed, opened her pussy. "This pussy stay wet, bring the dick in here."

Gerald came in. Pierre said, "Gerald, give me fifteen minutes bro. I got to work on this lion."

Gerald laughed, "hurry up!"

Ricardo and Crip were jumping Papaine while she begged for no more. Pierre slid in there and talked her into letting him fuck her last.

Syco rolled a joint for Janeka in the back as we posted there. Ricardo and Crip came back there. Waiting for the rest, I thought about what time it was, and me and Crip walked to the pay phone to call Mom. When we came back thirty minutes later, the bitches were gone.

Gerald said, "them bitches said all us Haitian niggas' dicks ruined. That Pierre had an extension when he was in the pussy."

Crip said, "that hoe Papaine said they never got turned out and fucked like that. When they left, they all said 'y'all Haitians the real ones. I'm going to tell bitches to stay away from you big-dick Haitians.' They love that money and the dick!"

We shared laughs about the process we just went through. Syco pulled out a stack of money asking how we were going to split it. We asked where he had gotten it from.

"That bitch Leandra's purse," he said, looking crazy with no smile. "We work too hard to give them hoes our money."

I asked to count the money. The girls had left with eight hundred dollars and two of our trophy purses.

Pierre said, "I can go for another round of bitches." We all laughed, rapping JT Money song out loud.

Life's a bitch so don't marry one. A nigga in love with a bitch is very dumb. I hate hoes, hoes hate me. I hate hoes…

CHAPTER SEVEN

The following Wednesday, we were all at Syco's house, except Pierre and Gerald, who left with a girl in her Honda Accord. We worried after six hours passed, and they hadn't returned. Ricardo's beeper kept beeping. The phone was off, so we walked with him to the phone booth so he could call his mom.

As soon as he got through on his call, his eyes grew wide. We sensed something was wrong. Ricardo got off the phone saying, "My mom just told me Pierre and Gerald locked up in the Juvenile Detention Center for grabbing pocket bags."

I said, "what?! Them stupid niggas must have got that bitch to take them grabbing books."

The four of us went to pacing right and left, round and round. Crip said, "you have to call your mom, 'cause it seems like Gerald's aunt already know what's up with him."

"She going to kill me," I groaned. "Literally, kill me for real on this one. Fuck walking round and round, pacing. Why couldn't it be me? She going to kill me. Syco, can I sleep at your house? I won't be home when she comes. Damn, she going to see we haven't been to school in a while. Oh, she going to kill us."

Syco had my back. "Come on bro, you know you can stay as long as you want to. My dad not trippin'. But you need to call her to get Pierre out. He's under 18 years old, so someone got to sign him out."

"Yeah, well I'm going to call." With reluctance, I picked up the pay phone and called Grandma Julia's house. I disguised my voice as much as I could. "Is Mrs. Adam available?"

"Yes, this is she," Mom answered. "Who is this?"

I said, "your son Pierre is in jail for strong-armed robbery and you need to sign him out."

"Who's this!" Mom was frantic. "Who's this! My baby!"

I hung the phone up and told the boys what Mom wept out. I had done enough, she was now on top of it. We went and got the little that Pierre and I had at the apartment and brought it to Syco's.

Pierre and Gerald had to do twenty-eight days before they went to court. We were still grabbing pocket bags and after saving a few thousand dollars, we got a Chevy Suburban truck. It was comfortable and big enough to sit eight people with ease. Going shopping every other week was mandatory. We got some new Jordans for Pierre and Gerald, for we thought they

would be released on the 28th day, which was tomorrow.

Next morning, around 11 A.M., Pierre knocked on the door. I hugged him real long, looking him over and asking what happened with Mom. He said, "they released me to go to some program for community service. As soon as Mom pulled up to our apartment, I jumped out and ran here, 'cause you already know.'

"I know bro."

Syco came out with a new pair of Jordans. Pierre got hyped. "Oh, damn! That shit look good. That's me?"

Syco handed the shoes to him.

"Thanks, Syco. And whose truck is that out there?"

"That's for all the boys. We saved to buy it. Now tell me what the fuck happened?"

We listened and shook our heads. I still couldn't believe they let themselves get caught slipping. Gerald came three hours later with Crip and Ricardo, and we gave him the same welcome. Over the next eight months, I had been to jail four times.

Pierre, five more times, Syco, one, Gerald, five, and Ricardo, three. Crip was the only one who had yet to be locked up. With so many of us going in and out of lockup for different things, we were getting raised by the state. The last time we went looking for tourists to rob, it was me, Pierre, Ricardo, and Syco. All of us were riding in Syco's hot Camry. A tourist had left the rental place with two ladies. We followed them to South Beach where they pulled into this gas station. Me and Syco jumped out. But it was a decoy. The police rushed us. It had to be at least twenty of them. They beat us real bad. I couldn't believe we got set up like that. One of the officers told us how a dude recently got forty years for grabbing pocket bags.

"They don't have to worry about me doing that again," I grum- bled once we were all put inside the bull pen.

Syco kept telling me we need to kill the rapper JT Money for telling the police on his CD's how to grab pocket bags and where all the best spots were.

"Syco, why? I'm not fucking with that shit again." Ricardo was on the same page. "Me either bro."

Pierre disagreed. "I'm with you, Syco. This pussy nigga getting all kinds of niggas sent away 'cause of his mouth."

Judge Peterson gave us yet another chance. When we walked outside, Mom took us to Burger King across the street. She told us we were moving with Grandma Julia, that she was moving everything that weekend. After we ate, Mom messed around and went to the car to get some papers that the school had given her about us, to chastise us. It was the perfect opportunity. My brother and I were out the other side of the door running fast. Pierre and I would send Aunt Marie some money at times.

She felt badly about our expressions of rebelliousness, but the two hundred dollars in American money was well-needed.

Our group wasn't grabbing pocket bags anymore, so all of our money was being spent up. We had gone to the dentist to get gold teeth. I dropped eight golds on the top. I was about to be 17 years old in one month. I kept a perfect fade haircut. My brown skin complexion with high cheekbones stayed fresh and clean. My leadership qualities earned me a lot of respect from my friends and the streets. I became the one whose input was sought the most.

Crip, who I was closer to, dropped six golds to the top. We called him babyface. He was able to cut alarm systems in a matter of seconds, could drive like a pro, and was constantly aware of our surroundings. He was someone I could think and plan with and not just say, fuck it, let's do it.

Gerald, AKA Gee pretty-boy gangster, had dropped eight gold teeth to the bottom with dreadlocks growing to his neck. If he pulled them straight down, the ten big doo-doo dreads bounced around high in the air when he walked. People could see he was a gangster by his outer appearance and the fact of him really being a G.

Pierre, who dropped thirty-two gold teeth, and Ricardo, who got ten, were the life of the party. People would not know that me and Pierre were brothers unless we told them. He was as black as the rapper Flavor-Flav with a big ego you would expect to find on Denzel Washington. Ricardo may as well have been Haitian to us. Even his mom would just be amazed to hear him speak fluent Creole. He had six gold teeth to the top and four to the bottom.

Syco, who had six gold teeth to the top and six to the bottom, was still a lunatic. People would look at him and know he was crazy. I loved Syco's ways of doing things we asked him to do. It was strange to think like that, but when we told him to go a certain way, he would, with no hesitation. But he might overdo things at times, and his mark of throwing a bullet at people he hated was well known.

We went everywhere together. Once I had a girl named Michelle that I liked, we went out to eat, to the movies, or anywhere else. She always complained about my boys being there. It was the same way the others went out with their girls. I remember chilling outside many times, waiting for Ricardo to go talk a girl into letting him fuck her. We would be outside with the A.C. on, smoking, and the boyz never let me put the window down. I had to accept second-hand contact because the dark tints had to stay up.

One day, I picked Michelle up and let the boyz know the bitch was pregnant. I wasn't for that. I went to take her to the abortion clinic. She came outside acting up. "I'm not getting in that truck anymore. All y'all act like you fucking each other or something."

Syco threw a bullet at her, hitting her in the stomach. I grilled him, "nigga, what the fuck wrong with you?!

"That bitch tried us. Plus, you going to have to have an abor- tion right now anyway."

I didn't like the way that went. I rushed in the back to fight. Syco and I threw punches at each other, not really leaving a mark, but getting things off our chest right then and there. Watching Michelle going up the sidewalk, I told Gerald, "let's go grab this bitch."

We got out, with Ricardo acting like he was behind us. Michelle stopped and gave up, saying she didn't want no prob- lems with my Haitian posse.

We started going to the clubs, Pak Jam and Carver Center. The Pak Jam was in Little Haiti, which was considered our backyard. The Carver Center Club was in Liberty City. We would go dressed in all black. Among strange crowds, we never usually got out of character. We did not slam-dance or pin young girls on the wall, slow dancing to Jodeci, Keith Sweat, The Isley Brothers, and many more artists. Most of those other crews doing things we only did in the house when we had some bitches over.

At the clubs, we stood in the same corner by the door every time. People saw us exactly the way we wanted them to, as 100 percent gangster. Plus we had a "hate Americans" chip on our shoulder at times because of their treatment of Haitians. We would see the Young 12th Avenue Boyz, Overtown Boyz, Pork-n-Bean Boyz, and Match Box Boyz. But they saw us too.

And as long as nobody crossed our line where we stood, we were cool.

The Pak Jam was the club where Luke Skywalker came through and turned them little hot bitches out sometimes. We would sit back and watch from a distance. Not wanting to move, we had to be choking to get a drink. Smoking weed is all that was going on among us.

At Syco's house, we complained about being dead broke the last month. At times, in order for them to smoke weed, they had to try and get twenty dollars from Ricardo's and Pierre's girls. Crip was the only one to pull out ten to twenty dollars most times. Occasionally, they asked Syco's dad for ten dollars. He freely gave the house up and kept complaining that we all had to pay some bills. I knew that was coming soon.

We knew we had to do something. Staying broke brought arguments amongst us. It was bullshit. The boyz slept at Syco's house. Me and Crip spent the whole night talking about differ- ent things we could do. I decided it was time for all of us to have a meeting right then and there.

The boyz came to the living room. Gerald dragged to get a quick bowl of cereal. Pierre started rolling a joint.

After everyone was sitting down, I stood up. "Look, shit rough fam. And we not going to do nothing stupid to go back to jail. I been thinking for us to get money, we got to be ready for war with anybody. That means we going to need some more guns. That 9-millimeter, 45-magnum, and Glock shit is not going to cut it no more. I seen a spot in Broward called 'Big Al's Gun,' it's on County Line Road. They got guns in there for armies. Me and Crip going to scope it out and do an all-day investigation at the gun shop."

Gerald said, "Hell yeah. And you know them ten young Haitians we met at jail who from Lincoln Field projects? We can take that shit over."

"Let's talk about that another time. Anyway, the shop, Crip said he went there with Syco's dad before. It has three people working in there and a buzzer. We don't got nothing but three guns, so let me know if y'all down. If one don't agree, then that's what it is."

Silence. No one responded. Ricardo finally spoke, "let's do it fam. We need some shit out here. We can rob banks and armored trucks with those guns."

Crip and I watched the gun shop for two whole days. It opened at 10 A.M. and closed at 6 P.M. A young man about thirty years old, always left at 2:30 in the afternoon. We followed him and noticed his consistent pattern of picking up two kids at a school and coming right back to the shop at 3:20 P.M. with the two kids.

There was a buzzer and two cameras outside. There were three people in there. Crip suspected, and all had guns inside easy to reach holsters.

On the third day of our investigation, Crip made it known that he had seen what kind of alarm system the gun shop had, and he could clip it from the light pole. "The camera is easy. I'm going to need a ladder. There's a second one that I think will relay twenty-five minutes after the first one."

"You think?" It wasn't exactly what I wanted to hear. "That's not good enough, Crip. Give me at least the amount of time the second relay will hit an automatic 911."

"Ten minutes."

"Well that's how much time we got. Let's go tell the boyz." The boyz were eager to hear what we were going to do. I was sure to make them understand that one mistake would mean we were fucked. We mapped out the time to do it. The highway was clear from 2:45 P.M. till 4:00, and there was a man who left at 2:30 everyday. This left only two people in the shop, both having 9MM handguns on their waist. I was sure one of them was probably in the head of the guns. One was about 47 years old, another about 42. We were unsure as to whether or not

there would be customers in the shop when we hit it.

There was a sign on the gun shop's door saying, "No bullets allowed inside."

I said, "Ricardo, you walk in there. Crip is going to have the cameras and two alarms cut on cue. Syco and Pierre and you, Ricardo, will have the guns. Me and Gerald got the bags and duct tape. I will grab the video tape out the VCR. Okay? Any questions?"

Silence.

I finished up. "Tomorrow at 2:00, me, Crip, and Gerald will be in one car, the rest of y'all take the other low-key car."

The next afternoon, we pulled off from the house at 2:00 P.M., heading to the gun shop. We got there around 2:25 and dropped Crip off at the light pole with a ladder. We watched one gun shop man leave at 2:30. Pierre drove around the corner to the gun shop parking lot at 2:35 waiting for

Crip's cue.

We waited.

Gerald and I stayed with Crip for the cue to drive around the corner. We waited.

Crip came down with the ladder. "Both the cameras and the panic buttons are cut."

Gerald blew the horn rapidly for Ricardo to go in the gun shop. Catching the signal, Ricardo entered the store. Crip put the ladder on top of the truck and got in the front seat. He drove to the gun shop parking lot. Ricardo saw the truck and headed to get buzzed out the store, walking past the only customer that was there. He had told the gun shop owners a tale about forgetting the clip to his gun in the car. He wanted to show them exactly what caliber of bullets he had inquired about.

The door buzzed open.

Syco, Pierre, Gerald, and myself rushed into the gun shop. "Don't make me shoot!" Ricardo yelled, with his 9-millim-

eter to one guy's head.

"Syco went all the way, pointing his gun at the other man, working his way to getting the gun inside the man's mouth.

I grabbed the customer. "Don't be no hero, heroes die."

The customer was perfectly still, too scared to move. Gerald started cleaning out the assault rifle racks. Pierre went for the handguns, breaking glass cases with his gun to get them. I duct- taped one of the store owners and threw a bag to Syco so he could go get rifles. Then I duct taped the second store owner.

"We got 30 seconds!" I announced, grabbing the video tape.

My watch beeped and we fled the store. Pierre was last to come out. The fifteen-minute drive was still and quiet.

"We good family," I said. We had made it to Syco's house, which was in a different county from the gun shop we hit.

There were three heavy army bags we had to drag into the house. Smiles finally crept onto our faces. Once the door was closed behind us, we celebrated.

Gerald said, "that shit was sweet. We could have slipped in and out the White House the way we handled that."

I grinned. "I don't know about the White House, but it was sooo sweet."

Pierre said, "Anything outside?" Crip looked out the window. "No."

We went to Syco's room and emptied the three bags onto his bed. There were five mini 14's, three AK-47's, three street-sweepers, two Caliber 15's, one calico, seven AR-15's with grenade launchers, nine .45 Magnums, eight 9MM's, ten

.357's, two Desert Eagles, seven Glocks, and four .38's.

We looked at the bed in quiet, picking handguns and favorite assault rifles. Looking at all this shit sent a shock through all of us.

Syco said, "we ready for war!" We screamed, "yeah! Yeah!"

Pierre picked the grenade launcher mimicking a Scarface scene. "Say hello to my little friend!"

I was ecstatic. "This Glock and .357 going to be my girlfriends." Crip said, "damn, this Desert Eagle is heavy."

Ricardo grabbed the AK-47 saying, "I'm old school and need target practice."

Gerald got the street-sweeper. "This shit right here don't make no sense."

I said, "look, take some to your house, Gerald. Crip and Ricardo, y'all do the same. And please get both of doze grenade launchers out this house with Syco in it."

Syco smiled. "Just leave me one." Ricardo said, "I think I can sell one."

That sounded good to me. "We need the money to get some more money, but nothing else gets sold."

"For nine minutes, we got a lot of shit," Crip said. "I thought someone would be an asshole and go in the register to take the cash."

Pierre said, "that little shit ain't nothin'. Let's get some money!!"

Still high from yesterday's perfect crime, Crip called us into the living room early the next day. "Come look! Come look at the news."

The news anchor, Rick Sanchez, reported that there was a robbery mid-day yesterday. Four black males went into Big Al's Gun Shop and robbed for five hundred thousand dollars worth of weapons that could be spared to the streets of Broward and Dade County. Sources had reported to Channel Seven News that the gun shop had ties with the Mob and could have staged the robbery to divert the true purpose of the gun shop. "The FBI, ATF, and local authorities confirm the gun shop is under investigation and has no more comments for the public. If anybody has information, call 305-555-TIPS. A twenty thou- sand-dollar reward is available for any arrests, and your name can remain anonymous."

Crip said, "we don't have no five hundred thousand-dollars' worth of guns here. What the fuck was he talking about? I don't understand nothing he said, but four people, it was really five." I nodded. "I think they robbed themselves also and it's crossed them up. But don't worry. Don't worry at all. Just

keep your mouth closed and die with what we did, alright?" "Yeah, Jean."

"We good."

"They got nothing then, right Jean?" "If you say we good then we good."

"Die not saying nothing at all."

"When can we start talking about some money?"

Being in the house through the week talking amongst each other is what we mostly did. Ricardo sold one of the AR-15 grenade launchers to his dad's friend. The money kept us afloat, but would last long.

We ordered four boxes of pizza, chicken wings, bread sticks and sodas to come to the house. Some of us were watching the Houston Rockets play the Orlando Magic in game four for the championship. We were going for

92

Houston Rockets because we always assumed Hakeem Olajuwon was Haitian for some reason.

We hadn't spoken about the robbery since watching the news earlier in the week. We remained confident in each other. The guns had put an extra chip on our shoulder. If anybody crossed us we would damage the person.

Pierre walked around with his old Superman shirt. He really felt like Superman with all the firearms that we had at arm's reach for any fuck-nigga.

I sat out by myself on the back porch, pulling grass from the ground and throwing it around. I was thinking about life, how to get some money, my new family inside the house, Mom, and different events that had happened. My seventeenth birthday was coming in the next week.

Gerald came outside. "What's up Jean? Why you looking like that? You didn't get a slice of pizza yet?"

"I'm coming in there bro, I been thinking about my family that I lost on the Freedom Boat. Life in the U.S.A. is noth- ing I thought it would be. The boyz is my family and I love you, Gee."

"I got love for you too, bro."

"The U.S.A. is full of racism. These people that run the government are 55, 60, and even 70 years old. Their people were part of the growth in slavery. Now they learned how to switch slavery from a physical aspect to a mental aspect. The blueprint is written throughout every neighborhood that has a Martin Luther King Street. Only the governors, mayors, and congressmen put out permits for McDonalds, flea markets, payless, car washes, liquor stores, and restaurants where I still can't understand how a chicken breast and leg gets so big."

Gerald laughed. "Yeah, you right." Crip walked out and joined us.

I continued. "The schools got thirty kids with one teacher. The illusion of watching sports gives hope, but there's not eight thousand blacks throughout the birth of football, basketball, and baseball. Not even eight thousand. And forty million blacks supposed to have hope."

Crip said, "that's true, and there's not even a thousand blacks worth over ten million dollars, so how can we help forty million blacks?"

"Me and Gee was talking on the aspect that mental slavery is even worse then physical slavery. I would rather they tell me, fuck me, to my face."

Gerald said, "shit, for all we know, when they see a chance to keep us bumping heads, they do a good job of keeping us that way. They always got some more guns to spread in the hood." "Exactly. The shit is a new form of genocide of our people. So it's kill or be killed, and that means it is what it is. That's the life handed down to us. We got to be careful and stay tight with each other. I got love for you, Crip, please know that bro. I see you no different than Pierre, plus you reminded me of, God

rest his soul, my brother Joe."

"Pierre always says that. And I got love for you too, brother. You a real Haitian to the core."

I said, "I think we prophets sometimes, to see how our Haitian people starting to step up and claim who they are to people. I heard Haitians calling themselves Haitian Posse. We stepping up after the first black country to overthrow Napoleon and the French back in 1804, Toussaint Louverture. So our soul and blood are just as tough as the other blacks, and they going to give us some type of respect around this motherfucker."

Gerald laughed, "let's get some money before you start the Black Panthers, Malcom X shit."

Crip said, "what's up? Let's talk about robbing a bank, taking over Lincoln field projects."

Gerald stood up. "I'm going to get some more chicken before Pierre eat it all."

Crip said, "oh, Hakeem Olajuwon and the Houston Rockets won the championship."

"That's what's up."

94

CHAPTER EIGHT

Syco, myself, and Crip went by Lincoln Field projects on 62nd Street which is Martin Luther King Drive. There was a gate on the main street and back of the projects. Lincoln Field projects consisted of about three hundred apartments.

About four different older crews ran around the projects. None really stood out. The Duke Boyz were led by Duke, who was known for having a lot of bodies under his belt. He was feared in Miami by many. His crew of fourteen sold crack and powder cocaine. They hung in the projects almost everyday. He allowed the other crews to sell weed. There were a crew of about ten Haitians, we met in jail that we used to boost their heads about being Haitian. We told them that nothing could stop them. They looked up to us. They were mostly 13 to 14 years old and talked about Duke like he was some type of king or something. All of them were in jail for running a truck into the back of the mall, trying to get away with a bunch of Tommy Hilfiger and Polo clothes.

Whenever a hurricane storm came through Miami, or a race- riot started, they would get two or three U-Haul trucks and run it in back of the mall.

The group of about ten Haitians sat there in amazement, smoking. The one who took most of the leadership was named Bam-Bam. He said, "we some real young Haitians, and them motherfuckers don't let us get no money around here. They heard about all of the Haitian Posse. They don't want no prob- lem with y'all Jean."

I gazed in the direction of a small crew of dudes. "That's them over there, right?"

"Yeah."

"Which one is Duke?"

"The one with the big gold cross on his neck, that's their leader I told you about."

"Leader, huh? We don't got no ladder among us, Bam-Bam, everyone is their own man. That's how we going to treat all you young niggas when we move in. They seen us coming to talk to y'all for the last three days."

Bam-Bam said, "yeah, probably, but I know they don't want none with y'all."

I said, "I'm going to be back tomorrow to holla at Duke."

The young crew marveled with smiles and made rejoicing comments.

"Se sa."

"Deme."

"No pa ka ton."

"A ke lae whapvene."

"Jean um cone ng say yo no per no mose e."

Going to the house, Syco started to tell everyone we needed a meeting. Most already knew that we were soon going to execute on some kind of money-maker.

Mean-mugging, Syco said, "so what up? What's really good?"

Crip said, "fuck that bank shit for now, we going to move in on Lincoln Field harder than Nino Brown in New Jack City."

Pierre said, "that's right! I want to move Nino out."

I took the floor. "Look, this how I think we should go at the situation. There's a nigga named Duke that all of us heard about. I'm going to go there tomorrow with them young niggas too."

Syco interrupted, "by yourself? Hell naw. Hell naw."

I said, "check it fam, hear me out. I'm going to give them an option first to let us eat on them young niggas' side, that we don't drop nothing but crack. We won't sell no powder on them young niggas' end. I'm going to walk over there with the youngsters to talk to Duke and all his boyz."

Pierre said, "I don't know Jean. That don't sound good." "I'm going to be strapped. Plus, the young niggas is going to be strapped."

Gerald was skeptical. "That don't mean them young niggas going to shoot!"

Ricardo was concerned also. "We got all this shit and you talking about going there by yourself my nigga?"

"Trust me fam, I need you to trust me on this."

Crip said, "how about we be in three cars with the AK-47's on the corner, and you don't go past that wall we saw. That way, if they jump wrong, shooting at you, we can follow-up and shoot back."

"What y'all say?"

"I want to jump out with my AK-47," Syco said.

"Look, we not going in like that, headfirst, so what's up? The way Crip say, is cool?"

Silence. Then Syco spoke again. "But if your body language even look a slight bit crazy and we don't like your facial expres- sion, I'm jumping out."

I said, "well we got a lick to execute tomorrow brothers."

The next day, I told Bam-Bam, all nine of them didn't need to go with me. I had five guns there, so I only wanted five dudes. He understood. "Jay, Sergo, Eric, and Steve, let's go."

We walked across a long field. The Duke Boyz could see us coming from a distance. They hung under the second floor between a stairway to their left, and the entrance to a thirty-step exit sign along their backs. On the first floor were about sixteen apartments. I observed them reaching around their waists, with Duke looking crazy at us. The young'uns walked two steps behind, avoiding the wall Crip suggested as we approached the Duke Boyz. I gave them view of us from their distance so they could see there were no guns in our hands. Duke stepped in front of his boyz. I stayed ten steps away from him. "Duke, can I talk to you man to man for a minute?"

He frowned. "What the fuck you want? Talk so everybody can here."

"I don't really want to make my ultimatums to you like that, my nigga."

"Ultimatums! I heard you Haitian Posse Boyz around town. You letting them stank-ass young Haitians, who probably came here on a camel, boost your head up."

His crew laughed behind him. They said for me and my "Dirty Haitian" posse to go fix a cat-burger with some coconut juice and go sit down somewhere.

In my head, I thought over how the streets had given our clique a nickname, and I thanked goodness Syco wasn't next to me to get me killed. "Duke, for real, the young niggas have just as much to serve in Lincoln Field as you do. They just want to sell crack and that's all. They not going to step on your money-maker which is the powder."

Duke looked as if he couldn't believe my nerve. "Look, if I even think anyone of them little Haitians got cat-crack rocks over there, I'm going to make them check back in school or check in a grave. Now get the fuck out my face, ugly-ass Haitians."

We turned to walk back to the young dudes' area. I heard some of Duke's boyz continuing to say disrespectful things about us, about Haitians period. When I took the guns from the young niggas, Bam-Bam voiced agitation. "I told you Jean, Duke don't play, I told you he won't let us sell over here. He be trippin'."

"I hear you but check this, tomorrow, they might blame all of you for some shit, so I want all you to be inside the bowling alley, where there's cameras at from 10 A.M. till 3 P.M., you hear me?

"Yeah, Jean."

"And look, I'm not the type to repeat myself. So if I ask you something, either say 'yeah' or 'no.'"

Jay said, "we going to be there for sure Jean. What the Haitian Posse about to do?"

"Haitian Posse, huh? Nothing. I'm thinking about this Hai- tian Posse name. But look, meet me at U.S.A. flea market at 7:30 P.M., the day after tomorrow."

"Alright," Jay said.

I jumped in the car with Pierre and Ricardo. "So what's up? Ricardo was curious.

"We got to kill Duke tomorrow, he trippin'."

"I knew it, the way his hand was pointing at all of y'all. And it looked like they were all laughing when you was talking."

"He took the whole thing for joke. But at least we gave him a chance to let us eat in peace."

Pierre was pissed. "We should just handle that buster right now, talking shit out there, man. He think it's a joke?"

I calmed him, "tomorrow, we going to slide right in their chest. I looked all them in the eyes and could tell they're not their own man. What Duke says is final. But there's one that wasn't laughing. I thought he was going to say something when he stood up, looking dead in my eyes, but he didn't. The way I see it, once Duke fall, the rest just going to go down like twenty dominoes. When they're standing one behind the other, the first will knock the rest."

We pulled up to the house and walked inside. "So what's up?

Gee asked immediately. "What's up with our dope hole?" "Duke got to go tomorrow."

"He didn't bite?"

"Nah, he didn't even give it a thought."

"I was watching him real good. He about twenty years old with dreads and that big cross around his neck with a bracelet on too. That's my man."

Syco said, "that's our man."

Crip commented. "What about them young niggas?" "They lack some heart, but if they hang around us, we will

help them bring their Haitian roots out of them. They been around these Americans and they been beating them with their mouths. I told them to go to the bowling alley tomorrow. Crip, go around there tomorrow and walk with an extra bad limp in your step. Make sure the dudes go to that bowling alley. Overall, them boyz was iced-up out there, getting money. Look like that spot makes a million dollars a year, or more. Soon it will be our spot to put down weed, base, and blow. But we got to think of a name to put on the weed."

"Ricardo said, "HP, for Haitian Posse."

Gerald agreed. "Yeah, that's it nigga. Haitian Posse. The Geto Boyz said, 'GB,' but it's HP."

None of us disagreed.

The next morning, we went Lincoln Field projects. Gerald led the ambush on the main street with a hand signal. All of us had masks on our faces. Duke and seven others were outside. Gee ran close to the open crowd catching them off guard and shot Duke right in the face. He fell. The others ran.

I said to the whole Haitian Posse, "look, there's only one way no one can snitch on each other, is for all of us to put bullets in this motherfucker!"

With no hesitation, Syco came and shot seven times, boof, boof, boof, boof, boof, boof, boof. I went over and emptied two from my Glock. Ricardo let loose four times with his 45 Magnum, standing over Duke's body. Boom, boom, boom, boom. Crip, from a distance, planted his good right leg and let the loud thundering Desert Eagle go four times. Bow, bow, bow, bow. Duke's right leg flew at least three feet in the air, the head was wide open. His gold chain stood on his chest with a bullet hole in it. Blood spread all over. Screams poured out through the projects. I thought Pierre didn't need to shoot because he was the only one with the assault rifle. But Gerald told him to let that bitch ring and Pierre went around the dead body in a circle, watching blood squirt on his mask as the big gun rang real quick and loud, tap, tap, tap, tap, tap. We ran around to the cars and left the projects yelling for nobody to come to Duke's aid. We knew he was halted anyway.

Both of the stolen cars we were in were taken to the Pork- n-Bean projects and dropped off there. Our truck had already been parked close by waiting for us. When we got to Gerald's apartment at Scott projects, we put all the guns up and grabbed handguns that were not used. Posting outside of Gee's crib, everyone focused on me.

Crip said, "what's next, Jean?"

I answered, "let's move in the projects next week. I'll talk to Bam-Bam them tomorrow to hear what happened. But we need some start-up money, somehow."

Ricardo looked at me. "Jean, holla at my dad, you know he's doing his thing, and he always talk about you in a good way to my mom. I know your word is good with him."

"I don't know about that, Ricky. Your dad is going to look at me different."

"Yeah, if you don't get his money back, but Dad will give you one chance. I done fucked up with him ten times already, but it's worth a try." "Well if you think so, I'll give it a try tomorrow."

"I know he will do it, watch, Jean."

I hoped he was right. "In fact, I'm going with you tonight to sleep over your house, that's cool?"

"Hell yeah."

I addressed the whole crew. "Nobody go to Syco's house.

Stay out of Little Haiti for tonight, Haitian Posse."

They all laughed, Syco said, "damn right, we Haitian Posse." At Ricardo's house, we went to chill in his room. When his mom came into the room. I kissed her on the cheek. "Hello,

Mrs. Malando."

"So, you the Jean my husband and son be talking about?" She said pleasantly. I been looking for someone to explain to me how this boy learned all this Haitian talk. He don't go to school, he don't give me no money, and he stay high as a kite."

I laughed, "I told him to stop smoking."

"Oh, you don't smoke? You a very polite boy. Don't let nobody hurt my son. I pray for him all through the day. I know he's not going to do right. He's like his dad, always into some shit."

Ricardo interrupted. "Mom, stop talking so much. We hungry."

She smiled. "Oh, good. Jean, you going to be here that long? I will cook."

Ricardo said, "Jean is spending the night."

Mrs. Malando had no problem with that. "Make yourself at home son." She then left.

Shaking my head, I said, "your mom is real cool. My mom could hear not one line of those comments without going crazy."

"Yeah, she cool."

We watched a video on MTV. A group called Cypress Hill was singing a popular song.

Here is something you can't understand, how I could just kill a man...

Later we sat at the table with his mom about to serve us. Ricardo and I spoke Creole to each other. His mom looked at us strangely. "I want to know what you two are talking about. Speak English. Why Jean don't speak Spanish?"

"Ricardo don't want to teach me Spanish." "Cause I'm Haitian, nigga."

The food was the spiciest food I ever ate. To be nice, I ate the mountain of rice, plantains, and chicken. It was around 11 P.M. Ricardo's dad hadn't been home yet, so we slept till around 4

A.M. Ricardo woke me up saying, "Dad just pulled up, Jean! Dad just pulled up."

"You didn't get no sleep?"

"Nah, I been looking out for Dad." "Damn, what time is it?"

"4:12 in the morning."

"Man, I'm not going to approach your dad at 4 A.M. to talk to him."

"Look, he's going to come in here and I'm going to say, 'Dad, Jean wants to talk to you.'"

"No, don't do it like that."

Mr. Malando walked in the room. Ricardo said, "Dad what's up? Jean is sleeping over, and he needs to talk to you."

I said, "Mr. Malando can talk tomorrow sir, I know it's late."

He waved a hand. "Let's go out back and talk, I feel like smoking before I eat my wife's spicy food."

A smile crept on my face. "Okay sir." I stopped by the bath- room to pee, then headed to the back-door stoop where only our four feet took up all the space. We stood close to each other while Mr. Malando rolled a joint in a white rolling paper called "1.5." He said, "what's going on, Jean? I talk to my wife about you all the time. I tell her that Ricardo is with a good soldier. I want you to know, I trust you with my boy."

His words put me at ease. I said, "he's my brother. I see him no different than my brother, Pierre."

"How is Pierre doing?" "He's okay."

"So, what's up? What you want talk about?"

"Well, Mr. Malando, I got a way to make some money, but I have no start-up money. The place where I'm going to do my thing at, will make instant money."

"How much you need?" "About twenty-five thousand."

"You know how to cook crack?"

"No. How you know that's what I'm about to do?"

"When we were in that INS facility and you chose doze two knives, I said to myself, 'now this a serious boy who has the mind of a man.'"

"Thank you, sir."

"Listen, I need to cook some crack cookies, so I'm going to teach you and Ricardo how to cook powder cocaine to crack. And I will give you a kilo, plus five thousand dollars. Is that okay?"

"Yes, sir."

Mr. Malando spent the whole morning teaching me and Ricardo to cook crack in forty-five minutes, at least three different ways. I told him, I'm going to use the "straight drop" method he'd taught us, which he smiled hearing.

After getting the money from Mr. Malando, Ricardo and I went to Gerald's apartment. He and Pierre told us what the young dudes had said, that the Pork-n-Beans boyz were the ones who killed Duke. That was the rumor in the projects, that Duke's boyz were not seen yet.

"Where's Syco?" I asked Gee. "At Crip's house."

Within five minutes, Crip was parking the car. He and Syco got out, greeting us all. I lifted my shirt in front of all of them, saying, "look, I got a kilo of fish-scale powder cocaine. And I got five grand. Ricky's dad looked out for us."

They jumped up celebrating.

Gerald said, "I know he could get it, but he didn't trust me with it after I done fucked up so many times. He trusts Jean, though."

I got right down to business. "Look, we got to go cook half of the coke and bag the rest."

We went inside the apartment and gave Gerald's aunt two hundred dollars to let us get it for the rest of the day. When we were done, we had cooked eighteen cookies, straight drop. They weighed twenty-eight grams each. The remaining coke was bagged up.

Syco and Crip went to the Jamaicans next door and bought two pounds of weed. They came back with the weed and we bagged that up too, till there was a mountain at least four feet high. All the packages were stamped "HP." The powder was stacked even higher than the weed with nickels, dimes, and quarters.

I address my boyz, "the weed will be for the young dudes. We'll start them off and let them take it from there. It's going to be a lot of tension in the air when people see us hanging around there through the months. But we going to treat the projects like family. People already screaming 'Haitian Posse,' so to be down, they going to come by to see what we made of. Some might even try to rob the spot. That's why we got to get some of the bitches in the projects to keep our ear to the streets. Don't get comfortable at all. Syco, you get two young dudes and make them gunmen, okay? The little nigga Sergo, he got an edge to him. Crip and Gerald, y'all keep the spot supplied at all times. Only keep twenty-five-hundred-dollars' worth of work at a time, rotating it constantly. Pierre, the young Haitian, Jay, make him and someone else be the lookout boys to stay posted on Front Street. They should already know to yell out every time they see a police car or anything funny coming in the projects. Me and Ricardo will cook and buy the kilos to keep it rolling throughout the spot. Tell little Bam-Bam they got to keep the weed rolling and buy it on their own. Gee will be the best person to oversee sales to the customers. No robbing any customers at all, or beating them up. That's a no-no! I'm already thinking this shit is a headache, so I want to bounce from this shit in nine months. For now, me and Ricardo going to look for a lawyer and a bondsman, because shit going to happen. Gerald, run the whole thing in three different shifts around the clock, every day. It's ten young dudes, and Ricardo will pay them every week."

Gerald said, "I like the nine-month plan. Then we can move somewhere else to another project."

I expounded. "Just selling drugs alone, I don't want to be doing, but if that's what we keep the fam eating, then that's what we do my nigga. Tomorrow, the same place where Duke and them used to hang at, put four young niggas there to start up. Question them about what police or detectives be coming to harass people over there in the projects. I know we all broke and got bills to pay, but we got to get Mr. Malando's money back ASAP. That's a Haitian Posse goal, you feel me?"

Everybody had equal understanding of our mission to get money. Crip said, "I want to get a Haitian flag, and put right in the middle of the field in the projects so they will know this our territory."

"Ha, ha, yeah, we got to do that," Ricardo grinned.

Pierre said, " I bet it's a lot of hoes in there, and they need to get ready for some of this Haitian dick. I'm going to be given them the business. And I mean BUSINESS."

CHAPTER NINE

January 14, 1990. On a Monday, we went to the eight-story project apartment complexes that made up Lincoln Field. They were shaped in a box form big enough to put a half of a foot- ball field in the middle. A brick wall was spray-painted to read, Haitian Posse Territory.

Bam-Bam and friends smiled seeing us jump out of the black Suburban truck heading towards the youngsters who stood in front of three different apartment doors, spread out with chairs and crates. Everyone stood up to greet us saying, "sak-pase, Haitian Posse."

I'm the only one who responded. "Nap-boule, little homies. Well, we going to start getting money as we planned. Seems like the Pork-n-Bean boyz made all our jobs easy. I got some guns we need to spread in some of your apartments. I also got six thousand dollars of crack, six thousand dollars of powder cocaine, and three pounds of weed for your clique. It's start-up money and all profits are yours, but you must keep the HP stamp on the bags."

Bam-Bam replied, "no problem, Jean, I say cool, but there's no need to just be standing here. We got some money to get family!"

I pointed. "Look, grab two chairs and some crates, Bam. Jay, you, Gerald, and Pierre walk to the other side of the field where Duke boyz used to post up at. Go chill over there. Get a radio so you can listen to some music while you post up, my niggas." Gerald and Pierre, both with dope stuffed in their pants,

headed to the other side of the projects with Bam and Jay. The rest of us stayed where we at, smoking and talking.

Five minutes later, the first customer went to Bam-Bam to get some dope. "Look at our first customer," Crip said, and we both laughed.

Mr. Malando had taught me well about cooking. He taught me the power of not stretching the dope, but straight dropping the cocaine into crack. In my mind, I knew that straight drop- ping was the path to riches, and I was determined to only use the way of cooking my crack for HP customers. I was thinking about the long-run money, and not the short-run.

Three hours later, people began to look over the railings to see what the new thing was that was going on in the projects. Some went to the laundry room to get a better view.

One thing I learned going to Carol City High School was that people don't judge character, all they judge is money. Schem- ing to get money out of the ones who have it is the ultimate goal of boys, girls, women, men, grandmas, grandpas in the hood. Times were bad. The way the Duke Boyz carried a chip on their shoulder in the projects, not looking out for anybody, was not what HP was about. In my natural understanding of being a good leader, I knew that the best way to succeed at doing anything illegal is to keep the loyalty of the people. And the best way to keep the loyalty of the people is to treat them good and look out for them.

The three-shift day consisted of nine to five, five to one, and one to nine. We watched mini lines in our first shift that ended with Bam and Jay coming back with three thousand dollars.

"The dope heads love this shit," Bam said, with excitement. "Oh yeah?" I said, collecting the money. "What else was going on over there?"

"There's a girl named Annie who stay in one of the apart- ments we stood in front of. She about twenty years old. Her and Pierre were going back and forth."

"What were they saying?"

"She wanted to know what all of us were doing sitting out in front of her shit. Pierre told her we were just posting there with our little homies. She wants to get money too, and the last nigga who promised her she would get paid wasn't doing nothing but giving dick to her. Annie good people, I know her. She got two aunts in the same building. I know both of them too, and Annie got some type of influence in her hallway. Pierre caught her checking out his gold teeth and put her at ease. He told her she'll get paid, that all she got to do is give us whatever she got to sell. He sweet-talked her, so she's down with us."

I was impressed. "Sounds like them boyz got that side on lock

107

already."

"She was all in Pierre's mouth like she was counting all thir- ty-two of his golds."

We all laughed. Crip and Eric went to pick up some Chinese food that was ordered. Little Bam-Bam pulled out three dice wanting to play some C-Low. It was a three-dice game based around points from one to six. One was a dick. Two was a shorty. Three was a bitch. Four was a Haitian. Five was a police. Six meant you head-cracked the motherfucker right in their pocket. It was an old famous game recognized in Florida and a few other states in America. There were other little tangibles to the game, but mostly you roll all three dice till two numbers match. The other number is your "point."

Little Bam opened the game with eleven dollars, and Ricardo got down and played with him.

Two youngsters came across because they were out of dope.

They gave me the money they had made already, which was three thousand dollars. There still were four hours left on the second shift. I didn't know it would all move so fast. One young- ster stopped to stuff a new six thousand-dollar worth of dope in his pants and walked back over to Pierre and Gerald. I watched it all with my mind racing, "Ricardo, I'm going to see Papi sooner than we thought. I want to get him out of here as soon as possible, and it might be this week."

Picking up the dice, Little Bam became nosey. "When we were locked up, I told you we were going to be more than a family." He rolled a three-three-six. "Head-crack!!"

I said, "you must be a psychic, 'cause you pulled them dice knowing you were going to get in Ricardo's pocket, keep your eyes on the prize Young Bam, keep your eyes on the prize."

Crip turned the corner with our food in his hands. I'm eating chicken and beef fried rice thinking of how sweet the crack game was. If crack were on the stock market, it would definitely be the number one commodity in the world. Quickly making 140 percent of your money back is unheard of, but there we were, doing it. Me and my homies were going to have a great year ahead of us.

Around 2 A.M., one hour into the third shift, we heard two girls yelling, "stop! Stop!! Get out my shit!! Get the fuck out!" We all watched the dispute coming out of an apartment right above where Pierre and Gerald stood. The fellas looked up towards the second floor, then turned their heads towards

our crowd.

Bam said, "I thought that was two dudes from Duke Boyz walking through the second floor hallway."

I said, "this is why we got to start the lookout from day one." Me and Ricardo went running up the stairs and down the left hallway. Making a right we came up on apartment number 222 where, without asking, we went through the opened doorway, both pulling out our guns. "What the fuck going on in this motherfucker?!"

One of the dudes in the apartment said, "look, we don't want no problem with Haitians. This is Trina and Biya, they our bitches. We not thinking about the spot, yo."

The bitches got frantic. "We not fucking with these faggot niggas no more!"

The other dudes slapped the girl Biya. I dug my Glock right in his forehead with five hits to the dome. Ricardo matched me with seven. The bitches yelled as they too hit the dudes. "Get your ass out of here! Go slap whoever shot Duke you pussy! Want to hit on some bitches but won't avenge your homeboy."

I looked out the door seeing Syco was coming our way. "Man what's going on?"

"Everything is cool. We going to escort these two niggas out the gate." I looked back at the two beat-up dudes telling them that when they got outside, if Syco even thought something stupid was on their minds, he would handle it like we just did.

They were too scared to resist. "No problem, Haitians. No problem at all. Fuck these bitches."

Trina kicked the nigga in the ass who had hit their friend. "You bitch-ass nigga. I see why your name is Hollywood."

We walked buddy and them out, telling them our ears were to the street. Ricardo and I planned to go back to the youngsters' corner, but first we were going to check on the bitches.

Ricardo said, "look Jean, you heard the tall dude calling homegirl Trina, don't even think about putting your eyes on her, that's me right there, bro."

"No pressure. Both them bitches fine, plus I think I was beat- ing Biya's man."

"Good, 'cause I got to have Trina, you see the ass on that red bitch?"

After coming up to the apartment number 222, we knocked on the door. The girls opened up.

"Is everything alright with you two?" I asked.

Trina said, "yeah, everything good. This motherfucker pulled out some of my hair and hit my girl, that's about all."

Ricardo looked Trina in her eyes. "I'm Bob and this my brother Burger."

Biya sucked her teeth. "Why you got to be telling lies already? I hate a nigga be lying. Your name is Haitian Ricardo and his name is Haitian Jean."

I said, "where the hell did you hear that from?"

"The streets talk, plus, we see all of you and your homeboys posted up in Pak Jam, not giving a bitch a chance. Y'all be look- ing crazy in the corner like there's a rope tied around all of you."

Ricardo changed the subject. "Damn Trina, you don't know how to approach a real nigga. Women holla at men too."

She looked at me. "Do it look like I need to holla at any dude?"

He said, "look at me, don't I deserve to be approached by a fine girl like you?"

"Yeah, come to my room. I got to find out why they calling a Chico, a Haitian."

"Baby it won't be no lies, and must you shake that red ass like that? Moi chere."

I glanced at Biya. "I guess this leaves me with what I been looking at from the time I stepped in this crib."

She said, "boy sit down. Let me get us some water, my throat dry." She left to go get two glasses of water. "Them dudes straight pussies. They man, Duke, died, and they know the Pork-n-Beans boys did it, but they not doing nothing about it. And I see the Haitian Posse notices a perfect time to move in the projects. Without Duke, them ducks will be broke. Them some bitch-ass niggas. But what' up with you? I heard you the leader of the Haitian Posse."

"Listen and listen real careful, Biya, "I got up to walk in the kitchen toward her, not extending my hands for the glass of water. "I never led a dude in my life to do something for my personal use. I got a family that I live with and brothers that I love like they came out my mom's pussy. Any crew, and street dude who got to follow a leader, not street dude to me. Plus, you see dude in the room with Trina? Two days ago, he punched me in my mouth for calling him a Chico."

Biya wasn't convinced. "Whatever. I'm going to make a sand- wich, you want some peanut butter and jelly?"

"Yeah, I was eating some good Chinese rice, till I heard you screaming like somebody was trying to rape you."

She said, "oh thanks, if I didn't say thank you already."

Feeling comfortable, I strolled into the little living room from the kitchen, looking out the blinds. "So, you don't got no dude?"

"No! And I never messed with a Haitian before. But I heard Haitians some good dudes and got big dicks."

"Damn, baby, that's all Haitian men are known for? What about our passion, devotion, and respect for women, Bee?

"That shit sound good, but I'm twenty-one years old and know hood is hood. It's just that there's real niggas who do and say real shit and don't have to lie a bitch either."

"Stop calling yourself a bitch girl." "I'm just saying."

Ricardo came out. "Bro, I'm going to chill in the room with Trina for a while. Call me if the boys need me."

"Alright fam. I think I'm going to take a two-hour nap right here. This girl done put something in this peanut butter and jelly sandwich."

Biya and I chilled in the living room watching Martin on

T.V. I dozed off for about five hours. Then I jumped, feeling my Glock on my waist. Lustfully, I looked between Biya's cleav- age with my ugly face. I knew Syco and Crip probably hadn't slept, keeping their eyes on apartment number 222. I knocked on Trina's room barking Ricardo's name. He said he would be out in two minutes. As we walked out the door, Biya told us to not be strangers.

Ricardo said, "nah, we all family around here baby, we could never start acting like some strangers." Coming down the stairs, Ricardo hit me on the shoulder. "Did you fuck already?"

"Nah, bro. I just got some rest."

"Yeah, me too. But that Trina smelled so good in the room, I was about to try her. I just didn't want her making all kinds of noise to wake you and Biya up."

"Whatever nigga."

As we walked up on the boyz, Crip said, "I got everything." "Okay," I answered. "I know all of y'all got to be sleepy." "Yeah."

Syco said, "I'm good, I found a nice spot on the roof to look out for the police with Little Sergo. I took a nap up there while he held the gun for an hour."

Crip gave me eleven thousand dollars for the night shift and let me know they had started the next shift. Ricardo and I went and switched places with Gerald and Pierre. Pierre was like, "this a million-dollar spot, man. They love that fish-scale dope, over and over."

I said, "yeah, Mr. Malando got that dope that make the friends run back."

Changing the subject, I told them about Biya an Trina. "Them bitches fine from head to toe."

Pierre said, "oh, by the way, stay away from Annie.

When I leave, that's my homie."

Okay, that's what's up bro. We all need to get a girl in the projects to keep our ear to the streets. And soon we got to use their spots for our personal use. We might have to give them a little here and there, just to keep afloat a good face around here."

Gerald and Pierre left to go get some sleep. No longer than forty-five minutes after Ricardo and I were at the main dope selling spot, Annie poked her head out the door. "Damn boy, I know you not no Haitian too?"

Ricardo answered, "Baby, Haitians come in different shapes and looks and that's what you looking at."

"How you know my name? Little Bam, you talking bad about me?"

Bam-Bam said, "why would I do that? You never showed me nothing but love."

Ricardo backed him up. "My little homie just like to keep his eye on the prize."

Annie blushed. "Damn I was hoping to tell Gold Mouth something."

"Pierre know you gave him a nickname yet?"

"No, and don't tell him I did, we got business to take care of between me and him, with that cute accent."

"Alright, alright, he will be back soon."

"That nigga didn't even say he was leaving, already doing shit fucked up." She closed her door.

I was glad me and Ricky stayed through the shift and spent most of the day talking to the dope-heads. At times when Little Bam gave me a cue, I gave them some extra dope. I asked them what their names were, how far they walked from, if the coke made their nose bleed when they sniffed it, and most of all, if the high was lasting long enough. One female said, "this my third trip in six hours. I bought eighty dollars worth every time. I couldn't even feel my face for two hours. Keep it coming and I won't spend money with nobody else."

I said, 'I'll be sure to tell the boss to keep it mixed the same way." I gave her thirty dollars' worth. She leaned close to try and kiss me. I avoided that. "A hug will do."

She hugged me briefly. "I like you boys. The last ones always talked bad to me when I spent my hard-earned money with them. I got lawyers and doctors that spend seven hundred dollars sometimes. I mean, I look crazy right now, but in high school I was the prom queen. All the big heroin dealers were wanting to marry me. You know Robert Hawkins or Bear? They used to be shooting at each other for this pussy. My tits flat right now and my ass is gone, but I'm not gone lie to you."

Bam tried to cut in, but I looked at him with an expression that read, shut up young dude.

The dope-head continued, "I'm the type to ride in Cadil- lac sedans with thousand-dollar shoes. When I hit Vegas in the winter, my mink coat is down to my ankles, costing about twenty-five thousand dollars. Anyway, I got to go. I can't stand here talking to you handsome boys with all this traffic coming in and out. Bye."

Ricardo started eating his chips and honey buns. "I thought she was going to tell us how she lost her teeth."

We laughed. Trina and Biya came down the stairs and the hallway with plates of food in their hands. Biya winked at me, handing me the plate she had. Trina gave Ricardo her plate. "We know both of you must be stank and hungry. And Ricardo, if you had some clothes at my house, I would have warm water running out the shower for you Chico."

I looked at Ricardo with eyebrows raised. I never heard him not go off from a girl calling him Chico.

He kept his focus on Trina. "Baby, I like how you approach a real nigga with hints boo."

She said, "don't get big-headed 'cause it's not what you think, we family remember?"

"You like jerk chicken?" Biya asked me.

"Yeah, bee, I love jerk chicken. Thus going to hit the spot right here."

Bee looked at the other boyz. "I didn't know them three were here, we would have made more."

"This enough to spilt with us five, thanks."

"Alright, see you two around. And go take a shower because you both smell like a bear." They waved. The two light-skinned girls walked away in their booty shorts. Biya had at least five tattoos.

I nodded in her direction. "She got to get my name on that."

Ricardo said, "where I get my name, nobody will see it but me."

"Watch yourself bro." Eating from the plate of food, I took four bites and passed it to Little Bam-Bam. "That's the nastiest food I ever ate. She never heard of seasoning. I need a Haitian girl that can cook like a five-star restaurant. I got to show her how to cook if I get some time."

Ricardo ate with quick bites. "Jean, this some Houston res- taurant. To me, it taste like lobster juice in this rice."

Five hours later, Gerald, Crip, and Pierre came walking toward us. We were bopping our heads to Scarface's song Mon- ey and The Power.

Money and the power. Money and the power. I'm not falling short 'cause I got money and the power

Crip turned the volume down looking seriously. "You see we got to up the shift package from six thousand to about ten. Me and Gerald been checking shit out and that's what we think." I said, "let's walk towards the field. I think that girl Annie be eves-dropping on our conversation outside her window. But yeah, I was thinking the same thing. You think ten thousand would be enough for one shift?"

"Well, we can put twenty-five hundred to the side, but it's got to be at reaching distance."

"Yeah, you right. I got to lock in that girl Biya's apart- ment. I don't want to put the youngsters close to reaching hands of the shift package."

"We going to get this rotation process going like a sewing machine, sooner than we think. I can't wait till the meeting to see the first week numbers."

"Crip, you know to take money out the package-money to write it on the books."

He grinned. "I just want to see the amazing numbers." Ricardo said. "I got to change clothes and take a shower,

plus I'm sleepy."

I said, "I'm good, but check on Syco to see if he going to take the car."

Ricardo walked off, telling us to call him if we needed anything.

The plate of jerk goat that Crip brought had hit the spot in my stomach. I walked to the candy lady's house to grab a couple of sodas. When I got back, Annie's head was poked out the door. Her aunts were coming out the next door. They had some clothes they wanted to sell. Though they stayed on opposite sides of Annie's apartment, they both emerged exactly at the same time with the bags of clothes as if they had been on the phone talking about coming out to sell them to us. We looked closer at them, seeing they were identical twins. Goodness,

Lincoln Field projects got some bitches, I was thinking.

Pierre took charge. "Baby bring them bags over."

We don't do much talking, we let the stacks of money that he held in his hands do the talking for us.

Annie went off, "watch your eyes and mouth, Gold Mouth."

Gee smirked sarcastically. "I'm glad that I'm a free-man up in this project. Bring the bags over here twins."

The twins smiled bringing the bags over.

"Hold up," Gee said. "Before I open up any one of these five bags, what's yournames?"

One spoke up, "I'm Lily and she's Biggie." "How I'm supposed to know the difference?" Lily said, "that's none of your business."

"But what if I want to holla at you, I can find a differ- ence then?"

Annie and all of us watched them two go back and forth with slick comments that had all of us laughing.

Lily changed the subject. "I got bills boy. I'm trying to sell some of these clothes in these bags."

"Baby check this out, I want all these clothes. Just tell me there's no Michael Jackson jacket in one of these bags."

"There's nothing but Polo clothes in these bags boy. A bitch don't fuck with that cheap shit nigga."

I whispered for Crip to move in on Biggie. He said, "I got it fam, I got it."

Gerald was still going through it with Lily. "How much you want for everything?"

"You sure. 'Cause this not no Swap Shop where we going to go back and forth."

Crip pulled out a stack of money, while everyone turned looking at him, pealing twenty-five hundred dollars, passing it to Biggie. "That's twenty-five hundred. That's cool?"

Lily took the money out of Biggies hand. "Yep! That's good, and there's no refunds around here."

Biggie said, "I got four hats inside my apartment, I'm going to throw it in with that, alright?"

Crip said, "Okay, want to go get them now?"

"If you want to, but you don't have to follow me." "I want to follow you, though."

"Come on then."

Pierre finally intervened. "Lily, what kind of Haitians you thought we was girl?"

Annie said, "I need to talk to you, Gold Mouth, 'cause I see you need to be checked about getting in people's business."

Pierre walked into Annie's apartment saying, "I'm about to get checked, Jean, you believe this?" He closed the apart- ment door.

Gerald said, "I like these black Polo gloves. My man Syco going to love these, but what am I supposed to do with these Polo-looking panties?"

Lily answered, 'I think I got some bigger sizes in my apartment."

"Well, can I come in there?"

"Yeah, I don't do kids, so there's no problem boy." "My name is Gerald, Ms. Lily."

I sat in a chair chilling and overlooking Syco, who had a clear birds-eye view of us. I wondered how much longer one of the boys would take to come out of the apartments behind me. When Crip came out four hours later, I said, "damn, I thought something happened to you."

"Nah, I was just vibing with Biggie in there. She cool people." "Everybody forgot I been out here almost three days straight.

Let me get some clothes out that bag. I'm going upstairs to Biya's crib and see if I can shower over there." I pulled out an outfit and headed straight up to Biya's apartment.

She opened the door saying, "I hope you want to take a shower 'cause you smell."

"Yeah, I smell like money. Let me take a shower Bee. I just got some clothes from Lily and Biggie, so I thought you would let me slide in the shower."

"Oh, you met Lily and Biggie? Them some boasting bitches there, but they cool people. We been around each other since we been eleven years old in these projects. Let me go run the water and get you a towel and wash cloth."

The water felt good. I showered shortly and got out, putting on some ladies' Speed Stick, and the new Polo outfit.

Biya said, "put that black Dickies in this bag." "You can throw it away."

"I'll wash it in case you need it instead."

We sat down in front of the T.V. in the living room while the Oprah Winfrey Show was on. We talked for a few hours. I thought Biya's info on the projects was even more calculated than Bam-Bam's outlook, especially on the events with the police. "A jump-out team of police officers named Kitchen and Polite, who lead a downright dirty team would stick us up, set us up, and give us a case."

I asked about the people in the projects, and it was what I thought. Money-hungry Biya told me about her daugh- ter who came from time to time to spend the weekends and holidays, but she stayed with her grandma in Homestead. I told her I stayed with my mom and my dad passed away, but I didn't want to talk about it. When I mentioned that I was born in Port- au-Prince, Haiti, she said my accent gave that away. I tried her by asking if I could leave my gun in her room.

"No problem," she said without a blink. "But come get it if my little girl comes over."

I took a nap and woke up about five hours later to see Biya walking around with a folder in her hand with papers in it. "I tried to tell you to get in my bed, 'cause you going to get a crick in your neck if you keep sleeping, sitting up like that. I cooked some spaghetti for me and Trina but there's enough for you. You want some?"

"Yeah." I looked at the time on my beeper. Going to the bath- room, I gargled some water in my mouth and spit it into the toilet before going to the kitchen.

Biya put a nice hot plate of spaghetti in front of me. I twisted some around my fork and chewed, mumbling in disgust. There was no way I could fake it, that shit was nasty. I looked at my beeper locking eyes with Biya. "I got to go, Bee!"

"Take the plate with you, just bring it back."

"Cool." When I got outside, I gave Little Jay the plate. "Make sure you bring this back to Biya."

Crip said," Jean, we made eight thousand five hundred dol- lars in the first shift and eight thousand seven hundred fifty dollars in the second."

"Wow! We got to have a meeting at Syco's house with all of us for at least an hour every Friday. That way we can break this money down in order."

"I'm going to tell everybody. Your brother came out for two hours and went back in the house with Annie."

"I hope he getting some valuable info out of her instead of talking shit all day. I got some valuable info out of Biya."

CHAPTER TEN

January 18, 1990. Five A.M. Everybody was at Syco's house, leaving Little Bam-Bam in charge of the youngsters for an hour. We talked about different events in the projects and all the progress we needed to get done to move safely in a bigger aspect. I said, "look brothers, we done made one hundred sixteen thousand dollars in our first five days. That's good. This is what we work for. We got a lot of expenses to take care of. First, before we split money between the six of us, Mr. Malando got to get thirty thousand dollars. We each will put five grand on top of that to get two kilos at fifteen thousand dollars each. Me and Crip went to this law firm. They said we got to leave a retainer fee of forty thousand dollars to be able to have and to even look at any case we bring to them. And the forty thousand dollars don't go towards the cases we bring them. Any questions before I keep going?"

Gerald barked, "there's more?!"

"Yeah, we got to leave twenty-five thousand dollars with the bondsman, Pat, to put whatever to the side and bond out whoever we want first on his personal calendar. That money goes to the bond until we reach five thousand dollars. We have to re-up the holding fee for special service bonds."

Pierre said, "that's a negative nine thousand we got exactly, plus what we done took off the books which was a petty sev- enty-five hundred dollars."

Gerald said, "man, Jean, you keep bad news. I'm starting to not want to hear you talk, 'cause you keep bad news. I got all kinds of things to do, but you right about everything. We got to do these things. I can't wait to see what you come up with next week."

I said, "next week will be here quicker than we think bro. I only know one thing we should do together, but that's next week's talk."

Pierre screamed, "fuck!!! Fuck!! Man I got shit to do, and lawyers getting forty thousand dollars without a case. We working for them."

"Yeah, yeah whatever yo!!"

"Look, before we go back, let's go have dinner at this nice Haitian restaurant called Ce Ce Bon."

Ricardo joked, "can we afford it?" Everyone grinned at that.

When we got to Ce Ce Bon, the owner saw how we ordered ten plates to eat and ten plates to go. He personally served us with a lot of kindness. We had conch salad, stewed chicken, steaks, fried chicken, fried pork, fried goat, mac-n-cheese, white rice, brown rice, freshly squeezed lemonade, and the best hot sauce in America called "Pekles." We laughed the meeting's sorrow away. The restaurant owner had to be wondering why Syco grabbed his food and went outside to eat it.

Gerald said, "soon as I get back to the projects, I'm going to try to have sex with Lily."

Pierre said, "you didn't hit yet?"

"Nah man, I really didn't try to hit her, I thought her period was on." He got some plantains with pekles on it. "She kept on some tight pants in the apartment."

The rest of us all admitted we didn't get no pussy from the girls either. Ricardo said, "that Trina got to be bow-legged. She walk around the apartment like a spider."

Gee said, "I already see I'm going to have to slap Lily two times a month about her mouth. But she see that Haitian gang- ster vibe and can't take her hands off me, cooking twice for me already. Plus, she going to be mad when she find out I ate already."

Crip said, "we should order some food for them too?"

I agreed. "You right on that." I told the owner, whose name was Ken, to give us eight more plates of a little of everything.

"No problem, Jean."

We finished eating and walked out the door.

Ken said, "make sure you come back, and Jean, here goes my cell number if you need me."

"Thanks Ken."

Getting in Ricardo's Chevy Caprice, we all went to Cesar's Barber Shop to get touched up by our favorite barber, Cesar.

Well into our second week, Crip and I spent a lot of time together catching up on some politics. The radio host, Rush Limbaugh, that we loved to listen to, was mostly the topic. In our eyes, he was the only one that told the truth about the mental slavery of the minorities in America. He was a big- ot, no doubt, but he never lied about how he felt, no matter how controversial it was. His right-wing Republican ideology helped to lobby the stop of food stamps, health care, funds for public schools, and his great win under Ronald Reagan to make federal prisoners do 85 percent of their sentences, gave him his first bragging rights in 1988.

We learned some things from Roy Black & William Barzee when we put down the promise retainer of forty thousand dollars cash. Their hopes to never meet our brothers was genu- inely expressed, as was our desire to never need the firm. Mr. Barzee passed me both his and Roy's phone numbers to their cells and homes and told us the things to look out for, that tele- phones in our business was worse than a woman with a disease. Most diseases can be cured, nine out of ten, but a wiretap don't lie, ten out of ten times. I would keep that in mind around my "construction company." The lawyers wanted us to come watch them represent a case in court. Shaking their hands to leave, I let them know we would think about it.

The normal had went on, with us sharing rotation, basi- cally never leaving the projects. The shifts made nine thousand dollars to eleven thousand five hundred dollars, which were great in our eyes as bills stayed out the way.

Chilling with the girls in the projects, meeting with Malando to get weed from him also made the week speed through like a sewing machine. It was Friday, around 4 A.M., and we were having a meeting between the six of us. Gerald jokingly said, "hold on Jean, I got to sit down to listen to this bro."

Let me pop a Tylenol first," Pierre added.

I said, "look, everything is good, fam. We made one hundred ninety thousand dollars. Taking out pay for two weeks for all the youngsters came up to thirty thousand dollars for all of them. And I think we need to help the tension in the projects some, so thirty-five thousand dollars go to one hundred fifty mailboxes there. And in two weeks, we'll put that same amount in the other one hundred fifty mailboxes. It will keep us out there without too much hate from people. We all got twen- ty-five thousand each to ourselves fam. Any questions?"

There were none.

Crip pulled the money out giving Syco his first, then around the table to himself being last. Everyone was happy. It was decided that we would go to Ce Ce Bon to get something to eat and celebrate. I stopped Pierre to the side and told him I was sending Mom three thousand dollars and sending some money to Aunt Marie too, one thousand five hundred dollars. He gave me three thousand dollars to chip in.

Syco wanted to talk to me on the side. He told me that he knew all the money he got was his but he wanted me to hold it for him. He wanted to get a Chevy like everyone else, so he was going to take five thousand dollars out but I was supposed to hold the rest.

"Syco, you sure? Your dad could flip some of this." "I got him on the next one."

"Alright bro, but if you need it, I will have it in reaching area bro."

"Cool."

We had unexpected guests in the projects. Syco and Little Sergo had three watch-outs on top of the building on point when Kitchen and Polite came running into the projects with an army of police. Those who were in the dope-hole heard Syco blow the whistle he and Little Sergo had. Through the open window of Annie's apartment went the dope package and money. The police beat Gerald, Pierre and whoever else they caught, asking why they were not signed up in school, that we would soon be locked up in prison doing ten years or better. The harassment kept coming.

I was sleeping in the room at Biya's house. She woke me up once. "Baby, baby, the police are back in the projects!"

I got up and looked out the window to see Pierre and Ricardo handcuffed going to jail. I immediately called the bondsman. He told me he was on it, that he would call me back. When Pat called me back, he asked me if Pierre was sixteen years old. I confirmed Pierre's age asking what that meant, only to be told that someone over twenty-one had to sign both Pierre and Ricardo out.

I said, 'look, I don't want my mom to sign Pierre out. Don't worry about Ricardo, his mom will come and get him. Mat- ter of fact, a girl named Annie will be calling you, she's 21 years old."

Annie was fierce when the police came to knock on her door. She pulled out her phone saying that if they came in there without a search warrant, she was calling 911 on them, that she didn't know what was going on outside her home. All of us had our pictures taken by Polite and Kitchen's boys. I came out of Biya's apartment once I was about to get in the car. Kitchen pulled up and arrested me, putting me in a group-home pro- gram, even though I was about sixteen and too old for it. He thought I was supposed to be living there. I stayed maybe two hours till I knew the police were gone and got picked up by my homies. We went back to the projects.

After that, Biya would always run out telling the police that we lived together and that I was seventeen years old and she was allowed to have a boyfriend my age. But the police did what they wanted to do.

Polite caught Crip and swiped him right in the bad leg. He was in the hospital for three days. We called the law firm to file a case against the city of Miami police department. Some- thing about the rich law firm changed things. Calling them was something we should have thought of months ago. The harassment slowed down. Crip told me that Kitchen caught him and Gerald walking to the store and pulled up telling them not to run. He told them that we young dudes were some smart dudes, and he was going to have to up his game with the Haitian Posse. "I like your law firm you put on the case Crip, but it won't work. All you did was buy some time."

Gerald pulled his phone out quickly, "I'm about to call my lawyer. I'm sixteen years old and don't have to go to school or listen to you talk, so get out my face bitch-ass cracker!"

They said Kitchen pushed Gee like a little boy and put his hand on his gun. Syco told me he saw everything, and he was about to let the gun loose on Kitchen if he would have shot Gerald. I told everyone not to let the cops press them into doing something stupid. The lawyer told me to tell everybody to just call them when one of us got into a problem.

At least three young dudes had gotten caught with drugs on them. Some went to jail for twenty-eight days, some for two months, which their moms handled their situations. We gave their moms their pay to keep their mouths closed.

Payday flew by. We went to pick up all our cars at once. The best car-painter in Miami was a dude named "Perfect." We asked him to lock down his paint shop for six old-school Chevy's. He told us it would be expensive, which made us laugh in his face, wanting to just hear the price for all six cars being done immedi- ately. Perfect played with his calculator for three minutes and got up to walk to his supply room and call one of his workers, asking him if he could work overtime for the next month. We shook our heads watching his work at pricing the paint job work. There were rims on all the cars already and at least five thousand dol- lars or more worth of music in each car. When he came back in the office, he went to punching more numbers on his calculator.

We waited.

Perfect turned his calculator towards us without saying the number. It read 61,742.75. Gerald and Pierre dropped twenty thousand dollars each on his desk in all twenty-dollar bills. Gee said, "we out. We will be back in a month."

Perfect watched all six of our backs walk away. We knew he must have thought we were some serious young dudes, and he had to impress us with his work so all the dudes in Miami can come to him.

When we got back to him in a month. Perfect said, "I think I underpriced you guys for all the work it took to finish all of the cars. My men worked around the clock and I forgot to charge a security fee. That would be another four thousand five hundred dollars."

I said, "no problem," knowing he wasn't getting a dime.

Ricardo whispered to me, "He was speaking some funny shit in Spanish, like, 'I can get more money out these black dudes.'" Gerald said, "mmm, mmm, mmm, looking at his '73 four-

door Chevy Impala. It was cherry-cola black with five coats of thick paint that changed chameleon colors in the sun to bright dark-pinkish. The eight speakers could start a party on any block. The car had all gold Dayton rims on it. "Perfect."

Pierre marveled, "I'm going to name this my African Queen." The '73 convertible Impala was all-black with gold trimming around the emblems and gold. "You can match my mouth marvelously."

Crip said, "how many colors in this paint? It goes from maroon to purple, or just plain rainbow." His four-door Impala went well with the all-gold insides, rims with silver on the outside, and front grill.

I looked at my convertible '73 Impala. "I need a drink." The root beer paint job on the car with it's brown rag-top showed greatness, with the gold silver rims. "I got to patent this color right here."

Syco got in the car yelling at Perfect, "I hope everything still working like I left it." He jumped in the yellowish-gold painted car with all-gold Daytons, hitting switches to three- wheel motion. "Okay, everything looks good from up here in the air."

Ricardo said, "this one right here got to be the car that carry a Haitian flag five feet wide." His 1970 Impala was royal blue with gold rims.

Pierre said, "It's calling for the Haitian flag to wave in front of the pile, Ricky. The royal blue look like the water in South Beach."

Gerald jumped up and down, "we about to kill it tomor- row, driving through the Martin Luther King Parade on 62nd Street."

Crip added, "if there's a hood in Miami, we going to ride by there tomorrow letting every nigga see how it's supposed to be done in the hood."

The Annual Martin Luther King Parade was the biggest hood day in Miami Dade County. It was our hood Super Bowl gath- ering where everybody who thought they were somebody, and 95 percent of Miami thought they had a name, had to be dressed to impress. It didn't matter if you had to get there by bus, train, four-wheeler, dirt bike, pedal bike, you had to get to the parade. Around five in the evening, D.J. Uncle Al got the music going on 15th Avenue, which was our version of Crenshaw in L.A., but more rough. Fifteenth Avenue went from 62nd Street. To 71st Street adding all the terrace roads.

It was sixteen blocks with crews on each side. There were at least twenty crews with only three of them having some notoriety. The Haitian Posse cared less about that.

Our cars got washed early in the morning, ready to ride through Miami. Lincoln Field project's dope-hole was closed for the parade. Too many people walked in an out of there. Ricardo led with the flag flapping high in his convertible. Our youngsters spread two each in every Chevy car. The AK-47 I had was laying between the seats. As it laid there, I mean-mugged with a head-bop that said, try something nigga.

Pierre looked real crazy with the AR-15 in his car. We begged for war.

We rode down 183rd Street going up 27th Avenue turning down 151st Street and making a right down 22nd Avenue, then a left down Ali Ba-Ba Street where we stopped in the "Tank." That's where we jumped out to get some Backwood cigars.

Coming back out of 22nd Avenue, we cruised through West- view projects through the blocks of Robin Hood. Bitches started following the six Chevys blowing their horns at us, but we stopped for no one.

128

Shit was serious

Darkside and Lakeside hoods must have thought there were two parades the way twenty cars followed Haitian niggas. Rid- ing down 79th Street, we saw the flea market was jam-packed with people pointing at us. I could read one girl's mouth saying, "I want one of them Haitians."

Gerald, in the second car in our line of six, threw some money in the air. Bitches and dudes went crazy. We rolled down 32nd and made a left on 46th Street. Brown Subs had at least forty blocks to ride down and we didn't miss one, even going into the one-way in one-way out Manolia projects. Dudes recognized real was real. In their eyes, we Haitians had came a long way.

THAT.

Passing through, I put a peace sign in the air to my homeboy Dewey Hound I knew from juvenile jail. He, and his twelve homeboys threw a peace sign back. Coming out and passing Jackson High School, we turned left down 46th Street to 7th Avenue making a right. We sped up the short highway letting the pipes holla.

Slowing down to make a left on 20th Street, we entered Overtown 12th Street, 11th Street, 10th Street, and 9th Street, all had to feel Crip's Chevy, which was the only one with all the limo-tinted windows up.

Passing through Wynwood, the Chico's embraced us. They jumped in the air with excitement as Ricardo stopped to talk to two of them, Mick and Fu-man. They shout out to my car. "I see y'all boyz Jean."

The Little Haiti affect was definitely a parade atmosphere. Stopping in the middle of 54th Street and North Miami, we got out of our cars yelling, "yeah, the pain is over."

Gerald turned on a Haitian song by Sweet Mickey, pulling the pole with the flag off Ricky's car, dancing in the streets with it. That gave us personal affection to get out of the character with our people. They smiled as if a million dollars was handed to them. I personally never hugged so many people in my life. Forty-five minutes later, after getting drunk off the Haitian whiskey a man gave us, we kept slow-riding through Liberty City down 62nd Street passing "The Wall." We drove past the Ward family, who threw peace signs up to us. John Doe Block blew smoke in the air looking at us. We shot down 18th Avenue's long strip. Big Herb, while bumping cocaine, waved us down to say, "Gee, Jean, you young Haitians go hard. These niggas

don't want no problem with the Haitian Posse.

Gee's system was banging Scarface's "Gangsters Make the World Go 'Round."

While coming up on 15th Avenue we made a right looking at a crowd of thousands of people. Ricardo turned, leading with the flag. Gee turned right, bumping the music. Little Bam-Bam was next to me in my convertible, mugging everyone with black jogging hoodies, covering our heads under the all-black Dickies set. Pierre's mouth made the bitches say, "damn!"

Syco hit a right on 15th Avenue being last in the lineup, hitting a three-wheel motion that came to a stop as we all blew our horns like a bunch of crazy Haitians. Syco moved up some, then dropped the car on all fours, making a loud noise.

Shit was real.

We parked to the right, in the front of the Pork-N-Beans projects, back to back. Then we got out twenty deep to stand along the six Chevy's. We saw girls pass us. Most of them waved. When nobody waved back at them, one of them stopped. "Who's Jean?"

Nobody answered.

"Well whoever is Jean, tell him he must be scared of this pussy I'm trying to put on him."

We looked, smiling and shaking our heads. I started to wonder why nobody walked down the sidewalk where we were at. Everyone went on the streets to walk, at times stopping to take pictures of the cars. Some went under Syco's car taking pictures of the way he left it in the air. I draped my arm around Syco's neck. "Syco, you belong in that Chevy, homie."

He smiled. Syco didn't really ever smile, so it was cool to see.

Gerald said, "now talk that Black Panther shit. We done put on for our people. I'm ready to die after what we just did."

I said, "not yet bro! It just started! It just started fam!"

About two hours passed. We were chilling, smoking and drinking, when a crew we didn't pay any attention to started making noise. Some dudes came out. They were the 61st Street Boyz. Their leader, Flune, grabbed an American flag and started to hold it up in the air. I put my hands in the air. "Let's go!" In my head, I couldn't understand why they wasted their chance to really start representing by raising an American flag. If they would have gotten an African flag, we would have had to say, "that's what's up." Real is real.

Our pipes hollered, coming out of 15th Avenue and turning right on 66th Street. I said, "let's go by some clubs."

The National Guard Army Club was packed out there, so we rode by Pak Jam Club. Officer Kitchen stood in front of the club looking at us. He shouted out loud, "everyone, there goes the Haitian Posse! You want to be seen, huh? You boys left a lot of bullets in that boy Duke."

All we heard was the tires screaming as we peeled out of

N.E. 2nd Avenue.

Kitchen had fucked the rest of the night up. We parked out- side Lincoln Field projects and chilled in Biya'a and Trina's apartment playing some Wu Tang. "Cash Rules Everything Around Me."

Gerald walked to check on Lily and came back. We talked about all the girls that were out there around the parade with their spandex pants on. We laughed through the whole night about the historical day that Dade County would talk about forever.

The police continued to jump out on us, but they mainly took our pictures and let us go. Crip expressed to us all the time that the spot was getting hot with all the police dressed in street clothes. The money still came at a great rate on each shift. We still were with each other around the clock. At times, we lost track of Syco, but his new approach of watching out while laying under a car, making friends with the old people while watching out their window and sitting in dark tinted cars, all gave us a worry of his whereabouts.

Biya and I didn't argue much. I kept her at a need to ask me for money, which was often, but her information on the streets were priceless. She knew any and everything surrounded around the Haitian Posse. The news about last month's parade had her come home with a tattoo of "Jean" on her lower back, and she brushed her teeth and chewed my dick early in the morning, looking up at me, sticking out her tongue and drink- ing all this Haitian cum. Papaine's sneaking into the projects to Little Bam's apartment to be with Syco was shocking, but not unbelievable. It was through her that I met Luke Skywalker.

He had came to take her and Trina on tour to shake their asses. Ricardo would try to stop Trina, but she didn't accept nothing he was protesting. We all went to hood restaurants, movies, and clubs, but to think about it, I don't think we ever took one of those girls outside the projects to any kind of outing, not even walking to the store. When Annie signed Pierre out of juvenile, he jumped in the car with us while she left with the bondsman. Biya told me that there were three Haitian boys in the hood of Coconut Grove. Tampa, Jacksonville, and Daytona Beach. They called themselves Haitian Posse.

"It spread that far?" I asked.

"Yeah, even Luke has been begging to talk to you. I been telling you that."

"Keep all dudes away from us, that's our number one rule to you and all them girls in Lincoln Field. Pierre and Annie stay putting their dirty laundry in the middle of the field. They argue out in the open and no one better try to stop them or they'll turn on them"

We pulled the toys out, riding on the weekend, but the attention was too much. We would be followed all the time. When I drew my Glock out, I would feel like an innocent person almost got shot. And we took no chances, guns on our laps was mandatory in our minds.

Biya came in the room. "Wake up, wake up, the jump-out boys are back."

I jumped saying, "it's three in the morning." Watching out the window, we saw Pierre and Annie in handcuffs. Officer Polite stopped in the middle of the field next to Officer Kitchen, who put two bags in the air calling out, "we got it, Jean! We got it Gerald!", while pointing at Biya's place and Lily's place. Biya wanted to go out, but I told her to chill, that we would get them out.

I called Ricardo and told him not to come back yet, because the spot was hot. Six hours later, Syco and I, went to go see Pat. He told us, "look, they're going to direct-file Pierre to Dade County Jail to be tried as an adult."

I said, "I'll go talk to my lawyer about that. What about Annie, she got a bond?"

"Yeah, it's one hundred thousand dollars." "That's a lot."

"I will have to give you ten thousand dollars only, but I got to get her out today."

"And there's no way you can get Pierre out?" "No."

I got in the car and called Mom, telling her I had to go check on Pierre. Finally, I gave her a number to contact me if she could do anything. Ricardo called me saying that he, Gee, and Crip were together. I told him to meet me at the lawyers' office in one hour.

I got to the lawyers' office without an appointment, telling the secretary that my situation was important. I waited thirty minutes because the lawyer was in a meeting right then. Syco went right past her and I followed, walking in his meeting. He leaped up out of his chair. "Jean, what happened?"

"I need to talk to you right now. I been calling you and a bitch kept picking up the phone on the numbers you gave me."

"Please give me twenty minutes, Jean." "Twenty minutes!!!"

The boyz came in the lobby snapping. Gerald said, "this lawyer better have something good to say."

I said, "he told me twenty minutes, and it's about an hour."

The secretary walked out with two people. "Mr. Roy Black will see yougentlemen."

We walked in. Roy Black held up some papers. "Jean, Crip, when you called, I got on it to see what's going on. What I have here is a charge for Pierre Adam and Annie Williams for felo- ny possession with intent to distribute one kilogram of crack cocaine."

Crip mumbled, "man, wasn't no kilo of crack brought over to the spot."

I said, "so what that mean?"

Roy Black went on. "He will be direct-filed to the adult jail. Annie is already there with a bond of one hundred thousand dollars. I'm going to go see Pierre tomorrow and ask him what he wants to do and contact you or Crip."

"Alright, sorry about earlier, we were just worrying about our brother."

"Please, keep the attitudes outside gentlemen, you scared the hell out of my secretary."

We went to Syco's house to talk. I said, "she got to go."

Crip said, "as soon as possible, she going to scream, if she not screaming already."

Syco said, "bond her out and we kidnap the bitch and take her for a ride to Alligator Alley."

I partially agreed. "Yeah, that's what we might have to do, but let me see if I can go see Pierre first and tell him the plan." Ricardo was all for that. "That's cool, see what he says first."

Three days later, Mrs. Malando called me saying that her son and Syco had been locked up for coming out the projects with an AK-47. Syco had that charge and a separate charge of throwing AK-47 bullets at an officer. I told Mrs. Malando thanks and let her know I would be calling the lawyer.

I met up with Gerald and Crip. "I called the lawyer and the bondsman. There's no bond for Ricky or Syco either. Mr. Barzee and Mr. Black is on the case, but they said to bring them sixty thousand dollars."

Crip said, "what we going to do about Annie?"

"Oh, Pierre called me last night. Some chick officer was on him real hard when she found out he is an original Haitian Posse. She let him use the phone. He kept saying this case could be beat, that they didn't have nothing. I told him we think Annie got to go, but he went to talkin' bout, "naw, don't touch her, I got her, I got her. He knows Annie, she's 100 percent with him. He taught her well and she was raised by G's, so I'm saying right now, she can't be touched. What y'all think?"

Gerald struggled. "We got to respect his mind."

Crip wasn't as accepting. "I want to smash her, man. He'll get over it."

I maintained control. "Let's give it some time. If we hear anything crazy, that bitch got to go. Close the spot down. Call Little Bam, Crip, and tell him he can sell his weed, but nobody should be selling no dope at all, or they have to answer to us."

Gerald said, "I think they going to respect that. They can't get that same kind of dope nowhere else."

"Let's go give the lawyers this money and chill in a motel for a while on Biscayne somewhere. And I already talked to Syco's dad and told him to get on the lawyers, starting tomorrow."

We were holed up in the hotel for a week, only coming out to get some food and maybe hit a movie. Not having three of our boyz was a downer, but we vowed to keep money to the side for them when and if they get out. All the toys were put in the back of Syco's house.

Gerald and I were going to pick up some food at Jumbo's Restaurant. Crip said he was going to stay and watch some T.V. We pulled up to Jumbo's and walked into the restaurant.

While in a line of three, we looked out a big window to see Lily and some nigga getting out of a yellow '73 Chevy Impala. I put my hand on Gee as he headed out the door confronting Lily.

"Damn, I been gone for a week and you got a man? It's all good." I walked outside as Lily and the dude walked towards the door meeting Gee.

Instead of her responding back, the dude, whose name was Lab, a leader of the Two-Two Avenue, said "young nigga, I don't know what she was doing with you in

the first place."

Gee flared up. "Buddy, I'm not talking to you, I'm talking to her."

Lily tried to keep peace. "Lab, let me go talk to him for five minutes, then I will be right back."

He barked, "fuck this dude! You don't have to explain shit to him!"

Gee said, "you know me, yo?!!"

Lab pulled away from Lily. "Let me go get my gun."

I had my gun on me and was reaching for it. Gee had his gun on him too. When Lab took two steps towards his car, Gee pulled out his Glock and emptied three in his head. Lily stood still, screaming. I made it to the car. "Let's go Gee, let's go!"

He got in and we jetted east, down the back roads. Gee kept saying, "he made me do it, Jean, he made me do it."

"He dead?'

"Yeah, I think so."

"Good, dead men don't talk." "He was going to get his gun." "I know Gee, I heard him."

After telling Crip what happened, we decided to go to another hotel. The next day, the lawyers kept calling and I didn't want to pick up. So I called them from a phone booth.

 Mr. Barzee said, "meet me and Roy at the park in Carol City." "Which one, Risco Park?"

"Yeah."

We drove in the park's parking lot. A beige Mercedes-Benz came up. We rolled up next to it and got out.

Barzee said, "your mom called us Jean. She said the police had an arrest warrant for you for first degree murder."

I shook my head, "shit!"

"I called the station asking questions and they told me they have proof that two people participated in an M-1. I'm going to advise you this, but you don't have to do it. I want you to turn yourself in to the police station. But I want you to call Officer Kitchen to come get you. Here goes his phone number. Call him and tell you want to turn yourself in. He would love to get the credit for it. Or you can run, run, run, but they will catch you."

"Give me the number, we got to go."

"If you do turn yourself in, make sure you bring me eighty- five thousand dollars."

Gerald asked, "what, you just make those numbers in your fuckin' head? Can you beat a murder case?"

"I can promise you a good fight only."

We left the park. Crip said, "I know where we can run to." I was open to hear his idea strictly out of curiosity. "Where?" "Venezuela."

"What the hell you know about Venezuela?"

"I been reading about it. They got no extradition and we can catch a private plane, I read about it in Forbes magazine. We should try it out."

"That don't sound too good. We going to leave the boyz here. I don't know about that."

"Jean, I want to free you, and take care of family."

"What, you done lost your mind? What you think we got lawyers for man? When you was whining about the lawyer fee, I was prepared for this day right here."

That's some weak shit you saying."

"Look, I think we can beat this case. Let's go to your aunt's house and tell her to call the police so we can turn ourselves in. The lawyer got a plan on Kitchen. We done filed three harass- ment suits on him and a lawsuit that Crip got. Crip, we going to need you to stay low and pass us some chips from time to time. We can beat this, Gerald, it was self defense."

Crip started crying as the reality set in that we were leav- ing. I hugged him. "This wasn't part of the plan, but we Haitian Posse for life. That's why we all got it tattooed on top of our heart."

Gerald came up making it a three-way embrace. I told them we had to have faith while repeating the word, "rebuke."

CHAPTER ELEVEN

Being in jail for three weeks was mentally stressful. Gee and I were hoping Judge Peterson would keep the case in juve- nile court, but at the conclusion of his hearing, he direct-filed our case to be adjudicated in Dade County for us to be tried as adults. My mom had pleaded with the judge not to send me over there with those grown men. The judge assured her we would be housed with all juveniles who were being tried as adults.

Gee and I basically just stayed together in the cell watching the way everybody moved. The cells were on four different wings on the tenth floor of the Dade County Jail. The "A' wing that we were in had four cells with fifteen people in each one. Being in A1, we could see what A3 and A4 were doing if we looked close enough. The small hallway where the Warden, Captain, and Orderlies walked through, could fit only two people comfortably side by side. The food came in a brown tray with a large area for the "main course" and three small areas to put corn, beans, and string beans in. It all got passed through an open slot in the cell doors that had a keyhole to open and shut it. The trays would get picked up thirty minutes, if not five minutes, after they had been passed out. Medical was the best part, getting to see a nurse come around to take blood or administer tuberculosis tests. We would have to stick our hand between the bars of the closed cage. The officers were supposed to do walk-throughs every two hours. Many times they didn't walk through during the whole shift of their job. Sometimes we were basically there to govern ourselves. To get a Tylenol, we had to scream and holler for at least thirty minutes straight to get somebody to come in the back. Not having any kind of cameras, we wondered if they cared if we killed one another in there. But the inmates were all we had for it was our current home.

Me and Gerald kept asking officers if Pierre, Ricardo, or Syco came up there yet, since the lawyer told us they all got direct- filed to the county jail, too. The answer was usually, "no." We had been noticed by two dudes in the cell, who asked if we were Jean and Gerald from the

Haitian Posse.

Gerald had said, "yeah. Why, what's up?"

But they didn't jump bad, they only offered Gerald to watch the one T.V. if we wanted to watch anything in particular.

We loved soap operas. All My Children was our favorite after- noon show to watch and we were going to do a lot of catching up on it. As we watched our show everyday, we noticed how things been running on the tenth floor of the Dade County Jail. One day, I saw the lawyer and was told that my brother was there. We knew we had to get the boyz on the unit with us somehow.

Gerald said, "how we going to do that?" We done asked them over and over, and over again. They keep lying and saying they're not up here. They must don't want all us together for a reason."

"Look, Gee, when they pass out lunch we taking the orderly job to pass the food trays back to the officer and demand our homeboys get put in the cell with us, okay?"

"Let's do it, Jean."

The tasteless food came. It was as bad as Biya's food which was really bad. The two officers came rolling in pushing a tray buggie. When they got to our cell, we told the orderly to back up. He looked like he didn't understand what was going on but felt my hand on his chest pushing him to the left, out the way. The officer, Anderson, looked every bit of three hundred sixty pounds and about six foot three inches tall. He was the size of any average offensive lineman in the NFL. He said, "you two just came here, don't start no trouble. This floor been running

sweet, so don't make us come in there."

I said, "my name is Jean, you fat motherfucker," and spit on him. "I want my homeboys in the cell with me now!"

The other officer, Garcia, told Anderson to hold up, that he thought they should get the Lieutenant before he killed us young cats.

Gerald and I barked with anger, "fuck you, get my homeboys here now! Bring it, bring it. We want to see what you made of!"

They left for five minutes. We got all the trays, throwing the leftover food between the hallway. They came back with the Lieutenant and eight other officers. We took a step away from their reach. I said, "Lieutenant, get my three homeboys here."

The Lieutenant shook his head. "I can't do that, okay?" "Are they here?"

"I know your brother is here. I don't know about the rest." I yelled out their government names. To that, the Lieutenant said, "look, first, pass me those trays, then come out here and

clean up this mess."

Gerald said, "tell your mother to clean that shit up!" The keys came out and the door slid open. We put our backs to the wall. They rushed us. I knew I got one good punch on the front-line officer before we were wrestled to the floor getting kicked for at least seven minutes straight. Sitting in the medical unit on the third floor, I could see Gerald with lumps on his forehead. He also threw his backbone out of place. I felt the same way, even more with losing a gold tooth from the side of my grill. I wanted to sue them for that shit. The pain medicine they gave us felt real good that night. Early in the morning, four officers escorted me and Gee back to our same cell in A1. We stumbled inside.

The other dudes in the cell were watching T.V. when Gerald straight-up grabbed it, trying to yank it off the wall. The T.V. wouldn't come down, so he used the mop handle to bust the screen on the T.V.

The officer said, "oh, you didn't have enough, huh?" Without getting the L.T.. they came in and jumped us again.

I said, "you hit like my mama you bitches."

They left us on the floor, bleeding from the nose, mouth, and head. My thigh couldn't move for a hot thirty seconds before I finally felt feeling in it.

Gerald grabbed three mattresses, tearing them up. I already had to take a shit, so I shitted in my hand and threw it between the bars. The three dudes stepped up saying, "hell naw! Fuck them Haitians up over there!"

The three that stepped up, me and Gee punished them bad. I kicked one dude in his mouth till I saw a tooth come out. The ones across the hall talked loud as shit, but they didn't want none for real. The other nine justified our going off say- ing, "Them boys want their brothers in here so they can fight their cases better." They said they felt us and where we were coming from.

Gee and I shared buckets of water that we threw in the hall- way at the dudes across from us who started throwing water back at us.

Through the days, we waited on the last meal and finally kept the trays again. In my head, I prayed that they didn't come in there and beat us again. I couldn't take no more, but I knew we were at war with the L.T. and his officers. I got a chance to call Crip and tell him to let the lawyer know what was going on. Through the night, every time they sent a group to come clean the hallway, we threw water on them till they refused to clean it up. I couldn't believe they let the night go without cleaning up the shit that we threw in the hallways and on the bars. I couldn't even inhale the air, and it was my own shit stinking. Gee kept telling me I needed to be flushed. "This don't make no sense," he said.

Early in the morning, L.T. came with four officers. "Adam! Adam! Come over here."

Me and Gerald went and stood in front of the bars. "What's up!" I challenged. "Bring your army in here motherfucker."

L.T. smirked, "so you guys are the Haitian Posse? Well, we the Take-Down Haitian Posse Crew right here. We done took down the best of them and you jits is going to be the easiest.

Gerald cut him off. "Man, what's up with our brothers motherfucker?"

I held him back. "Let him talk, Gee."

L.T. continued. "I'm going to bring your thug brothers over here, but there's one that showed me the same tattoo that you two got. But he looks Cuban to me."

"What, the man told you he was Haitian?" "Yeah."

"That's definitely the right person you talking about. He's our brother."

"I don't give a fuck about those high price lawyers you got. If you fuck my house up, I will give you what you want, you little bad motherfuckers."

Gerald said, "so when they coming?"

L.T. spoke to one of his officers. "Bring them here so I can talk to all of them together."

I breathed more cooperative. "Lieutenant Miller, we don't want no problems. We just want to be with family in this hell hole."

Ricardo, Pierre, and Syco came through the door down the hallway. Loudly, I said, "Haitian Posse! Haitian Posse!"

Gee said the same.

The boyz started repeating it.

The inmates all around us went to clapping their hands at the three approaching us. Lieutenant Miller hollered, "no, no, no! Shut the fuck up, before I bring all three of you back to where you was!" Once our boyz were in the cell, L.T. finished his talk. "Listen, listen, this is my house right here. If I hear any one of you give my officers any kind of problems, I will make sure you pay for whatever you do. You young dudes need to get a book and study your case. Stay low and out the way. All of you, some inmates, but none of you are true convicts or you would know how to handle a situation in jail…blah, blah, blah." The man wouldn't stop with his lecture. "Get someone to clean this mess right here, Officer Anderson." He then left. We all hugged each other asking the dudes if we could get the set of bunk beds in the back so we could vibe together. We told the boyz what we went through. They looked over at us

and saw how fucked up we were.

The officers gave us a T.V. when they came by. The Lieu- tenant came two days in a row, at least five times each day, sticking his head in to see what was going on. I told him my little brother Bam-Bam was coming up to the tenth floor and asked if we would please bring him in the cell with us. He said he would think about it.

We mostly kept to ourselves while the others were disre- spectful to each other. Americans didn't understand us from the outside looking in. They would call each other bitches and pussies and hoes. We never understood the Americans idea of friendship. When four of the boys would be playing cards and ask me to get them some snacks and fix them a tuna sandwich, the others would look like something was wrong with that. Before eating, we held hands and prayed over our food. We sat on each other's bed at times switching from top to bottom and bottom bunk to top. Seeing Gerald hand-wash all our clothes, even underwear, brought on curious eyes from the outsiders. But we took turns at everything we did and loved each other like blood brothers who had nothing but each other. The second week of us being together, the T.V. man put another T.V. in our cell for us.

Syco looked around and noted that there was more Haitians on the other end. He advised us to make our cell a Haitian- only cell.

Pierre sprung into action on that. "Who want to stay in this cell, 'cause this just became a Haitian-only cell!"

Ricardo said, "I want that Spanish dude right there. He been looking at me crazy."

I calmed things down. "Man, L.T. going to split us up."

Syco said, "how? Plus, I'm tired of hearing all the fun you and Gee had."

Ricardo squared off with the Spanish dude, but because he didn't want to fight, we jumped the Spanish dude and told him to bang and yell for the C.O. Pierre kicked another dude in the face telling him to pack his shit and bang too. Three others didn't want no problem and went to bang on the door. Officer Anderson finally came forty-five minutes later wanting to know what was going on. The dudes all made it clear they wanted to get out of the cell.

"I can't move unless you fear for your life."

They all said they feared for their lives, and all of them were moved out the cell.

Officer Anderson went and got four other boyz who were a clique of Robin Hood Boyz. They came in and we thought the officers had us doing they dirty work. We squared off with the dudes. I announced, "today your lucky day boys, you get to pick which one of us five you want to fight.

A big dude picked Syco. Syco went head-to-head with buddy punch for punch, coming out on top by knocking him out. I grabbed some water and threw it on. "Wake up!"

Pierre and Gee, who loved to fight, went for two dudes knocking them out with one punch for Gee, and one kick for Pierre.

I then made the niggas bang on the door. They banged and we yelled for the officer for them. When they came and got them. Officer Garcia said, "look at you clowns, done got fucked up by some Haitians and was just talking shit about the Haitian officer Jableb."

A week later, Bam-Bam and two Haitians came in our cell. We took care of all them with hygiene items, snacks, and three- way phone calls. It was all Haitians just like we wanted. We met four new Haitians and the rest were already family from the projects.

Ricardo told us how he got stopped in his Chevy Impala when he pulled out of the projects. As soon as he was about to make a right, Kitchen and Polite jumped out on him. He tried to get away but when he got blocked in a little traffic jam, Kitchen got on foot and got right in the convertible. "We put our hands in the air when he pulled his gun. When they didn't go in Syco's other pocket they screamed for him to not move!! Syco reached in his pocket to throw four AK-47 bullets at Kitchen. He was mad and hit Syco with his billy-club right across the neck, and I caught one just for the hell of it on my back. The shit wasn't funny then but I'm glad we can laugh now." Pierre said, "Syco, you crazy dude."

We missed the dudes that we put out the cell. We had fun with the fake thugs who probably were only hard with a gun in their hands. In two months of being together, the word of how Haitian Posse was acting crazy and wilding on the tenth floor spread through the jail house, and the streets. A Haitian officer lady had snuck a cell phone to us. Crip had given her seven hundred dollars for the one hundred fifty dollar-phone. I talked to Biya who told me the streets said we were going off and acting crazy in the jail.

Crip told me he mostly stayed at a hotel and really didn't push to keep it running like it was when we were out. He did a little here and there with Little Sergo. But he mainly chilled at home and the hotel. He always said he missed all of us. It was likewise, because we felt his presence.

The rest of the boys got their weed in through Annie and Trina who visited Pierre and Ricardo twice every week. Being able to wear street clothes in jail, we kept two pairs of Jordans and a pair of Clarks with all Polo sets. Some of my best times was when the Nurse Brant came around to the hallway and A1 wing. We five would run to the bars pulling our dicks out while she watched, pointing. "I can tell you two brothers. You Spanish boyz not working with much. You other two definitely Haitians." She would look at the dick like she wanted to eat it, till all of us came in our hand. I personally fell in love with her. I wanted to make that nurse my girl when I got out but the others said the same.

We would be so bored in the cell, tired of smoking, tired of T.V., and about tired of each other. Sleep was out of the question. When trying to sleep, someone would say, "sleep when you die or bond out!" And make a bunch of noise.

Gerald was trying to sleep one night when Pierre kept talking loud with Annie on the phone.

Gee said, "sucker for love-ass nigga. I'm trying to see." Pierre said to Annie, "Boo-Boo, I'm going to call you back."

I laughed. "Hold up, let me grab some popcorn. I want to see this fight."

Gee said, "I know that kicking shit real good. I'm going to knock you out."

146

Pierre was unmoved. "I got two hands too, Gee, you got me fucked up."

Syco said, "hell no, you two don't fight. We brothers."

Pierre shrugged that off. "We going to hug like brothers after we fight."

I got my popcorn. "Man, hands only, no kicking allowed."

Pierre said, "you know about these hands Jean. Shit, you can be next."

"Whatever little bro. I got my money on Gee on this one." Ricardo chuckled. "Pierre, I got my money on you."

Syco shook his head. Gerald and Pierre squared off taking shit for a while. Gee then hit Pierre right on the cheek.

The whole wing said, "OOOoooh!!"

I leapt up throwing popcorn all over. "Stop the fight! Stop the fight!"

Pierre sucked it up. "That shit felt weak, nigga. Annie hit me harder than that."

They stood in the middle of the floor again. In my head I knew Pierre was lucky Gee didn't follow up. They went to each oth- er's face, hitting back and forth like one Mike Tyson against another. Blow for blow, blow for blow, it was a stand-up brawl. Pierre stumbled real bad going backwards and came with a kick to Gee's chest. All three of us ran in the middle of them breaking it up. Gee, with a busted lip said, "we good. Let me give my brother a hug." He kissed Pierre on the forehead. "I love you, nigga."

Pierre said, "me too man. Good one."

I went on the bars looking at the other side of the wing. "This how real dudes do shit! You see with your eyes how we do shit, soft niggas!"

We went about our day as Pierre and Gee teamed up to play a game of spades. The next day. Officer Anderson brought two people and said they were going in our cell because there was nowhere else to put them.

Ricardo bucked, "man, you trippin'." We don't got no room. Them three empty beds taken over by Haitian caspers." He walked away saying, "if they say they fear for their lives, we will move them, but for now, they stay right here."

I said, "is this a trick?"

One said, "you guys are Haitian Posse right? We heard about you making noise on this end. Didn't you hear us making noise on the other side?"

"What's both you dudes' names?" One said, "I'm Bobbie, he's Bam."

"Check this out man, we won't fuck with you if you bang on the door and tell them you fear for your life."

Bobbie said, "that's never going to happen, first of all. We can fight all day, just don't jump me. I can go with two of y'all, then the rest."

Bam said, "when he rest, then I'll take on whoever, then rest." Pierre said, "I'm first."

I said, "hold up, hold up, Gee, Pierre. Real fucks with real. They want to fight, so we not going to do it like that as both stands for their manhood like these two right here."

Gee said, "man, they not Haitian."

"We not on some Haitian shit, we on some respect Haitian shit."

Bobbie said, "the C.O.'s using y'all to check dudes, but we told them it's whatever."

Pierre said, "oh they think they can't get it, huh?"

Bam said, "I been waiting to set it off on them, but only me and Bobbie was ready to get at them. We not stupid. They jumped us once already, about five deep. We heard they jumped somebody over here too."

Ricardo said, "oh yeah, I heard they got two dudes last month."

I said, "well, let's give them a run for their money." I turned to Bobbie and Bam. "I got some snacks, y'all want some?"

Bam said, "nah, I just need some soap and shampoo to take a shower."

Little Bam-Bam threw them two clean towels. When they got out the shower, I said, "we got to get one of them officers real good."

A week later, we caught a good time to start a fire. The sprin- klers went off on the whole top tenth floor. The officers came to our hallway fifteen-deep. We stared them fourteen-deep.

L.T. Miller said, "you got five minutes to get on the floor!"

Bobbie put baby oil all over the floor. "Come in bitches! Come on in!"

Syco threw paper tissue bullets at them. They all looked at us and saw nothing but fire in our eyes. We thought they were coming in when L.T. motioned a hand signal, but three officers came with gas masks.

"What the fuck they got that on for?" I asked.

L.T. Miller said, "you got two minutes to all get on the floor or I'm spraying this cellblock gentlemen."

Our thug motivation was too high. Looking like a mon- ster, I said, "we can eat that!!"

Bobbie said, "that's all you got?! Stop talking so much, L.T., and come in!"

Miller was not bluffing. They pulled out three fire extin- guisher sized canisters full of mase and sprayed it all in the cell. We hollered, "AAaaaa!"

But we never sounded weak.

"Come in here bitch!" Pierre screamed. "Damn this shit burning. It's burning bad!"

They turned off the water and continued to holler. I heard Little Bam-Bam calling for help and grabbed him, wanting him to shut it up. That mase burned real bad. I heard them all laughing in the hallway watching us like a herd of chickens slipping on the baby oil, falling onto the floor. I blew into Syco's eye's and he blew into mine. Everybody was either blowing someone's eyes or having theirs blown. The pain was so excru- ciating. Those bastards let us burn for seven hours straight before bringing us to medical to check our eyes. I told Bam, "L.T. got us real good. I didn't even think about the mase."

"This pain lasts longer than them kicking us." "I don't know how we going to sleep tonight." "I can't sleep in the hell-hole anyway."

The weekend was painful. Everyone, including the other three cells, caught side effects of the mase. We took five show- ers a day to slow the pain of our itchy eyes down. The whole wing was cleaned by hands with washcloths and anti-itch soap powder.

Monday morning hit and the best breakfast in the world came rolling in the hallway. The officers put extra trays in the breakfast holder for us in A1 to keep us calm. We called it the Cadillac because the way the pretty trays came through the slot looking pretty with corn beef hash, scrambled eggs, biscuits, oatmeal, two pancakes with cheap syrup, and a small orange juice twelve-ounce pack. The whole A1 prayed and dug in the breakfast that tasted like Grandma's cooking. There was never any complaints on Cadillac day. There were even enough food for Pierre to get full, and Pierre never got full.

Most of us hit our bunks to take a nap. Two hours into my sleep. Officer Garcia woke me up for a lawyer visit. I got up and put my Bally shoes on and all-beige Polo set. Grabbing my law folder, I told the boyz I would be back.

Seeing both Mr. Roy Black and Mr. William Barzee gave me a sense that they were devoted to all the cases they were fighting for us.

"What's up Mr. Black, Mr. Barzee." I greeted them.

They wanted me to stop being so formal and call them by their first names. Roy was curious about appearance. "What's wrong with your eyes, they're blood-shot red and you're miss- ing a gold tooth. You okay back there?"

"Everything's good in here, I want to know the truth and only the truth about my brothers and me. After that, I got no problems except I turn eighteen next month and they're saying I'm going down stairs to the sixth floor away from my brothers. Is there anything you can do about that?"

"No. You can handle yourself in there. You're turning eight- een years old and that's not considered a juvenile in the eye of the state. We have a few things to go over for the next four hours. First, I want to tell you we are not allowed to disclose other clients' info to you."

"Don't start the bullshit up in this place, motherfuckers."

Roy said, "we're going to tell you, but we had to state that line so we can get going with all the cases."

"Okay, go ahead."

"The case with Ricardo and Ganeo is the easiest. The state government has an offer for six years, but we are telling them to fuck off. Our client was pulled over and illegally searched and seized. A judge, seven out of ten, wouldn't even go through the process of picking a jury. We think they would play hard for a couple of years, so tell those boys buckle their knees and wait it out. I don't even want this on their record. They threw out the charge of throwing the bullets at the officers. We thought that was funny as hell. Both lawyers chuckled at the thought of it. Now, to a more serious case. You and Gerald are charged with first-degree murder. That's a significant charge Jean. It's beat- able, but I think you may have to go to trial. They're offering twenty years, which we didn't indulge in a conversation with that. The best factor on your side is that the dude died right next to his car where they found a loaded Desert Eagle with an extended clip holding twenty-seven bullets plus one in the chamber. It proves with this guy's violent record, he meant to kill you guys. The self defense case you paid to represent you and Gerald on will be researched front and back a thousand times if we have to. You turning yourselves in to the authorities shows sympathy with the previous filing of harassment on the city, it's an overall great look."

"So you think we can beat the murder case?"

Barzee said, "you have the best fighting team on this case Jean. Right now, you would have to trust us."

"Alright, we're all in here keeping our mouths closed about the situation."

Roy nodded. "That's perfect! That's what we need you to do. We don't need any new surprises coming up."

"I want you to know twenty years is not even in me or Ger- ald's thoughts. We ready to pick twelve and go to trial, sir." Looking at Roy and Barzee in the eyes, I said, "that's the only option on the murder case."

Again Roy nodded. "That's clear. Now we will have to talk about a gun shop robbery and some other things I don't want to mention right now. But we told the D.A. none of our clients would sit down with them for a lower plea."

"I'm glad you said that. Now, what's up with my little brother?"

"Well, Pierre and Annie is a case where the police claimed to have seen Pierre with something in his pants which they thought was a gun, so they ran after him. They went into Annie's residence with no search warrant, finding one kilo of crack cocaine. We asked for the videos, search warrant, and for them to put the drugs on a scale in front of us. They did neither. The offer for fifteen years for Pierre and five years for Annie was declined by both of them. This case may also go to trial the way the process is going, and both clients are willing to go to trial."

"I'm not sensing the same enthusiasm as the other two cases." "Well, the young lady had been to our office three times a

week saying Pierre's thinking about taking fifteen years for the whole case if they let Annie go. I talked to Pierre. He wants me to ask the prosecutors on his case to see if they're willing to do that. But I told Barzee we should go over it with you before we talk to the prosecutors."

"Hell no. By no means should you ask the prosecutors that stupid question. If he goes to trial, she goes with him. If he's adamant about the fifteen years and the case gets stronger, we will talk about it. But for now, if he goes to trial, she goes too." "I have a feeling she wants to go to trial. It's Pierre sending

her to ask those silly questions." "Oh yeah."

"Yeah, but just don't explode on nobody. Keep it to yourself and if we plan on making any kind of move of any sort on that case, we will talk to you first before talking to the state pros- ecutors." He slid me six pictures of Annie completely naked.

"Thank you very much Mr. Black and Mr. Barzee. This dude is a tender dick about Annie. Is there anything else? I got a headache now."

"Well, there's more Jean." "Give it to me."

"It's about the fee on the cases. We forgot the civil case against Crip versus the City of Miami. It's a case that can take almost ten years, but as long as he goes to all his doctor's visits it should pay in the end. Also the fees have gone past what we estimated. We need seventy-five thousand dollars to keep going to hire some needed help around the office. And the private investiga- tors on all three cases are handing us all kinds of extra expenses."

"Crip will come see you early tomorrow morning. Is there anything else?"

"No. And Happy Birthday, if we don't see you before then." "Thanks." I shook their hands. "Come see me if anything

changes." "Alright." They left.

When I was escorted in the cell, all the boyz came towards me. Gee said, "why you look like that Jean?"

"Everything good. I just feel like we took over Lincoln Field projects for them two white boys. They want seventy-five thousand dollars more."

"Oh hell no. Hell no, I hope you told them we will give it to them when they beat all three cases."

"They got us cornered, I can't snap on them. But if they lose any case, we going to kill them two crackers."

Syco said, "I would enjoy killing the one with the blue eyes. He look like the old President Jimmy Carter."

Ricardo sucked his teeth. "Shut up. What the fuck you know about Jimmy Carter?" We all were about to start a political debate when I said, "I'm going to the back to call Crip." I grabbed the cell phone hidden in my deodorant box and got Crip on the first ring. "What's up?"

"Chilling at the hotel with this bitch."

"Check it, the lawyers need seventy-five thousand dol- lars more."

"Damn, they want more money?" "Yeah."

"So what you want me to do?"

"Bring them fifty-five thousand dollars tomorrow. We will stall them for the rest and cry broke. Stop wearing jewelry over there, they think we rich."

"Jean, money is real low, real low."

"I know bro. This should be the last lump-sum we spend while we in here." I told him what was really going on with the cases and fell back and went to sleep for the night.

During my last three weeks on the tenth floor, we all basically worked out doing push-ups everyday, playing cards, and me and Boobie talked about history, politics and life on the streets. He reminded me of Crip a lot. I told him that. Knowing I would be separated from my boyz was really killing me inside. If they were still there, they all would be coming down to the sixth floor the next year. I would have everything situated before they came down.

Waking up one morning finding the boyz playing cards together, I asked, "did any of you go to sleep last night?"

All of them looked at me crazy. "No," Pierre said. "We will sleep when we die."

"When we get out this bullshit, I don't know what none of you going to do but I'm not going near Lincoln Field projects. That shit is a death trap."

"What we going to do then if we get out of jail?"

"I don't know, but I'm not fucking with those projects at all. I'm not stepping foot in Lincoln Field."

Ricardo was skeptical. "I hope you and Crip come up with something. For real."

L.T. Miller stuck his head in the hallway. "Adam! Jean! I can't wait to escort you to the big boys on the sixth floor."

Gee yelled out, "tell them to be suited up with vests to come get Jean.

154

And we want some mase for dinner today."

"I can't wait to feed you some mase, but I got some new shit I want to try out instead."

I cut in, "it won't be no problems coming to escort me to the sixth floor, L.T. Miller."

"We will see. We will see."

Waking up early, packing and waiting for L.T. Miller to come get me, I hugged everybody. "I'm going to miss y'all. Send messages through the officers who got love for Haitian Posse if you got anything important to get to me."

Gee was upset. "Damn, I'm going to miss you bro."

"We can always call each other. Stop it, Gee." I hugged Boobie and Bam. "You two got to have some Haitian in your blood line."

Boobie laughed. "We might, Jean."

Little Bam-Bam and Jay, who were leaving the next week, had plead guilty to five years of possession of one hundred eighty grams of crack cocaine. I told both of them to make sure they write me and call Crip for anything that's an emergency. Hearing there was a group of Haitian Posse members on each floor, I knew the sixth floor would welcome me with open arms

knowing I was one of the original Haitian Posse.

L.T. came through the hallway with five officers, jaw-jack- ing. "Oh, I see you packed up. I was hoping you weren't going to follow orders so I could try my new toy. And don't start talking that shit when this door opens."

I said, "whenever you ready Lieutenant." "Let's go!"

On the sixth floor, I got greeted by seven Haitian dudes. Most of them were around twenty-two to twenty-five years old. Me and a wild dude named Biscayne mostly chilled together throughout the months doing push-ups and playing cards, and on some occasions, we fought a few dudes here and there.

The first year had went by when Syco came down. Two months later, Gee and Pierre came, followed by Ricardo, who came down two weeks after them. We were all growing up mentally to where we did not jump at every move, but thugging was just in us. Being hood was something we were born into. To even see Ricardo pick up a book sent shocks to my thoughts. Pierre still stayed on the phone trying to control Annie's pussy on the outside, which none of us chastised him about his love for her anymore.

I never called Biya unless I needed something. She complained that she didn't understand how I got a cell phone, but Pierre talking to Annie all day, messed that up. I thought the way Biya sucked my dick she could wheel any dude in Miami and didn't need me around. I thought she just loved being affiliated with the boyz. When Papaine visited Syco, he told us that she changed. "She's not fucking for money."

I was worried only about all of our cases. Mine and Gee's trial was coming up in about a year and a half. Pierre's and Annie's in two years.

The plea that Syco and Ricardo signed for six years was a bad one, but they chose not to fight it anymore. With having to do 65 percent of their time in Florida, they would be home in two years. Watching them go away to prison, I told both of them to keep their eyes on the prize and pray for the rest of us. Two months later, I called Crip. He told me Syco and Ricardo were both losing their good time acting stupid in Rayford State Penitentiary. The following week, Crip let me know that two dudes had rushed him at a red light trying to car-jack him. "Ain't nothing changed Jean. Gun on my lap at all times when I'm riding. I hit both dudes and left them right there. But I think both of them still alive."

"Crip, stay out of that type of shit, it's going to get you killed." "Why you talking like niggas been in jail too long?"

"Please homie, just stay on your P's and Q's. Syco and Ricky will be out soon and they both going to need you."

"I'm about to go chill with this girl in West Palm Beach." "That sounds great."

Me, Pierre, and Gee were talking about our white Olympic Jordans. We argued about who had more blood on our shoes. Gee said, "come on, Pierre, the only reason you might have more is because you always kicking people in the head like you see a soccer ball."

I had been telling Gee and Pierre to stay out the way. Me and Gee had trial in two weeks, and we didn't need that negative vibe around.

Pierre got wrote up for jacking his dick at the night-shift lieutenant. Three officers hauled him out of our cell. Gee woke me up cursing at the officers. I tried to get him to relax. "Gee, chill. He's going to be alright. We need a clear mind for this case. Our life on the line."

"You go clear your mind, I'm going to get him back in our cell."

CHAPTER TWELVE

June 15, 1993. I was 21 and Gerald was 20. We had done a little over four years in jail and the jury came back with a verdict. My mom sat in the crowd with Biya, Crip, Gee's aunt and two pastors. Mom had a bible in her hand and her mouth was mumbling something every time I looked at her. I knew it was prayers.

The judge asked the foreman to announce the verdict on our case. The six black, two Spanish, and four white group gave no sign of what the decision would be. They all had a poker face on. Roy's head standing so high was a confident sign to me. The jury foreman stood and said, "on the count of first-de-

gree murder, we find the defendants, not guilty."

I sighed with relief. Mom yelled thanking Jesus. The state marshals ordered the crowd to quiet down. My nerves were so raw that I didn't hear anything but first-degree mur- der. I looked at Gee and his big clown smile told me all I need- ed to know. I could feel the two prosecutors, Kitchen, Polite, and two other officers looking at our reactions as we shook our lawyers' hands. The journey finally allowed me to take a deep breath. I asked the state marshal if I could hug my mom. When I did, she prayed more, continuing to thank the Lord. I told her I loved her and winked at Crip.

Biya embraced me tightly. "Look at you, your chest is poked out. You done got taller and pit on some weight. Let me see that six-pack."

Roy said, "stay out of trouble and try to get that twenty thousand dollars you got for me."

"Keep your eyes on the prize. My brother and Annie is my true worry."

"We're preparing for that case. You just keep in mind that you had a nice jury and stay out of trouble."

My mom wanted all the clothes that me and Gerald had on and wore in jail. Crip had two outfits with two pairs of new Jordans for us. He took our clothes and shoes and gave it to my mom, and she promised she would burn the residues of the devil along with them. "Nothing in the devil's house is worth taking with you."

When I told mom I was going with my friends and would call her, she pleaded for me to stay out of trouble. She was going to see my brother that day and the next with the pastor. Mom wanted us to change our lives because we were still all she had left. And since I was missing one gold tooth, she wanted me to take the rest of that "nonsense" out of my mouth.

"I will call you Mommy. I love you." I kissed her, then left with Crip in his Chevy.

"What's going on bro?" He asked me.

"You done got smaller. Don't tell me you been stressing 'cause we been gone for a hot minute." I grabbed one of his cheeks and Gee grabbed the other one. "Tell me you miss me."

Crip swatted at our hands. "Get off me. Get your hands off my face." He then started grinning, saying, "not guilty!"

We chanted all types of shit with him about our freedom, and about Haitian Posse. Rocking side to side, we celebrated behind the window tints.

"Haitian Posse for life!!"

I was pumped up. "Crip, where we going?"

"Where the hell you want to go at?"

Gee asked, "I want to go eat at Ce Ce Bon."

I agreed. "Me too. After that, take me to the dentist to put my trophy back in my mouth."

When we got to our destination and sat down to eat, the owner said, "Jean, Gerald, where you been? I thought you guys found a new restaurant."

Gee answered, "we going to be in the hood eating your food forever."

Finishing up the food, I spoke up, "I can't believe we going to stay at Syco's house tonight 'cause I'm not stepping foot in Lincoln Field at all."

Crip said, "yeah it's on fire."

"What we going to do?" Gee asked curiously. "We will figure it out soon."

Crip said, "money is real low, Jean."

"I know, but we all been broke before. Let's just make sure the boyz' prison accounts stay right and stay on a budget. Biya going to slide to the house later. I'll be in for a couple of days."

Crip looked at me. "So we really going to let Annie go through with this?"

"Pierre insists on that and it's been four years plus a hundred percent gangster in my eyes. No matter what, we got to look for her like she one of the boyz. Pierre saw something I didn't see." Chilling late in the night with Biya, I felt like I was going backwards for some reason. "Jean, I got something to tell you," she announced. "What's up?"

"I don't want to go to jail, but I was at the jail with Annie doing some research and we think we might be able to find a way to pay a jurist once they start picking them."

"How?"

"They all go eat at a certain spot when they take a break. We was going to approach one on your case but we backed out at the end of it. Annie don't want to back out on her case. She just need the money when the time comes up."

"Just let me know. Don't tell nobody else and don't stick your nose too deep to be noticed."

"We practiced and told one of them you were my brother on your case and they were talking to us laughing and chilling with us."

"Yeah?"

That Saturday morning, Gerald and I took out one thousand dollars each from the pot we had saved up and went to buy some clothes for ourselves. We

160

also picked up a few things for Syco and Ricardo. Crip didn't go along with us to the 163rd Street Mall. The bullet in his leg was moving around again, causing him a lot of pain.

Walking with our pockets nice, wearing a gold watch, a chain with a cross on there, and my bracelet along with our expensive clothes, we felt like a million dollars. But we knew money was getting short around us. Gee had his big, wide, Mercedes-Benz piece, with a big king hat look-alike on his middle and index fingers. We both felt like billionaires, laughing and hitting each other while talking about nonsense. We walked straight in the polo store and were finished shopping in twenty minutes after getting everything we needed.

I walked to the register to pay for the items. The young lady grabbed everything and started ringing them up one by one. She stopped to glance at me. Her hair was in a ponytail. She had light make up on with green eyes, standing about five feet six inches. Her skin tone was so light she could go for a white girl, but her features made it clear that she was black.

She looked like someone I knew.

I pulled out my money and looked at the customer regis- ter screen that read the total to be seven hundred eighty-two dollars and forty-two cents.

The worker said, "Jean?"

"What's up Cathy?" "Oh my God, it's you Jean! How you doing? How's your brothers and uncle and mom and dad doing?"

"Good. How's Walker and your family?"

"Great, you look so good! You look like one of those rappers. Why you got all them golds in your mouth? You don't need that, you too handsome for that."

Gerald came up. "I'm finished."

Cathy looked at him and then back at me. Pointing at Gerald, she asked me, "is that your brother?"

"No it isnot."

Gee was confused. "What? What the fuck you mean I'm not your brother?"

"Nah, it's not like that Gee."

Cathy observed all the stuff Gerald had. "Where you working to buy all these clothes?"

Gee said, "That's none of your – "

I gave him a mean-mug that stopped him flat. Then I turned to Cathy with a smile. "I'm a construction worker."

"Oh yeah! I'm in college getting my Master's Degree in Polit- ical Science. Hopefully I'll get it in three years. I already have my Bachelor's."

Gee's eyebrows shot up. "I'm not your brother? What's going on here?"

"I will talk to your brother."

Cathy said, "You have to see Walker, he would love to see you, and the others."

"I would love to see Walker."

"Hold on, you not paying all of this for these clothes. Let me get my 50 percent off for you."

Gee wasn't confused about that at all. "I don't know what's happening, but that 50 percent off sound good to me."

"Okay then, but y'all have to hide these." She put her hand on Gee's big gold chain and tucked it in his shirt. Then she did the same to mine. "There's a lot of crazy people out here that could rob you. You must not have heard about the Haitian Posse."

Gee asked, "You Haitian? We are Haitian –"

I pushed him a little and he fell back three steps. He said, "I can't believe this shit I'm seeing. Thus is not for real, not you Jean."

"Trust me, don't say a word."

We got the 50 percent discount and Cathy wrote her number down and passed it to me. We paid the subtotal on both clothes. Cathy told me she wanted to come around to see me. She gave me and Gee hugs before we left.

Once outside, Gee said, "What's up with the friendly bitch?" "Don't call her that bro. I know her from Haiti. She knew me

since I was four years old on up to when I got to this country. She like a family member to me."

"My fault brother. Can I call you brother now?" "Why you trying to make it so difficult fam?"

"I'm just bullshitting. We got extra money to get four pairs of sneakers each. Let's go to Foot Locker."

"Let's do it."

When we sat down eating some pizza, Gee was talking, but I couldn't focus on his words. I was so far gone, he shook my arm. "Jean, what's up man? What you thinking about? I know it's about money. I know you going to tell Crip first, but I'm anxious to know, so what's the play?"

"Yeah, yeah, yeah, just chill, in fact, let's go to the house."

Grabbing the six bags, we walked a long way to the exit. Gerald approached a group of four girls standing in front of a women's clothing store. He talked to one of them while I sat back looking around to see if any dudes we had problems with were around us. Also, I was thinking about Cathy. Gee got the girl's number walking away. He asked me why I didn't get at one of the girls. I knew they would be around as long as he had one of them, and I could always get at a friend.

When we walked in the house, Gerald started clowning. "Crip, would you believe Jean told a white girl that I'm not his brother?"

Crip looked at me crazy. "What he talking about?" I said, "don't listen to that fool."

Gee grinned. "You still didn't really tell me nothing about her, but she's family."

Crip pulled out two shirts. "You got to let me get that baby- blue and white polo. I got a hat just for that."

Gee shook his head. "Nah." He threw Crip his medicine we had stopped to pick up. "You sick right? Well sick people don't need none of these new Jordans or new Bo Jacksons. And don't ask for a friend when this pretty little thing called Percila come see me with four other bitches."

"Damn, I should have went with y'all."

I said, "don't let pretty-boy Gerald hype it up too much, it's not all that."

Gee brushed my comment off. "What?" Did you see that pretty black girl with the little mole on her chin and under her eye?"

"I wasn't looking that close homie."

Crip was curious. "When you going to call them to come over?" I said, "I'm going to clean up this room and cook something for us. We on a serious budget. Soon we might have to pawn all this jewelry around here to get by till something come up."

I woke up in the morning at 10:00. I'd had the best dream ever, all about Cathy. I thought to myself, when should I call her? She said I look good, she hugged me. But she hugged Gee too. Maybe she just really see me as family and that's all.

I debated with myself about calling her and decided to do it. When I called, she answered with the sweetest voice. "Who's this?"

Jean. Is it too early to be calling you?"

"No." She yelled for Walker, then continued. "I was thinking why didn't I get your number. I wanted to call you last night."

"Well, you got a pen?"

"Hold up, here goes Walker." She called out to her brother, "It's Jean!"

Walker took the phone. "What's up Jean?" "I'm alright."

"Cathy told me she saw you and I asked her why she didn't get your number. I got to see you. Where's your Uncle Mike? Put him on the phone."

"He's out of town."

"What about your brothers?"

"Everyone left for a job out of town on a construction site." "Well did you tell them you saw Cathy?"

"I was waiting till they come back in three days to tell them. You know how Dad is about to work."

"Well Jean, I don't want to wait to see you." "I'll come to see you."

"Me and Cathy have a spot Dad got for us at Miami Lakes. The Mores."

"It's a house?"

"Yeah."

"Let me get the address and what time you want me to come."

"Now!"

"Okay, I'll be there in one hour."

"No problem. Cathy could cook some breakfast for us three."

Gerald woke up to see me getting dressed and asked where we were going. I lied, telling him I was going to see my mom.

"Everything alright with Pierre?"

"Yeah, you talked to him last night. I just got to calm her nerves some."

"Alright, let's catch up on some movies we missed while we was locked up later."

"Cool."

I left my jewelry behind and grabbed the cheapest car we had, a Ford Tempo. I got to Miami Lakes, The Mores, in exactly one hour. Walker and Cathy came to greet me at my car. Walker gave me a big hug. Cathy kissed me on the cheeks. Walker said, "you got tall and put on a lot of weight. You were so skinny, I could see your bones."

"You got a lot of muscles like you play football."

"I play basketball for the University of Miami starting at point guard. You have to come see me play."

"For sure, 'specially when Pierre get out." "Where's Pierre?"

"I mean when they get back, I just stayed in case I have to send some equipment to them."

Cathy said, "come eat, I cooked a big Haitian breakfast I love to cook."

Finishing up my oatmeal that had rice in it, I asked Walker how he stayed in shape with his sister cooking like this.

"I don't know Jean, truly I don't know."

We talked about Haiti and the politics of Haiti and how we all had to go back one day to live there. Then Walker said he had to go to basketball practice, and for me to not be a stranger, that this home was my home.

I thanked him. Telling so many lies made me feel bad, but I truly never felt comfortable talking about my dead fam- ily, except to the boyz. Not telling Walker and Cathy still felt uncomfortable. I didn't like for people to feel sorry for me.

Cathy said, "I'm off for the next three days. I got a big book to read, but I want to catch a movie."

"I'm free too, let's go."

I never saw a movie without the boyz and for a sec- ond I felt guilty. Walker left and Cathy and I got in her Honda Accord. I grabbed a hat that was in the Ford Tempo and put it on. We had stayed in the house for three hours talking. Cathy had to stop at the cleaners and do some grocery shopping. We went back to her house and had great conversation. I shared the little I learned from jail and tried to stay away from the personal questions. The way we horse-played was like we were in the house together for weeks. We went to the movies around 7 p.m. to see a movie called Poetic Justice.

In the end, Cathy gave me a hug and kissed me on the cheek, telling me to get home safe. I drove to the house and told the boyz I was tired. I talked on the phone with Syco and Ricardo and went straight to sleep. I slept the next day till about 1 p.m. When I looked at my phone I saw two missing calls. One was a girl that Gerald gave my number to. I talked to her for five min- utes the night before. The other call said "12:27 Cathy." I didn't even brush my teeth. I called right away.

She answered, "hey Jean. You just woke up?"

I lied. "No, I been in the Home Depot. The phone don't work there."

"Oh yeah? What you doing for lunch?" "Nothing really."

"Do you want to get a bite to eat?"

"Sure, there's a restaurant in Little Haiti where I stay called Ce Ce Bon. Want to go there?"

"I'm not in the mood for nothing heavy like that. What about Red Lobster?"

I was hood. I never went out that far. "That's great. What time?"

"Two thirty at the one on 79th Street."

"That's perfect." I thought Gee and Crip were about to grill me about where I was going. I took a shower, put on some clothes, and some cologne.

Crip asked, "what's up? Where you going, nigga? You plot- ting on something without me?"

"Naw, bro, my mom want me to go to a church with her." "On a Wednesday?"

"Yeah, but I'll be right back, it should be about an all-around five-hour trip. Tell Syco I'm going to call his dad to give him the money for this month's house bills."

Crip and Gee walked away telling me to kiss my mom for them. Then, as near afterthought, Gerald said, "you got your gun on you?"

I lifted my shirt. "You already know."

Flipping through the many cassettes in the Ford Tem- po, I found nothing but hardcore rap music. Not one slow jam was in the damned car. I put the radio on Hot 105.1, Jodeci came on.

So you're having my baby. And it means so much to me. There's

167

nothing more precious than to raise a family. If there's any doubt on your mind, you can count on me. I'll never let you down. Lady believe in me.

I rolled into Red Lobster's parking lot. Cathy pulled up seven minutes later. Meeting her at her car, I opened her door. She kissed me on the cheek asking how long I had been there.

"Not long." "Let's goin."

The water gave us a table outside with a water view. Once we sat down I began building myself up to ask her some questions. Ten minutes after the waiter left with our order, I said, "Cathy, where's your boyfriend?"

"I don't have one. I dated a black guy before and even a white guy, but their not being able to speak Creole made me feel empty at times. I love my Haitian men and feel comfortable around them. What about you?"

"I don't have one either."

"Living in Haiti. I know those ghetto girls love a man like you." "It's not like that at all."

"I used to always see how you looked at me when we were growing up. I knew my parents would object to dating you but I thought you were cute and too skinny since I was young. And Pierre's penis in the first one I ever saw."

We laughed at the memory of my brother constantly running around with no underwear on when we were kids.

I said, "to this day, he hates underwear. When we heard of boxers, he was hooked. I can't believe you noticed me like that, though."

"Even though you were young, all your uncles and brothers gave you a special kind of respect."

"I thought they took advantage of me, especially my uncles."

After a short pause, Cathy said, "make sure you stay out the way of those Haitian Posse guys I hear so much about."

"What you heard about them?"

"That they're gangsters and they're nothing to mess with.

They disrespect Haitian women and not the American women. They kill people, they steal, rob, just everything that's bad."

"You can't believe everything you hear. By living in a commu- nity like Little Haiti that's set up for failure, someone's hand can be forced to do wrong to survive just to feed their family. Like the very first John D. Rockefeller who started for his family and took people's oil lands. This is not Heaven."

"I love a smart man. There are theories that my dad took a lot of people's land growing up in Haiti to start his peanut butter company."

"So you know that, don't be hard on those Haitian Posse guys. They could be opening doors up in Haiti for their families or other Haitians."

"That's a good way to see it. I guess."

"Never forget how the great America was built with killing, stealing, slavery, and I can go on and on. It don't justify wrong, but I'm a firm believer in only fearing God."

"I fear God too, but stay away from doze guys, okay?" "Alright, Cathy."

The waiter came with the food. He placed our orders in front of us and left. I said, "I can't figure out how this pork and chicken get so big."

"I can tell you, we study that in political science. Can you handle it if I tell you now?"

"You already know Cathy! You know where I'm from! I can handle it. Teach me something, 'cause I been busting my head trying to figure this out."

"Well, it starts where they're raised. Meat is such in demand, the supplies have to be manufactured quicker. The factories use a bug to manufacture an antibiotic called bacitracin. It's a methionine, an amino acid-like lysine that promotes animal growth eighty times faster and bigger. The lysine is a bug in the body that causes you to be hungry when you're actually full. The Chinese are known for putting it in their rice. Scientists say no one knew where cancer comes from, but eating a real bad deformed or retarded chicken or beef, any meat can cause cancer in the blood stream. That's why I eat fish only. They throw AIDS needles in the ocean, but I have faith in knowing man didn't come up with salt water. I believe God blesses the fish. But that's my theory."

"That must have been the best pork I ever ate. It tastes like the pig been swimming in mud only."

"You crazy. I can make a better tasting pork chop, but Jean, you crazy."

"But you make a lot of sense and state facts. I hear even the vending machine snacks, cookies, cereal, a lot of things has lysine."

"Oh, you really did look into it? All you have to do is put a closed pack of cupcakes on top of your T.V. and five years later, it would remain the same. The bugs in it can last up to ten years."

"Alright, alright, alright you win. Where you going after this?" "I got a call to cover someone at work. But I want to play

hooky with you. So let's do something crazy." "Like what?"

"Let's go to Disney World." "Orlando?"

"Yeah."

"I think I'm the one going to play hooky with my family." "When does your family come back?"

"Don't worry, we can go tomorrow. What time?"

"Let's go at six in the morning and be back at midnight. Want to sleep over? We have an extra room."

"Oh, no. No, I can't sleep over. But I will be there at six in the morning."

"Okay, I will go get a rental car when I leave."

"Don't worry about that, I can get a truck from my dad's friend."

"Alright, Jean. This will be fun." "I bet it will be."

I didn't know what I would tell Crip and Gee. Cathy and I hugged. I paid for lunch and we both got in our cars to go our separate ways. Before going to the house, I stopped by a pawn shop and pawned my necklace, watch, and ring. I got forty-five thousand dollars for it all. I went home, Crip said, "you good? Where your chain?"

"Damn. I just walked in and you notice? I just pawned it. Here goes forty thousand to put in the pot. It should be fifty- five grand now, right?"

"Yeah, but you didn't answer your phone all afternoon."

"I turned it off not to hear my mom's mouth. Where Gee at?" "Locked in the room with that girl, Percila."

"Where your girl at?"

"She told me something about babysitting, trying to give me some kind of hint, so I let her leave."

"Listen Crip, I'm looking at a get-money plot by my mom's job. I'm going to leave around five in the morning to go check it out."

"No pressure. But leave your phone on, I been worried Jean." "After tomorrow it would stay on, just trust me Crip."

"It must be big if you not taking me to study the money-plot with you."

"I'm going to get some sleep bro. I'm tired and got a headache. And Crip, I need the Explorer tomorrow."

CHAPTER THIRTEEN

I sat in front of Cathy's house at 5:54 a.m. waiting for her to come out. Walker came outside instead. "I see you got Cathy playing hooky."

"It would be the last time Walker."

Cathy came out with a mini suitcase. I only had the clothes on my back. She handed me a breakfast she made and kissed me on the cheek. Walker told us to call him if we got in any trouble. The chicken croquettes with lamb and chicken in my scrambled eggs went well with the syrup on the biscuits. I felt sleepy and love-dizzy from watching Cathy's pretty toes on the dashboard and listening to her sing every Mary J. Blige song that came on from the 411 C.D.

The first two hours of the drive were love-dreadful. Cathy took over for the last hour and a half. We got a hotel, took showers, and went to catch the Disney World bus that picked us up. After getting the tickets we walked and Cathy grabbed my hand. I slipped my hat down and took a deep breath. I laughed to myself thinking of one of Ricardo's jokes he would've had for me if he would have seen me holding hands.

We went on a bumper car and it was so fun, we did it three times. I enjoyed the bumper cars, us trying to bump everybody and anybody till their necks popped. We took pictures with Mickey and Minnie Mouse. The candy apples and cotton candy that we fed each other was good. It seemed like everyone that passed by us would look at Cathy, who was drop dead gorgeous. They seemed to wonder how a girl as beautiful as Cathy could be holding hands with an apparent gangster. Cathy lit up the park with her shorts, Reeboks, and ponytail. The fact that she wasn't even trying was what made her beautiful.

We took a nice ferry ride through the whole park, picking at people in Creole. They looked at us not understanding a word we were saying. Cathy took me on a ride called Space Moun- tain, knowing she was setting me up. It was the scariest thing since the Freedom Boat. While going through Space Mountain, pictures were taken and I was holding onto Cathy like a bitch. We took a picture in Wild Wild West clothing, which was cool. We played basketball, played a game where we tried to throw a penny in a bottle, played Bull's Eye with a water gun. The bull ride that I jumped on by myself got a standing ovation from the crowd that surrounded me. We ended up with at least nine different stuffed animals.

Taking a break, we sat down on a bench, five kids ran to me saying, "Uncle Jean! Uncle Jean! Uncle Jean!" They were on a trip with two older ladies from Lincoln Field. The weekend parties in the projects where we stopped five ice cream trucks, got a DJ, and got a bounce house had built a bond between the project kids and the Haitian Posse. Cathy looked in surprise as I hugged each child. I introduced Cathy to the ladies. I was lucky I never went outside with Biya.

One of the ladies said, "since you Haitians left, I hate going to pick up my mail."

We both grinned at the inside joke. I walked over with the ladies while Cathy was playing and talking with the kids. After I handled the ladies five hundred dollars each, they left.

"Where do you know all of them from?" Cathy asked.

"We did some work in a project and it lasted about three months so we bonded together."

"I told you that you got a special glare that people love about you. But don't get too friendly." She hugged and kissed me right on the lips. It was something I had daydreamed about since childhood, and it was coming true.

It was about 11 p.m. We went to the hotel to leave. The day had been so exhausting that we decided to lay down for thirty minutes to get a little nap. I heard her get up in the middle of the night and call Walker. I thought of how I would deal with my boyz tomorrow. Waking up first the next morning, I said, "Cathy, Cathy. It's eight thirty. Let's go."

She was fully dressed, as I was, with her head laying on my chest. "Okay, baby."

I drove the whole way to Miami, only stopping at a Waffle House for

173

a quick breakfast. I dropped Cathy off at home where she kissed me on the lips and promised to call me.

I walked in the house at 1:07 p.m. meeting eyes with Gerald.

He said, "where you been bro?" "I slept at my Mom's house."

"Why the fuck you got to be lying, homie? Pierre been with his Mom for four days asking about you."

"You my daddy, nigga?"

"Motherfucker, you got your nose in that bitch ass from the mall. That Haitian bitch."

"Watch your mouth."

Crip said, "What's really up Jean?"

Gee answered, "he been acting funny since we got out of jail. I don't even think he care about his brother."

I became angry. "Fuck you, YO!!"

"No, fuck your bitch! Nigga you got a hookup to try to pay the jury and won't even follow up on it."

"I'm on it. But don't come at me with no bullshit."

"Jean, we never lie to each other, What's up?"

"Shit nigga!" Gee laughed at me. "I could never figure out what you and Pierre do alike. Now I know what it is. You both tender-dicks!"

"Fuck you nigga."

"Don't think I need you to get money." Gee wasn't even mad. "I can open up Lincoln Field or go find where the money is at. I did it before we met and I can do it after."

"How long that's been on your chest? I'm glad you let that out, pussy."

That pissed Gerald off and brought us close to fighting. Crip, with a bad leg, couldn't even stop us. He went and got a gun and shot into the couch. We stood back.

Crip said, "what the fuck, man? What the fuck with you two? Don't both of you know that you just beat trial a week ago?! They wanted both of you doing twenty years in prison! Now Jean, you lied to us so know when right is right and wrong is wrong."

I said, 'I'm going in the room. I'll talk to both of you tomor- row. I'm sleepy, I been on the road all this morning at Disney World since yesterday."

After getting some well-needed rest, I woke up at 1 a.m. to see Crip and Gee watching T.V. They were eating some chicken wings on the couch with a tight space between them. I dropped myself between them touching both of them in the process. Gee moved over a little. I said, "these chicken wings good. It tastes like Gee cooked them."

No answer.

I said, "what's up with the boyz, Crip?"

"Well, Lil Bam-Bam and Jay get out next week. I told them we will be there to get them."

Gee asked, "How you know all of us going to be free."

I said, "I hear you. But I want to tell both of you some- thing. I think I like this girl, Cathy. We go way back to when we were young."

"Pierre told us about all that on the phone, about you been crazy about her and he was surprised she gave you the time of day."

"But I really like the girl. I didn't tell her about Haitian Posse when she asked and I don't think I'm going to mention it to her. If she corners me, that's another thing."

Crip said, "we not the type to tell girls that anyway. But we both were saying that we happy you got a girl like that."

"Thanks. She think I'm a construction worker." Gee said, "what's up with getting some money?"

"That could take six months, a year, sometimes two years. We got to be smart at our attack moves."

"What's up with this jury shit?"

"I'm going to get with Biya tomorrow." "I'm about to go lay down."

Later, we picked up Lil Bam-Bam and Jay. They said they didn't want to go to the projects so they stayed in the house with us. Lil Sergo ended up joining all of us. Lil Sergo also ended up joining all of us. I spent at least three hours a day on the phone with Cathy. She thought I was out of town doing some construction work. We made a couple of three-way calls for Mr. Talkative Pierre, whose enthusiasm stayed at a high level. Biya, who could find information on Mars if she really wanted, told me one day, "I would love to take a picture with

Mickey and Minnie."

I would brush her words right by me, changing the conver- sation by asking if Kitchen and Polite were still jumping out crazy in the projects. She told me they were not. Biya said that some of Lil Bam-Bam's boys were posting up in front of

Annie's apartment. They still brought us money from time to time, but it would be around two thousand dollars a week, if that. I tried to keep Biya with as little information as I could. We talked about the next day's events that would take place in Pierre's and Annie's case. They were picking the jury.

Biya and Annie had been rehearsing over and over again just hoping to approach someone black. Annie and Pierre picked their jury. Annie had five strippers and two owners of two different strip clubs to come and defend her and claim that she had been stripping and prostituting for years. Luke Skywalker also would be testifying that she had won eight different dance contests with trophies to show. And everyone knew what kind of dance contest Luke had in Miami. All naked.

Pierre's defense was that he met Annie three months ago and only came to Lincoln Field projects to buy sex from her, and the massive foot traffic caused by her pathetic constant prosti- tuting meant anybody could have left drugs in her apartment. The defense lawyers research and arguments were para- lyzing how they disgraced Annie's and Pierre's upbringing.

The jury with five blacks, five Spanish, and two whites, none of whom were tipped off, found both defendants 'Not Guilty' of all charges. My mom and a whole of strippers were there jumping for joy outside the courtroom. Annie cried. Pierre held her and tongue-kissed her in front of all of us. It was an exciting atmosphere.

We all went to the Red Lobster that I chose. Having dinner with twenty-two people, we spent at least five hours sitting together telling jokes overlooking the water. I grieved not hav- ing Cathy around, but Biya filled in the empty space as best as she could. My mom even stayed with William and Roy sharing laughter with one another. Mom took pictures. Crip slid Pierre one thousand five hundred dollars on one side and turned to me, "how you know about this place?" "Don't ask, Crip. Don't ask."

"You and me need to talk Jean." I mumbled, "Biya, Biya."

Me, Gerald, and Crip went home while Pierre followed Annie. He said he needed two days to put a black on his Boo- Boo's pussy.

Gerald said, "Annie is straight certified in my eyes. I probably would be marrying and putting a baby in that soldier."

Crip frowned. "Marry? I don't know about that, but defi- nitely a baby."

I said, "he needed to get his life together."

The three youngsters came in with Red Lobster leftovers in their hands. Lil Sergo said, "man, we need to have more Beat Trial parties. You saw all them bitches? I got two phone numbers."

I said, "when Ricardo and Syco come home we got to go over to the Rolex strip club. We old enough to all go. Or we will tip them a little extra money to get in."

Ricardo's mom pulled up to drop Syco and Ricky off to the house. Pierre got to Ricardo first, lifting him up. "What's up Haitian?"

"Freedom!!! Freedom!!!"

I hugged Syco. "I miss you brother."

"Me too. We were tearing them people's prison up." "That phrase is

177

over, we got big dreams bro."

After all of us kissed Mrs. Malando, she said, "please take care of my baby and keep him out of trouble."

Crip said, "we will, Mommy."

Gee, Ricardo, and Pierre went in talking about all kinds of personal business. Me, Syco, and Crip chilled in the room talking. Lil Bam and Jay were in the other room talking about Syco's dad and what we had been doing since the rest of us had gotten home.

Syco said, "I need my bullets."

Everybody fell out laughing at that. I told him we got some clothes and sneakers for them and he needed to get cleaned up.

"Where we going?"

"The strip club. The Rolex."

"I'm not really on that, but I'll go with the boyz and go chill with Papaine tonight."

Crip said, "that's the plan then."

I said, "we too crowded in this house. We got to get some money."

Syco squinted. "I thought the plan was already in place. Why we don't go back in Lincoln Field?"

"Oh, no! That's not happening bro. Let's take you to get a haircut 'cause you look like a caveman with all that hair on your face. And you need to get something to eat. Call Papaine, 'cause Trina, Biya, Annie, and some of their friends coming."

"Let's do it!"

All of us walked in the Rolex about twenty-five deep. The girls stood with us for a while, then went to mingle. The boyz stood in a corner. Some smoked weed and drank out of the bottles of Hennessy. We stood there not even getting one dance. Personally, my knowing that most of the club knew me and I didn't know them made me feel uncomfortable. We never got out of character in public. Some dudes that we met in the jail system came by to say what's up, but we didn't go approach anybody at all. Annie was right when she said we were boring when we got in a club. But as long as all of us were together, we had a good time in our eyes. In fact, we stayed in The Rolex for about six hours.

Two days later, I took Pierre to dinner at Walker's and Cathy's house. When she opened the door she hugged Pierre and shook him around. "Look how big you got!"

Walker said, "Pierre, I see you got on pants."

When Pierre laughed showing his thirty-two golds, Cathy said, "oh my God!! Pierre what you doing with all those golds in your mouth? You look like a hoodlum."

"I love gold. You should see my necklace and rings."

Walker said, "wow! You have to come pick me up from school and walk around the school smiling. Make sure you say we cousins."

"We ARE cousins."

Cathy hugged me in front of them and kissed me in the mouth. "This my baby Pierre, don't get him in no trouble."

"He causes all the trouble."

I pushed him walking in the house. The twenty-five ounce steaks with rice and beans with papaya juice hit the spot. Walk- er talked Pierre into going with him to the school. They left around 8 p.m. to catch some fraternity party.

Me and Cathy decided to go for a walk on Virginia Key Beach. Walking in the sand, I held Cathy's sandals. We kissed a dozen times. The laughs felt genuine to me. We decided to get a hotel room at the Holiday Inn. It gave me a sense of the fact that we might make love for the first time.

We got in the room and Cathy went in the shower. I sat and watched T.V. Cathy came out the shower almost an hour later with her hair wrapped and wearing a Holiday Inn bathrobe. Her pretty feet made me aroused alone. I took a fifteen-minute shower and got out showing my six-pack with a towel around me. Cathy said, "Jean, why you have Haitian

Posse on your chest?"

"Listen to me Cathy. I really have feelings for you since I was four years old. I want you to have feelings for what I bring to you and say to you."

"Are you a gangster Jean? Oh God, I can't believe I fell in love with a gangster. How didn't I see this?"

"I'm a rebel. A rebel is disobedient to authority. I'm in search of utopia in America and shall die trying to receive that. I have had the best four months ever with a woman and I will always protect you. Just know I promise never to put you in harms way."

"But I hear all kinds of things and I'm not in the streets. Are you Haitian Posse?"

"I'm me, and love my family. My name is Jean Adam, that's what you know, and all I've shown you Cathy."

She sent pacing around the room. Lord I can't believe I love a gangster! Oh Lord, why?"

"Do you like to make society happy or yourself?"

With a river of tears flowing down her face, she said, "Jean, just stop what you doing. I can take care of us. Let's move to another state."

"Please feel protected with me, don't judge me with an evil eye. You know how far I came from. I want nothing but to love you back Cathy."

"No, Jean, no. I chose to break my virginity with you tonight before I get married and now I have a killer in my hotel room. " Her voice was now vicious.

"Get hold of yourself. You're twenty-one years old. I never brought harm to you and will give you the most genuine love that I can give.

"Yeah, one day you just will pick up and leave as soon as you get you some pussy, huh?"

"This is your choice. We can leave right now." I reached for my pants. She grabbed my hand and wept. "Don't you understand what

I'm telling you? I love you Jean. I been telling you that for two months straight. You have never told me you love me yet."

"Can you be you and I be me before you say I did it for sex? Now if I say I love you, what you going to think?"

"I fell in love with a member of the Haitian Posse. My dad will kill you and me."

"Sorry to tell you, but your dad had always been an icon in my eyes. The way he gave you a good upbringing was magical to me."

Still livid, she said, "your dad works just as hard, if not harder. Wait a minute, is your dad in America or Haiti?"

"We will talk about that another time."

"Oh, I forgot, gangsters don't speak from emotion, everything is bygones be bygones."

"Look Cathy, I'm leaving, okay? 'Cause you just want to scream." "That's not an answer, Jean. I kept wondering why I never saw a drop of paint on you. And in four months, me and Walker haven't talked to none of your brothers except Pierre, which was today, and none of your seven uncles. Where are they? In jail or dead?"

I screamed, "My dad is dead! My brother Joe is dead! My twin sister Marie is dead, okay? All seven of my uncles are dead! Okay? Okay?! You happy? They all died coming to America. You happy now? And my two aunts got eaten by sharks. You like that?!!"

She was stunned. "I'm sorry Jean. I'm so sorry." "Get your hands off me."

Her tears were heavier now. "I'm sorry Jean, I'm so sorry. Please hold me. Hold me Jean, I can't lose you. I love you with all my heart. Please love me Jean. Please love me. Let's leave. We can leave with Pierre. Where's your mom?"

'She's around."

"Oh, thank God. I'm sorry for being heartless and selfish. How have you been able to not tell me this for four months?" "I don't know. You brought emotions around that I thought

181

was lost at sea on a fucking Freedom Boat ride." "Please hug me Jean."

We hugged tightly. I said, "I will protect you Cathy, I will protect you."

"I love you Jean. Please don't let me go."

Cathy and I spent the whole night hugging each other. She cried over and over again when I explained about the trip to America that took my family. I told her the guys around me were my immediate family and would protect her in the same way as I would. Eventually she cried herself to sleep, resting her face on my naked chest.

Early in the morning we ordered breakfast. Cathy insisted on not going to school for the day. I was adamant on her to go, but she insisted on staying one more night. She called Walker and he told her of all the fun he had with Pierre drinking beer at a Delta Psi Beta frat party. I called Ricardo to tell him I was staying another night with Cathy.

Making passionate love to her that night was emotional from not fully being able to enter Cathy. I had scratches of blood on my back. By our fourth try, I was sliding in and out of her. The KY Jelly had been a great deal of help. Cathy moaned so soulfully that she spoke nothing but creole words to me. "Um vta toute chare, Je tamie mui na mue, woy woy, le au da me Jean, le au da me Jean."

The sex had fireworks all in the air. We stayed an extra day but on the last night I told her she needed to go to school. We would hook that weekend. Cathy agreed. She told me she felt she was walking funny and asked me if I could tell.

"Yeah, it's bad."

She patted me on the arm playfully. "For real, Jean?" "I'm for real.":

After our time together, Cathy got her books, gave me a hug, and headed out the door. "I'll call you Jean, I love you baby."

"I'll be waiting on your call, Kitty Kat."

She smiled and blushed. "I like that nickname, bye."

CHAPTER FOURTEEN

I pulled the cover up and saw blood on the white sheet, confirming that Cathy truly was a virgin. I shook my head in amazement. The hot shower felt good. While putting on my socks I watched the six o'clock local news and saw a bunch of police officers. The anchor on Channel Seven said, "the boats from Columbia and Bulgaria contained cocaine with a street value of twenty million dollars. Custom agents and Coast Guards were tipped off about two different boats entering the Port-of-Miami."

I got up to look out the window and saw a clear view of a lot of police officers, which I assumed were Customs agents and Coast Guards. A pair of binoculars would have made my view even more perfect. Catching the tail end of the news, I heard the reporter say, "The cocaine kilos should be all disposed of in the weeks to come."

I sat for fifteen minutes clicking my criminal mind together thinking of all different ends of logic that I knew could be regulated. Finally, I settled on an idea. I called Crip. "Listen, the seven o'clock news about to come on. You have to be hear by six fifty-five by yourself, now!"

"I'll be there Jean."

Staring out the window at the other six boats beside the boat that got busted, I marveled with a smile. After being so serious by myself, Crip knocked on the door. When I opened up, he said, "It's six fifty-two bro, did I make it?"

"Yeah, look out the window for a minute, Crip. See all them boats with their flags hanging high?"

He stared for five minutes. "I really can't put together what you see Jean. I need more clues."

"It's on, watch the news."

We sat quietly looking at the T.V. The news anchor did all the talking. "Again, as reported earlier, the boats from Columbia and Bulgaria contained a street value of twenty million dollars. Customs agents and Coats Guards were tipped off."

Crip walked to the window staring at the boats again. "They carrying drugs on them boats."

"Exactly. But doze two got tipped off. Usually they pass Cus- toms and Coast Guards and they got to pass Haitian Posse bro. If we see any boats like that arrive on Port-of-Miami and see them pass Customs and Coast Guards, we going to pay a visit with straight fifty-round automatic guns letting them know we mean business."

"That's it Jean, you seen all the kilos? They just said twenty million dollars worth."

"I heard it all and I'm leaving this T.V. or this room. I'm going to watch the eight o'clock, ten, eleven, twelve o'clock news. Go get the room for a week. Buy two telescopes, two binoc- ulars, and a book that can tell us what flags is what country. Anything coming from Canada, Europe, or China I think is legit. But Columbia, Mexico, Haiti, Panama, and a bunch of others getting their dope in through the Port of Miami."

"Cool. I'll be right back Jean."

"Don't tell the boyz nothing, not even to watch the news. Just tell them we busy and I stay home."

Getting comfortable in my new home in the hotel room, I looked out the window and wrote down anything that I knew we would need, like a stop watch, newspaper, names of boats, whistles, and gloves. I put the pad and pencil down. Fear, I thought to myself. That's going to be the most important thing. Fear, I knew we had to be serious with no games.

Crip came back three hours later with a couple of bags. He assured me that nobody had stopped him along the way. I pulled out the binoculars. "The Bulgaria boat is called Kebabcheta."

"What that mean?"

"I don't know, but I can see all in the boat. It all look like money to me. We need a language guide. We also need to know how much time it takes to get from the dock ramp to the boats." I held up the binoculars. "These are perfect, Crip."

"I got two sets."

"We going to look at this heavy through the week. Let me know if you sleepy and I will let you know if I'm sleepy my nigga. Just study this shit to the T with me."

Getting the newspaper in the morning, I had a good read. There was a full-page story about the two drug boats. When I read along, I saw that there were no arrests made. I told Crip that particular shipment was supposed to get caught for political reasons. The same night Crip woke me up to look at the dock. "Look what they taking off."

"I see it. What does it say? Sugar?" "Yep."

"That's all dope on the Panama boat. It waited two days, I know this because it parked two nights ago and passed Customs and Coast Guards."

"We supposed to get at this one right here now."

"I know, but study it. That dope coming in like a water foun- tain. Boats coming and going. Five left yesterday and two more came today. Damn, the hood getting pimped. It's probably George Bush's dope."

Crip laughed. "You bullshitting. It probably is." "I'm for real, fam."

The six days went by and I felt like I could work on the docks. We knew the movement of boats real good. "Crip, your driv- ing is going to have to be perfect. We got to go with trucks so go ride around and find a nice routine. I'll study it with you."

With Crip gone, I learned so many flags, I told myself I was going to visit all those places with Cathy. I even dreamed of us in Venezuela during a hot summer month. But the task at hand was my biggest concern. I continued studying the timing of the authorities and made a note to get a radio scanner to channel in the Coast Guards' awareness on the water. The sketch I had on the blackboard in the room maintained a time of fifteen minutes on the boat and being off the ramp by fourteen minutes and forty-five seconds. The ramps came down at 6:00 a.m. and went up at 11:00 p.m.

Crip came in and we went to sleep until 7:00 in the morn- ing, so Crip could show me the route to the house. He said, "the truck could park right at the end of the ramp. There's no cameras and the nearest police station is nineteen minutes away. Once we make a right down one block, we will get on the main road to go over a drawbridge that comes up for big fishing boats or boats with antennas on at least twenty feet high. After the bridge, we will be clearly out of view of Port-of-Miami."

"Sounds great! Let's go back to the hotel and pay for two more days."

Sitting in the room going over everything, Crip finally said, "let's order a bottle of Hennessey."

"No problem, but I'm not going hard. One of us got to stay up tonight."

Around 10:00 that night, I was watching the sea and saw the target. I woke Crip up. "They let it go! That's the one, I feel it! Look how that boat give me goosebumps." I showed him my arm.

The boat had a Columbian flag on it, coming on the Port- of-Miami looking proper. Crip said, "yeah, that's it. That's it, my nigga."

"We got to be up early to see when Customs lift the boat out the water and check on it, and Coast Guards go through it as well. We hitting it two hours after that bro!"

THAT!!!

Crip said, "We need to get doze big army bags that stand at least six feet to drag it down the ramp."

"Go get it tonight 'cause it's going to be a busy day tomorrow." THAT!!

A little Spanish man walked around with Customs agents on the Columbia boat called Por Avion, Air Mail. I said to Crip while both of us looked at the scene through binoculars, "that little Spanish man on the boat, that's our main man right there. He gots to be apprehended. We got to make him talk, he knows that boat too well."

"Look at him walking with those agents pointing at everything in their sight."

"It's two o'clock Crip, if the Coast Guards leave the port's premises we going in two hours later."

"Sounds good to me, Jean."

We later walked in the house with bags in our hand and the same clothes we had on for eight days. Gerald yelled to the boyz, "Jean and Crip here everybody!! They here! I love when you two spend nights together, it makes me sleep real good."

Ricardo, with a serious face said, "what's up Jean? What's up Crip?"

I nodded. "Everything here right?"

Pierre said, "yeah, Little Bam-Bam them could stay right?"

"They family. We going to need about ten of us for this one. Let's do a meeting right now!"

Gee screamed, "meeting! Meeting! Syco, let's do it bro! Meeting!"

Everyone stood silent, only fueled with energetic urgen- cy. I said, "me and Crip been scoping out the Port-of-Miami at a Columbian boat called Air Mail in Spanish. Now today we seen Custom agents lift and search in the boat, and the Coast Guards got on the boat as well while it was surrounded by Coast Guard boats. All those government motherfuckers is gone. Now they got to be searched by Haitian Posse."

Everybody reacted with excitement, but I quickly regained control of the situation. "My main thing is putting fear of God in anybody on the boat. I want everybody to have auto- matic fifty-round weapons. I'm only going to have a .38. Crip and Jay going to stay in both trucks waiting at the end of the ramp. I will lead coming up the ramp with Ricardo right behind me. We all got to carry one of these." I held up a green army bag for them to see. "When I say 'Let's go,' that means let's go. We all going to come right back to where we stand. And Lil Jay, I want you following Crip's tail never turning unless you have to. There's a bridge that you have to go over, but I will be in the truck with you fam. We leave in one hour. Put on your gloves, regular clothes and a hat. We'll get on the boat ramp at 9:45. Just follow my lead and point the guns and let me talk to the boat crew. Ricardo, your name is Chico for right now. Syco, Gee, Lil Bam, when I point, that means go secure all around the boat. Once I grab this little Spanish man, Pierre, Sergo, Toro, follow me. You other three go around the boat and tie whoever you see up with the AK-47's and come back to me. Is there any questions?"

Silence.

"Well let's do it!!! Me and Crip going to talk for a while. Just get all the guns, empty both trucks out and get ready. It's on my niggas."

The scene was filled with fast-paced movement. Both trucks drove over the bridge to turn left down the Port-of-Miami. They pulled up in front of the boat ramp where the Columbian boat of my interest was docked. I told Little Jay to blow the horn repeatedly if anything crazy came in sight, and pop the truck latch when we came down the ramp.

I opened the door leading the walk up the ramp with Ricardo, behind me and the others flanking him. We walked in view of each other with our guns on the side of our legs. It was 9:56

p.m. I hit the deck. "Don't move, motherfuckers." I pointed the boyz to go right and left. They jetted with guns high in the air. Finding the little Spanish man, I grabbed his shirt. "Where the dope, motherfucker?"

He spoke Spanish. "What he saying, Chico?"

"That's no problem, no problem. Ssshhh, Coast Guard." I said, "take us to the dope."

We took a long walk downstairs to an engine room. The Spanish man kept saying, "Ssshh, ssshhh, Customs."

Ricardo translated my words in Spanish.

We walked to a spot where the little Spanish man point- ed. I looked at my watch. "Fuck, it's been sixteen minutes."

"Ssshhh, please, please, no trouble. FBI. Customs, Coast Guards. No trouble please." The man begged.

The boyz caught on to us throwing bags of Columbian coffee in the bags. The knife I stuck into some of the coffee revealed cocaine. We stuffed some of the bags and Pierre and Ricardo left. We stuffed more bags and Gee and Syco left. We stuffed the remaining bags and Bam and I left.

The old Spanish man stayed unconscious on the floor from Syco hitting him with the back of the AR-15. I looked at my watch. Twenty-two minutes. Going down the ramp we saw there was not a car in sight. The latch in the truck was open. We drove off following Crip's truck with the rest of the boyz. When we crossed the lifting bridge I took a nice breath looking at the passenger seat's rear view mirror, seeing just regular cars turning behind us. The one police car I saw fifteen minutes into our driving gave not one indication that the trucks were hot.

We pulled up to the house with major silence, each person grabbing a bag to walk inside the house. Crip locked the door. "We got it. We did it. Is this it, fam?" We took the bags in the living room and gathered around them. Me and Crip stuck knives through some of the coffee-covered dope. I said, "it's about fourteen of them we done stuck. All kilos of cocaine. Let's count each bag to know how many we got. Here, give me that bag first Ricardo and everybody count with me."

One kilo.

Two kilos.

Three kilos.

Four kilos.

Twenty-five kilos. Twenty-six kilos. Forty-two kilos.

Forty-three kilos. "Give me the other bag." Forty-four kilos.

Forty-five kilos. Eighty-six kilos. Eighty-seven kilos.

One hundred twenty kilos.

One hundred twenty-two kilos. "Stop yelling, Gee, you making me nervous."

Two hundred twenty-two kilos. Three hundred five kilos.

Three hundred seven kilos. Three hundred eighty-nine kilos. Four hundred kilos.

Crip said, "damn, there's still two more bags." Four hundred eleven kilos.

Four hundred seventeen kilos. "Here we go, last bag. That's the fullest one."

Four hundred seventy-nine kilos.

Four hundred ninety-two kilos. "Kids we done hit the jack- pot!! WE RICH!! Five hundred two kilos!! We done retired homies!!!"

That's when we started celebrating jubilantly, calling out all kinds of things we wanted to buy.

"I want a island!!" "We RICH!!!"

Gee picked up one kilo and tossed it to Pierre. The rest of us jumped around like we were at Mardi-Gras. That priceless moment was like Christmas in October. The guns laid on the floor, the kilos of cocaine laid in a big-ass mountain. Knowing that we left some didn't bother us. We'd hit the jackpot.

After about forty-five minutes of celebrating I said, "chill, chill out everybody. Come back, we got a few things on our agenda to take care of as a group."

Everyone came to their senses and calmed down to hear what I had to say.

"Homies, we got some shit to handle. First, all these cars around here, we got to do something about it. You know Syco's dad is a pastor and a realtor. I'm going to holla at him about getting two warehouses to park these cars plus more that we might get. Put these guns up and we can chill. I need to know who all got to get a home to talk to Syco's dad about also. I say we get one six-bedroom crib for us all. And I might get a spot around the corner with Cathy. Now who all want to get a crib?"

Gee said, "I'm staying with the boyz." Syco said, "me too."

Ricardo nodded, "me too. I don't need no separate spot." Gee said, "You know what, I'm going to move my Aunt Boo." Pierre was like, "let me stay with you, Jean, with Annie." "Negative."

"Well, I'll get a place with her."

"Oh, we all will chip in to get Annie that Lexus 400 she wanted. She's gangster. All you young niggas can stay at this house here and you know the house we get is for the whole family. So five houses and two warehouses is mandatory. Now listen, and listen carefully, this depends on a group decision. We can sell all this shit at one time to Papi, but he going to want a price of twelve and a half for each kilo. Or we can slow grind this out with some out of town connect and get up to twen- ty-six and a half for each kilo."

Gee said, "sell that shit to Papi today!" Ricardo said, "yeah man."

Pierre agreed. Crip, Syco, and me all wanted to slow grind the coke and get the most money possible for it. It wasn't a conversation for the young ones. The vote was split 50/50. Gerald and Pierre went to disputing, we done took enough chances already, and we never been out of town, so we not taking a chance, when we could retire now?

Look my nigga, think about it homeboy, if we sell this five hundred two kilos out of town for, let's say for the low twenty thousand a piece, we can make ten million dollars fam. But if we sell it right here in Miami to Malando, we only make six million dollars, that's a whole four million extra my niggas, think about it Ricardo.

Ricardo said, "that shit sound good, but for-sure money is better than 'Not for-sure money,' I know my old boy can get us that six million dollars 100 percent for sure and you know that Crip."

Crip shaking his head side to side saying, "I don't under- stand how all three of you don't want to try to get this other four million dollars fam, we got five hundred two kilos and that shit sounds like we going to retire, but that's not even a million a piece after we break off the young niggas if we sell it to your old boy."

Watching Ricky, G, and Gold Mouth ball up their face, huff- ing and mumbling bullshit out their mouth. They complained so much, I said, "sell it to Papi, fuck it."

Syco and Crip went ahead and agreed for the fast move. I would sell all that shit one hundred kilos at a time to Mr. Malando.

When I told Malando I had one hundred kilos outside, he had a big eye and let me know he could sell it all by that day. I was amazed to hear that. By the third day Malando had given me six million dollars. Syco's dad talked to me and Crip with hunger in his eyes. At least Mr. Malando had asked if we were n trouble. Syco's dad just asked if we had more money, if we needed any cars, and if Syco had money.

We spent 1.4 million with him and not two weeks passed before he got us the big warehouse that easily could have held fifty cars if we had them. The nineteen cars we did have just rotated n and out. The warehouse had two offices we turned into bedrooms with cable T.V. It was the perfect place to stop and chill at.

The six-bedroom house had six bathrooms. We all got a room. The four-car garage always kept seven cars outside of it, or more. Little Bam-Bam moved his mom to Hallandale. Our six-bedroom Pembroke Pines house, and the three-bedroom home me and Cathy got around the corner were all-white neighborhoods. We never really felt at ease there and chilled at the warehouse and Syco's house. We still were too ghetto in our hearts.

The money split. We had six hundred thousand dollars each. I bought Biya a 325i BMW and she parked it right at Lincoln Filed projects with a front tag that read "Mrs. Jean." Cathy never asked me questions about coming home or what I had been doing for the day. She understood when I told her she was protected plus she loved the house we bought. Cathy begged for us to have kids and played mind games by buying a child

seat to put in the Mercedes Benz 500.

Pierre never got a house. He and Annie basically stayed at the boyz new house in Pembroke Pines. Syco looked thorough with his chain that had six gold AK-47 bullets. Ricardo bounced around with chicks. I told him Trina played him after he got her a David Yurman four-piece set, she went man-hunting standing next to Uncle Luke looking real shiny.

We went to the mall at least nine times a week at the Bal Harbor Mall. Gerald asked the Polo store owner to lock us in the store. After getting tipped one thousand dollars, he gave me and Gerald special membership cards in the Polo Clothing Club. Normally all of us came from the malls with about five bags in each hand.

We didn't do regular clubs, mostly strip clubs. The Rolex was our spot to go at every night. A girl Gerald was chasing named Pinky, had a party on a Monday night boxing fight day. The section in the back "in view" of us was our new spot. Far away from the normal door hangout we usually chilled at. I personally saw my homeboys' swagger come out of them so flashy. Besides dazzling the club with all kinds of the latest clothes, Pierre's seven-inch long gold and diamond-studded

H.P. piece stood way out. He had paid seventy-five thousand dollars for the chain. Th six bottles of Hennessey on three tables with Alize to mix up the thug passion did the job. There were at least sixteen girls around us chilling real glamorous. Pierre, Gee, and Ricardo rapped to every song with a hand full of money, the other hand with a bottle. To watch Syco dance side to side with a bottle in his hand while an Amazon Jamaican girl stood right next to him with her twin sister in front of him, made us all laugh. He drunkenly threw at least eight bullets at the bitches. Crip was sitting down on a chair to my right. He always sat the girl down on a chair in front of him and pulled out a flashlight, turning into a gynecologist. I would always ask myself what he was looking for while he put the flashlight in the pussy. He would look back and forth from the girl's eyes to her pussy, spread the clit out and measure it with his pinky nail, then look at her. He would turn her around looking in her butt telling her to open it and close it. "You feel this finger?"

At times he paid girls five hundred dollars to shave their pussy hairs right in the club. He wanted to see it all.

The young dudes got lap dances till their zippers caught their pants. They even pulled their dicks out and fucked some strip- pers right there. I mostly chilled with a Haitian girl "Sweet Pea." She has a big Haitian Posses tattoo with the Haitian flag on her back. Her caramel complexion, ass round as an apple, Busch Garden hair that covered her pussy from thigh to thigh, glossed the area where we posted at. Sweet Pea gave me a lot of information. I didn't want her to have to do all kinds of extra dancing, so I paid her to just stand there. I took her to the hotel a few times.

Crip called out, "wet, wet, wet! Wet!!

We all stopped with the girls we were with and had a mini auction with the bitch, Cookie, who Crip had been looking all up in. She acted scared as the boyz yelled out their bids, going from one hundred dollars all the way up to two thousand dol- lars. The two thousand-dollar bid was Ricardo's. "Baby I need you tonight. You say wet, wet, Crip?"

"Hell yeah."

Those moments were priceless.

Me and Pierre had gotten together and gave Mom one hun- dred thousand dollars each. When we had dinner with Mom, she mostly told us to be safe and protect each other, that the lifestyle we were living was not meant to be an everyday life. She encouraged us to go back to Haiti and building something for the future, that the money we gave her would always be around in case we needed it, but we told her over and over again we didn't need the money, it was all for her. We begged her to enjoy herself and leave that old lady. Not knowing when the next time she would see us, she asked us to go with her to dad's grave site. We couldn't say no in her face and went to spend three hours at the graveyard with dad. Dropping some flowers and hearing Mom pray made me personally think about the decision to go back to Haiti.

Me and Cathy's house became Mom's four-times-a-week hangout spot. I gave her Syco's dad's phone number and told her whatever she needed to call him for, and me, and Pierre would take care of it. The ten thousand dollars each we gave my Aunts in Haiti got us grateful voodoo blessings sent from Aunt Marie. She offered to send me and Pierre two red handkerchiefs and told us to eat a paper with our goals written on it, followed by a glass of chicken blood to stay protected. It would be in us for life. She advised us to buy a black cat to put in our home. We listened but denied going through it. Being from Haiti we never understood how the poorest people were voodoo priests.

The two bedrooms that Crip's mom and dad moved in was packed with the boyz in it. The kidney surgery that Crip's mom had was successful. We were full of loving compassion watching her four steps in over twelve years. The family party we had with Ce Ce Bon catering gave Crip a sigh of relief. Grief from his mom's pain was all in his face. Ricardo told him to turn around and let him take the money off his back and Crip did it. We gave him a toast while the room full of fifty people or more listened as I gave Crip a personal toast and speech, giving

him a well-deserved round of applause.

Cathy looked at me and said, "you speak so well when you want to. So, stop acting like you have an accent with me." We both laughed together at that.

We all were chilling at the warehouse hanging out watching Brazil and Argentina play in the World Cup soccer game. Syco called out for a meeting. All of us stood in front of Gerald's Audi 500.

Syco said, "look man, I've been thinking we need to do some- thing for our souls. Let's all go to my dad's church for Easter Sunday?"

All the boyz, including me, shook our heads, oh no. None of us wanted to do it, but in our heads, we knew Syco never asked us to do anything together. It was the first time he ever called the meeting for his own topic. Me and him were real close, he even gave me seventy-five thousand dollars out of his cut, which was more than the rest of the boyz who kicked me something on the side. It was something I took in deep one-on-one concern.

Pierre and Annie were dressed lovely for Easter Sunday. So was Gerald and the stripper, Pinky, he met. Ricardo took a girl named Michelle. Crip came with his mom and dad. Syco came with Papaine, and I came with my mom and Cathy.

Syco's dad set us on the pulpit overlooking a crowd of at least eight hundred in his new church. His new wife who was fifteen years younger than he was had big eyes and jumped on every loud voiced shout of the Pastor. We all called Syco's dad, Pastor, and Pastor was good. He preached with a lot of energy and heartfelt words. The man who took well over 2.8 million in cash deserved an Oscar.

I was scared of not being fully committed to God, so I rejected when he told the crowd that we 'boyz' came to change our lives in front of them. Pierre stood up and my mom cut her eyes at him making him sit down. But Syco, Ricardo, Crip and his family all went up in front of the crowd.

After church, our group of thirty went to Red Lobster to eat an Easter dinner. Nobody had cooked at home, not even Pastor's wife who had two lobsters in front of her. She quickly made it known that she loved to eat a grilled and fried lobster at the same time. The gathering was among family and Syco was determined to pay the bill by himself. The gesture was accepted by us. Pastor jumped in his blue Benz and his wife jumped in her red Benz leaving the parking lot of the restaurant. Syco thanked all of us for coming, telling the boyz he would never ask us nothing again.

Pierre said, "stop trippin' and let me see if you got any bullets in your pocket."

"Nah, I don't, but I'm strapped."

Cathy told me that Pastor was a little creepy to her. I said, "he's family." In my head though, he reminded me of Captain Baptiste.

I wondered why Cathy never offered me to go see her parents, but often asked me weird questions like when was I going to take the eight golds out my mouth. I always enjoyed he company. She was wifey to me, so I never questioned her.

CHAPTER FIFTEEN

During a meeting at the warehouse, Gerald, Pierre, and Ricardo went to complaining they were broke. The past two weeks I had been giving them two thousand dollars here, one thousand dollars there, and at times fifty dollars to get some weed. Gerald said, "look, Jean, why don't you and Crip show us how to plot on the love boats on the Port-of-Miami? We got to be able to hold it down too."

I said, "Ricardo, I don't understand how you broke, man you just went fucking every bitch you met."

"Man a nigga missed out on pussy for four years, plus I had a lot of making up to do."

Pierre laughed. "We all did. Seriously, Jean. We left a bunch of kilos on that boat. You even said when you studied the port at least nine different boats came every week and Coast Guards and Customs agents check them every trip. We just need a little trip or two so we can really retire."

Gerald said, "you know all of us except Crip and Sergo just got out and we're flat broke living way under our means. Now we just set ourselves up. The next one should put us over the top."

Ricky, Gee, and Gold Mouth complained for thirty minutes while the rest of us heard them out. In the back I could also hear a new rapper named Nas singing.

The projects is talkin' that somebody gotta die shit. It's logic as long as it's nobody in my clique.

I said, "check it for a minute. Everybody else not well off either my nigga. Syco got to buy bullets for all these guns in here. While he do that, me and Crip going to put something together but we got to be a little smarter."

Crip said, I think we should start a record label together."

Syco shook his head. "Let's go I'm tired of hearing these niggas cry all day."

While driving I said, "Crip we are all in need of money." "I know."

"We did just basically set ourselves up good fundamentally. Another one like that should put us way over the top."

Syco remained quiet in the back seat of the black Lincoln Navigator truck I had bought. Crip spoke. "Fam, I think if we go do research on another boat, we don't have to go in the love boat. Can we catch them coming off the ramp?"

"I think that's possible because we seen them bring the ramp out late night bringing something I guess was important off the boat. Or it must be when their Customs buddies tell them to do it."

"So, what's up? We doing it?" "Yeah, we doing it."

"We'll get the special hotel room and I'll get all the other gadgets we need to do this homework."

Syco got out to get some bullets. Crip said, "It would be better if we could probably clean them out this time."

"That's true my nigga."

"I love seeing that sign, Port-of-Miami."

We hit two boats in one month. The amount of cocaine wasn't near the amount of our first robbery. The money was well-needed. When I told the boyz we had to have some mon- ey with the law firm they all disagreed. But they knew deep in their minds that problems could come up and the lawyers have performed well in the past. They all eventually agreed unanimously. The retainer of five hundred thousand dollars was steep and left us a little over seventy thousand dollars each, which we put to the side. Another robbery brought us fifty kilos of cocaine which was the lowest amount yet. The plan of catching them coming off the boat wasn't lucrative as we thought. Malando had to give us a couple more thousand. We still were not well-off enough to retire. After picking up the money for the 50 kilos of cocaine, Malando asked me to come back by myself. He wanted to talk to me one on one. I dropped Crip off and went to talk to Malando.

He had moved to a big house in South Beach where taking ten steps would have you touching sand. He wasn't a man to let you know everything directly. As when we met, I thought at times he read my body language before and after he said what was on his mind. We sat down to have lunch prepared by his 25-year-old cook who served as a cheeseburger and French fries. He spoke about the racial tension in Miami, about the recent police beating that occurred. It took both our minds back to the INS facility, how we had went hard in there. The thoughts of how everybody stood together made us laugh remembering the way certain people stayed in their room and didn't participate in the riot. It was good chilling with Mr. Malando, but he gave me more anxiety as I stayed two hours in his home. He had not given me a clue of why he wanted me to drop Crip off and come back to see him alone.

He gave me some new slippers, "put these on and let's take a walk outside where I can talk to you about something."

I put the sandals on and waited for him in the sand. To feel the hot sand on my feet felt really rich.

Mr. Malando rolled up a joint and proceeded on by saying, "I want to really tell you some things. I want you to take it serious." "Okay, no problem!" I answered. He often wanted me to read

between the lines.

"I've been hearing some disturbing news on the streets of Hialeah. Did you ever hear of a family called the Medellin Cartel?"

"No."

"Well, listen carefully. In Columbia, there is a lot of different families, but most of all, there's a lot of people from overseas selling their drugs right here in Miami. Some big suppliers are Pablo Escobar, Manuel Noriega, Ochoa brothers, and a few more. These kinds of guys I really never liked because they play with drugs, with the police and the streets. I never think the two mix, but doze kinds of families kill a lot of people and then set people up to go to the feds. I was at a big chicken fight with some heavy hitters and a guy asked me if I know a way to find a crew in Miami called Haitian Posse. Now I never got in your business, but I've heard Ricardo mentioned that name a couple times in my house."

"There's Haitian Posse all through Florida from Pensacola to Key West."

"Right, it's something I just want to mention to you Jean." "Mr. Malando, we stay in the hood and truly never leave each other, we don't go out of our way to meet new people and have them around. We keep our mouth shut about anything we do." "Listen Jean, I don't need to know how you get money, or where. I just want all you guys to understand what I'm saying.

You're like a son to me. I watched you grow as a man right before my eyes. Just be careful."

"All right Mr. Malando, I understand you."

I took a bottle of liquor he gave me, tapped my Glock on my waist, and jumped in my truck to go meet the boyz to hit a club. I really didn't understand if he wanted in on what we were doing, or if he was trying to do the same thing we were. I told only Gerald. He and I both thought Mr. Malando wanted in.

"Maybe he's going to ask you to kill some Colombians for some money," Gerald guess.

I agreed with that theory and told him not to tell the boyz about it. We went to the new club that opened called Miami Nite's in Carol City. There was a comedy show first, then the club. I told Pierre that if Mom could see us in our pin-striped three-piece suits from Gucci, that we bought from Bal Harbor Mall, she would have a big smile on her face.

We took a dozen pictures at the club. The vibe was just sexy like the sexy-violent Miami we stayed in.

I spent four days straight with Cathy. We went to Disney World again and stayed three nights there. She was happy to have me around her all day and always said jokingly that we were soon going to Oregon and get a farm when she finished school. I would look at her sparkling green eyes, melting.

Dreams come true.

Around 1:00 p.m. one day, Biya called me over and over for an hour straight.

"What's up, why you are blowing up my phone?" I asked. "Damn, you hard to get in touch with."

"What's up Chewey."

"Shit, you won't let me get my pacifier, but I didn't call you about that. This nigga Uncle Luke want to talk to you about something. I told him I had to ask you, to pass the number."

"What he want, you got any idea?" "No. He won't tell me."

"Give him my number, Chewey."

"So that fake Jayda Pinkett look-alike got you all wrapped up around her pinky huh?" "What's up Chewey?"

"Nothing, we'll see who back up first, 'cause I'm not backing out. I'll be there till the end."

"That's good to know. I'll call you back." "Whatever, bye."

Ten minutes later, Uncle Luke called me. I said, "Yeah, what's up?"

"Jean, you so hard to find." His voice was raspy.

"Yeah, I'm in the hood everyday. You not looking hard enough.

"I want to talk to you about something. Can you come over to my house?"

"The house I seen on the Lifestyle of the Rich and Famous?" "Yeah. Bring your boys and some money. I got a pool party

with at least twenty-five bitches in it." "It's Monday."

"So?"

"I'll be there, yo."

I called Gee and heard all the boyz were chilling at the ware- house. I told him I would be there in forty-five minutes, that we were going to go visit Uncle Luke Skywalker.

I got to the warehouse to see the boys about twelve deep. I said, "nah, this not a meeting Syco. But Uncle Luke wants us to come by his house. He told

201

me he needs to ask me something, I don't know what it is. He also said he got about twenty-five bitches in his pool and for us to bring some money and come hang out."

Ricardo said, "it's Monday."

"I said the same thing Ricky, he said to come anyway."

We got to Uncle Luke's house and as soon as we walked in Gerald saw Pinky and barked, "bitch!! I thought you were going to sleep, hoe"

They went off to talk while Gee held her by the elbow. The rest of the boyz went to the back where the pool was. I went to an office where Luke sat behind a big table pulling out a fat cigar. I said, "so what's up uncle Luke? I've been telling Biya and Annie to give you my number. I wanted to take you out to dinner after the trial with her and my brother."

"Oh, that's your brother with all the golds in his mouth?" "Yeah."

"You two don't favor to me. Anyway, I got a little issue. I've been having problems with some dudes on the West Coast."

"What's up?"

"You heard of Snoop Doggy Dogg, Dr. Dre, and the Dogg Pound. They all signed to Death Row Records.

"I heard of them."

"Well, they've been disrespecting Miami and they coming to Miami for a show."

"I think I heard the song they disrespecting you saying, 'gap teeth in your mouth so my dick got to fit."

"Yeah, yeah, yeah, but we are Miami. They did say that shit and a lot more things. Overall the disrespecting the crib my nigga."

"All right, go 'head with what you saying."

"They supposed to perform at Virginia Key Beach Satur- day. I need some soldiers to shoot it up, but don't shoot them."

"Luke, we don't shoot in the air."

"Jean, please, you got a favor with me, plus I helped your brother."

"Look, we going to do it for Annie, but don't tell anybody we shot that shit up in the air, that's embarrassing where I'm from."

"Okay, I like you man. Just keep it between us." "All right Uncle Luke, now I got to get in the pool." "I got a girl in a room called Freaky Red for you."

"Yeah."

"Nah, that's not my type. I see my type out there, plus it look like Freaky Red got a mustache."

We laughed. I walked out of the pool. J.T. money came up to me. "What's up Jean?"

I had never met him. "What's up J.T. money?" "Nothing. Your man over there is crazy." "What he did?"

"He threw two AK-47 bullets at me."

I shook my head. "I want to holla at him about that stupid shit." I turned to Luke and said, "there's a new group I heard coming out called The Fugees. A couple of them are Haitians and I want to meet them."

"That's nothing Jean, just do that for me."

"I'm going to the pool man, you tripping about that petty shit." I stood there looking at his backyard with a pool full of bitch- es and thought this dude got the best life ever. We hung out

and had a ball.

The next day we went to Syco's dad's house and continued the party with about eight bitches. We had a walk-around naked party that Pierre wanted to throw. We felt a little uncomfortable by Pierre having Annie there with him. I used to wonder what Pierre was telling her. Sometimes I needed those words to use on a girl. Annie was the ringleader, saying, "bitches there's money around, get to sucking. And bitches, my niggas don't fuck KY Jelly, they want all-wet pussy, so get into it."

I personally fucked four bitches and for once I went outside and said, "Ricardo let me take a puff of that weed."

Lil Bab-Bam and Pierre were trying to hit a record by fuck- ing all eight of the bitches. I had told all the boyz about what Uncle Luke wanted. They laughed and said, "no problem." They all just wanted to keep coming to his house parties.

Crip kept one stripper named Vanessa for the night. He said she had the biggest clit he ever saw, that she had a mini pinky poking out her pussy, that the water fountain that poured out smelled like strawberries.

I said, "you trippin.'"

"Nigga, this is the true wet, wet."

That Saturday, after dinner at Olive Garden I said, "we don't need any big boy guns, just need some handguns."

Syco said, "man, let's test that damn grenade launcher out at the beach. It might be getting rusty."

I said, "my niggas, please leave that and all the big guns right here at the warehouse, please sir."

Pierre said, "I got an extended clip on this nine-millime- ter. I got thirty-two rounds anyway."

"Cool, why don't all of us not shoot except three?" Everyone looked at each other.

I said, "so nobody don't want to be the person not shooting?

Well, I want to shoot too."

We all laughed at that. I finished, "fuck it, everybody shoot, and get these West Coast niggas out of Miami. They must think because all these bitches in Miami and Luke keep making all this booty-shaking music, that Miami soft."

Syco said, "let me shoot one of them niggas." Gee gritted his teeth. "I want to hit one too." Ricardo said, "A leg shot won't hurt."

"Look fam, the man not paying, so we shoot nobody."

We watched the bus as all the rappers came out, Tupac, Snoop Doggy Dogg, Dr. Dre, Kurupt, Daz Dillinger, and Suge Knight. I said, "okay, the West Coast in town. When they hit the stage, we make them run like a bunch of chickens with no heads."

One by one the rappers all got on stage. Snoop said, there's only one way to start, and that's Murder Was the Case That They Gave Me, Miami."

Gee said, "man let's do it after this song, Jean." "Cool."

Snoop uttered another word, and Syco let loose, thump, thump, thump. Ricardo followed, and so did I. Gee, Pierre, Lil Bam-Bam, Jay, Sergo too, all let loose shooting out for five whole minutes. Riding in the truck with Crip, Syco, and Lil Bam-Bam, we laughed kicking our feet in the air, slamming our hands through the car like gun shots.

"Them dudes ran fast as fuck."

"You saw Dr. Dre hide behind Daz? Haaaahaa!!!"

"Damn, we should have gotten that damn jewelry, we slipped on that."

"What about Kurupt high-stepping crazy offstage?"

I said, "Suge might be street, but he dropped straight down and rolled off the stage like he was on fire."

Biya called me to let me know someone had told her about Haitian Posse fucking the party up at Virginia Key Beach, that Haitian Posse shot the beach party up. I was like, "who want to know? Tell them to get at us, we going to Little Haiti."

She said, "you crazy! I love you Jean."

"Hold on, let me put you on speakerphone. Now, what you say?"

"I LOVE YOU JEAN! Bring my pacifier over here! I will always be Mrs. Jean, so tell them hoes to back up. I've been there since day one."

"That's right Chewey, preach to the boyz."

"They know who the real one is that's going to be there till the end."

Lil Bam-Bam said, "hold up, let me get one of these bitches on speakerphone." A bitch got on the phone representing him.

Getting to the house in Pembroke Pines, Crip and Syco took most of the guns to put up back at the warehouse.

The month of November 1994 was the most inspiring month for me as far as education. The Pastor which we followed in my Lincoln Navigator, took us around to look at different options of businesses that were for sale. The fast-talking pastor showed us a Little Haiti Coin Laundry which we all voted that we could get. A nightclub he showed us was interesting. We thought to call it Sak-Pase Club. We passed on the car dealership, a dental supply store, a sports event spot and a few others. He was adamant about buying a lot of cheap land on South Beach, but we thought it was too far from the hood.

While all six of us rolled behind Pastor's Mercedes, Lil Bam- Bam called me. "Jean, somebody came to Lincoln Field and took the air conditioning unit out of the spot where Little Jay, Toro, and Pee Wee was at, and shot all three of them in the head."

Gerald, in the passenger seat, said, "Jean what's wrong? Why you looking like that?"

I kept listening to Lil Bam.

"They cut all their hands off, then burned the apartment with them still in it. They burnt the whole right side of the six apartment units on the corner."

"When this happened?"

"I found out five minutes ago, but it happened about two hours ago. I was coming to pick them up to go chill at the warehouse."

"I'll call you back. Leave there and pick up Little Sergo and go to the warehouse. Make sure nobody follows you."

I told the boys what happened and we all mainly stayed in a silent state of shock trying to figure out where this could have come from. Crip said, "chopped off their hands."

Syco said, "damn, that's a message."

We stayed silent. I pulled next to Pastor saying, "we got to go, Pastor, we will call you back."

"I thought we were going to do the papers on the Little Haiti Coin Laundry?"

"Bye man, I'll call you."

Putting my window up, I can hear him saying, "y'all just wasting my time."

I called Biya and talk to her for fifteen minutes. Pierre and Crip called their girls also. By the time we pulled into the warehouse the young niggas were in their chilling, looking mad. I jumped out saying, "Lil Bam Bam, I want to hear what you think and don't leave nothing out."

"I don't know what to think Jean, all I know is them dudes from down south called the Untouchables been scoping out the projects lately. They've been selling they shit in there from time to time, but I've been telling you about that."

In the midst of sadness, Pierre said, "that's the same theory Annie told me."

Lil Sergo said, "everybody around the projects screaming Jean and his Haitian Posse did that."

I said, "Sergo, now you know we don't got nothing to do with that shit man."

"I know, I'm just telling you that's what they saying. They said it's because they owed Haitian Posse some money. They around Jay's mom's house telling her all that crazy shit."

"Unbelievable, the checks stop coming and they turn on us like that."

Ricardo asked, "what's up with them dudes, Untouchables?"

I said, "Lil Bam-Bam get the low key, Lil Sergo get the other one. The rest of us, let's get them big boys and do our ritual to some of these niggas. Six different guns' shots in one body." The night was gruesome. We went to cemeteries of different sets. Pierre chopped dudes dick off and put it in his homeboys' mouth, putting the tombstone on top of the gravesite.

Putting the guns up at Crip's mom's house, we went and got a hotel suite to chill and read the streets of Miami through the phone calls. In the hotel we all considered getting away and trying something new in Georgia, New York or Los Angeles, somewhere. Miami had become too small for us. People knew our faces, but we didn't know theirs, losing each other was our main focus.

We came up with an idea to go on another drug boat. The sketch Crip drew on to show the rest of us was our new target to hit the love boat. We would retire out of town. Cleaning the boat would be what we did this time. I sensed all of us just getting tired of everything, the parties, the clothes, jewelry, just about all the bullshit that surrounded us and meant nothing.

Gerald said, "where can I put this jewelry at Jean? I'm tired of this chain, ring, and bracelet. I'm only going to wear a watch from now on."

Pierre added, "yeah, man, we got to slow down. I got five cars. Why the hell I need five cars? I want to sell two of them Jean." "We will do all that this week, but let's focus on this next boat we going to hit. If we move out of town, all of us just going to crank it up strong again stunting, flossing, letting everybody

know we Haitian."

Later we went to watch the University of Miami Hurri- canes football game right in front of the 50-yard line with the Hurricanes' basketball team. Walker got all eleven tickets for us. That break was well-needed. We screamed and hollered like the fans of Miami that we were. It relieved some stress that had been surrounding us.

I sat in the crowd next to Cathy and invited the whole bas- ketball team and a few football players to come and celebrate at

Red Lobster after the beating of 41-14 they gave Florida State. Me and Cathy ate at a booth by ourselves. The others includ- ing Uncle Luke ate at a table overlooking the water, about thir-

ty-five deep.

Cathy, who never got into my street business, said, "Jean, I have to ask you something. This has been on my mind since yesterday morning. The front page of the Miami Herald said Haitian Posse may be wanted for over eighteen murders."

"What paper?"

"The fucking Miami Herald Jean, now tell me why the fuck would they say that?"

"Cathy your own brother and two other guys on the foot- ball team has Haitian Posse tattooed on them. All them little Haitians doing that dumb shit, claiming their Haitian Posse. We can't stop people from claiming our shit. You and I know that's out of my hands."

A football player for the Hurricanes, Dwayne Johnson, inter- rupted our conversation saying, "hi Cathy. Hello Jean. You got five minutes?"

"I'm trying to finish this apple pie and ice cream, but go ahead."

"I've been drinking a little bit, I told Cathy when I get to the NFL, I still will be chasing her, and I'm not scared of you Jean."

"Please don't fear no man but God. Cathy is my girlfriend, so don't disrespect me in front of her."

"I'm gone Jean. I'm sorry, but I just wanted to say I told you so."

"No Problem, take it easy on the drinks over there." He left.

Cathy said, "that dude is so corny and talks too much. I've been telling you about him. He needs to be slapped."

"You know he might get sixty million dollars for three years."

"So, I'll be at a farm in Oregon watching his corny ass on TV cheering for him."

The waiter came and I told Cathy to give him a credit card. She kept wanting to continue talking about the same Miami Herald newspaper. I got up to say, "I'll be in the front with the rest, so catch up when you finish paying the bill."

"Jean, you not brushing this off. We got to talk."

In front of Red Lobster, I told Syco to let me get one of those bullets out his pocket. I took it and threw it to Dwayne Johnson. "Catch."

He caught it asking what that was all about. "For your knees, in case they get hurt."

He ran in front of me. "I'm sorry man, I'm sorry. I've been drinking too much. I won't ever bother Cathy again, I got a career ahead of me so please accept my apology."

"It's cool, just tackle dudes on the field, because you can't tackle bullets and walk away."

While me and Kathy were in our car ready to pull off, Uncle Luke came laughing to my window. "Hey Jean, that boy begged me to talk to you. I told him to leave that beautiful girl over there alone. I don't even look at her twice 'cause I love life."

Cathy said, "just tell him don't talk or walk next to me in school."

I pulled off, disrespecting Uncle Luke too.

Crip and I have been in the hotel room for three days straight looking at boats on the Port-of-Miami. I stopped watching for a minute to tell Crip that the room was where I first made love to Cathy and told her about the trip on the Freedom Boat from Haiti to Miami. Crip listened and didn't give no real opinion on the issue.

The boyz were all at the warehouse staying on cue in case they had to go to rob one of the love boats on the port. Late at night, around 9:30, we could see a boat with a white and sky-blue flag which had passed Customs and Coast Guards bringing out seemingly endless packages of rice.

Crip said, this the one, they must be trying to empty it out tonight."

"Let's pack up and go before the round go up at eleven. That's a lot of rice there."

"Let's go."

Getting to the warehouse, we briefed the boys on the event. They were ready. We all got into our designated vehicles and headed out of the Port-of-Miami. It was 10:42 when we were coming up on the bridge to turn down the port. The bridge was about to come up due to a boat wanting to pass underneath it. Before the bridge could go up, the two stoplights and tollgates came down. One of our cars had a chance to go around the tollgate. Me and Crip looked at each other. Together, Pierre and Gerald told little Annie-Poo, the car's driver, to go around the tollgate. I said, "them dudes too hot in the ass when they call me. Yo Gerald?"

"What's up Jean? It looks like the ramp about to open up." "Yeah." There was silence. "Wait on us."

"We going to get on and have everybody tied up for Ricardo can just be ready to hear the Spanish motherfucker's saying." "Alright man," we all wanted the bridge to hurry the fuck up with the slow boat underneath it. It finally went down. When Crip pulled over the side of the road, from a distance, we saw FBI agents, Customs agents, and Coast Guard officers surround-

ing the port and the boat. I got out the car and slammed both my fist on the hood. "Fuck! Fuck! Fuck! It looked like they got on and jumped in the water."

We could see the Coast Guards helping one of them out the sea. I said, "let's get the fuck out of here."

Syco was outside the truck. "Let's get the boyz! Something told me to bring the grenade launcher. It's in the back of the truck."

"We can't."

"why the fuck not!" He screamed.

"Let them handle this in the court system YO!!!"

"Why we got all these guns for if we scared of the police?"

As I walked to the passenger door, Syco threw a bullet on me. I looked at him breathing hard, listening to Ricardo say, "let's go Jean, let's go."

The whole ride back to Crip's mom's house was quiet. Inside the kitchen the three of us sat there while Crip put up the big guns. The silence remained with tension in the air between me and Syco. I was thinking in such a furious event that talking was the last thing I wanted to do. Crip came back to get my gun and Syco's, I didn't say a word or even look at him. He knew my answer and walked over to the TV and the living room.

The silence of tension in my head caused me to shoot Syco in the head. Then shoot Ricardo in the head, while putting shots in Crip and his family. Then blowing the world up. I shook my head saying, "rebuke these insane thoughts."

Ricardo became frantic. "What the fuck happened?!! What happened Jean!!"

Crip said, "hold it down, my peeps sleep."

I answered, "I don't know, I don't know bro."

Ricardo said, "my fault, Crip, I'm just mad but don't know at who."

Syco said, "not going to war with them crackers."

Crip said, "oh shit, look, they talking about it on the news." The news anchor was saying, "four black males were arrest-

ed on the Port-of-Miami for attempted robbery, attempted armed kidnapping, aggravated assault with a firearm in the commission of a felony. The four young men whose identities have not been released yet, each have lengthy histories with the authorities. We would have more history on this story in the coming hours."

We were already in silence before, now it was shocked silence.

For some reason Crip and Ricardo looked at me.

"It's ugly, it's ugly," is all I could come up with with. "You talked to the lawyer already, right Crip?"

"Yeah. Roy said to come to his office at eleven in the morning." Ricardo said, "I'm going to the room to lay down."

I got up. "I'm going to my crib and be here in the morn- ing." I dialed Cathy's phone number. "What you doing?"

"Me and your mom is watching a movie, you on your way? Or you staying at the warehouse?"

"I'm sleeping at the warehouse." I couldn't even look at the two of them knowing how easily they could read me.

"Okay, let me know if you want me to bring everybody some breakfast."

"Alright."

Crip said, "your mom over there?"

"Yeah, I'm about to sleep on the couch over here." "I'm going in the room with Ricardo."

Syco slept on one half of the couch and I slept on the other half. The aroma of breakfast that Crip's mom cooked gave me the only reason to wake up. Seeing her walk around gave smiles to end my thoughts of endless bad dreams. As soon as she walked out the door I got up. I went to brush my teeth and wash my face. Looking in the mirror, I said, "Fuck!"

Sitting down eating breakfast, the boyz came in one by one getting some breakfast.

At the law firm, only William was there to talk to the four of us. I told him not to worry about the other two, we had two other lawyers for them. "How much you think it's going to run us out of the retainer fee you got?"

With a full bold face, he said, "One hundred and twenty-five thousand dollars."

Syco said, "what, that's promising you beat the case?"

The lawyer kept talking, telling us all the charges all the defendants were charged with and there's no bond. "These four charges are very serious and I'm going to see Pierre and Gerald today. So far, the only thing good is that the feds didn't pick up the case. It's a gift and a curse that the state has the case, but I suspect officers from Miami will be at every hearing. And if it were the feds' chances at a 924.c robbery charge, starts off with twenty-five years. I want you guys to not talk on the phone with these two while they're in jail. I will advise them also when I see them not to call their friends and brother for you Jean. Now should I talk to your mom?"

"No, don't call her, just call me only about both of them." "Okay, I need you guys not to add onto this catastrophe I have

on my hands."

Syco jumped up, "how much to pay the judge? Just tell us, we some real ass niggas up in here."

William replied, "I don't do that. I worked hard for my bar exam, I'm not losing it for nobody, plus, I don't trust no judge. But as I was saying, give me and Roy two months before you come back to the office. I will call you Jean, or Crip, if anything of an emergency comes up."

Ricardo sat back in the chair. "Can it be beat?" "Everything has loopholes except when you're in the feds.

You better have only a gun case because that's all the feds let you win and that's because of the Second Amendment."

"Loopholes? Well, get it to the feds to try them for the guns." "Just give me two months to search through the case front and back gentlemen. I will answer every question that any of you have. Now please stay out of trouble because I sense someone is after you guys and I can't pinpoint who it is yet and that's a terrible thing."

Jumping in the car, Ricardo said, "that lawyer be talking Ebonics at times."

"I just talked to Annie and Pinky. They going to see the boyz in jail. They got a lot of questions, so I told him to call you, Ricardo, to answer any questions about money, the case, or whatever they need, while they in Dade County jail."

Eating a meal amongst the four of us at Ce Ce Bon Restaurant was so depressing without Pierre and Gerald, we took four or five bites and took the rest to go.

The next three months we mostly stayed at my house and the warehouse. I had told mom, because Gerald's Aunt called, to inform her on what happened. Telling mom in her face at my house caused her to snap by throwing things and hitting Syco, Ricky, and Crip. "My baby, my baby, my baby." She cried over Pierre asking Jamie if I was trying to kill her with a heart attack. We all promised her when they get out there will be a change.

She believed us. All four of us attended a weekend swap shop with her. I told her we all were going to sign up in night school, and she smiled. "I never heard you say that Jean, please do it, or go to Haiti."

I told her not tell Cathy, I would tell her myself. She agreed. During most of our days we went to the Port-of-Miami to scope on a boat, I personally showed no interest and no enthu- siastic participation investigating in a boat. We all agreed every-

one had to feel it, and when we would choose a boat, I would say, "I'm not feeling it." It cost mainly me and Ricardo not to see eye to eye, but Haitian Posse law was that everyone had to agree on a mission.

I enjoyed scoping out an armored truck leaving the Miami Heat basketball arena. We all agreed on hitting the truck. It had three people jumping out with two bags in each of their hands. We recruited Bam-Bam and three others, but an unexpected event of a police car that followed the truck on the robbing day caused us to retract, even though Syco kept trying to convince me and Crip that he would take care of the police officer in the car.

Taking Cathy back and forth to school had her questioning me. "Something is wrong, you never really let your friends stay at the house and where's Pierre and Gerald at?"

I sat Cathy down, eating lunch at her school with her. When I told her about my brothers. She exploded, "I'm done! It's over! I can't take this gangster's girl life no more." Yada, yada, yada.

I told her they were set up, but she just wouldn't believe that. The next day I took her to Bayside in Downtown Miami to give her a promise ring, promising that I would stop what- ever I was doing and that I love her with all my heart. It was something I never told her, "I love you." I took her there while playing some Lionel Richie and Diana Ross, "Endless Love." That always cheered her up. I also got her some flowers and chocolates while walking the deck on a music-boat that rolled around Bayside Downtown with mostly couples on it.

There were about thirty people on the boat, and I tipped the host well. She had a microphone in her hand, and thought the promise ring was an engagement ring. I didn't debate with her and said, "yeah, that's what it is, an engagement."

After about fifteen minutes on the boat, I looked around and saw about five young couples, but I didn't think the dudes were enemies, which was usually my concern. Being strapped, I real- ly didn't care.

I gave the host a cue, they slipped Lionel Richie and Diana Ross in the music box and I dropped down to my knees in front of Cathy. "Baby, I love you and I will stop what I'm doing."

She screamed, jumping up and down. "I been waiting eighteen months. It's March 14, 1995 and you said you love me Jean. I love you too."

"You been counting?"

"Just keep saying you love me boy."

"I love you, I love you Cathy. I'm not going to hurt you baby." The boat crowd cheered for us. The host brought the micro-

phone to Cathy and asked, what's the response?

Cathy said, "Yes!"

"So, when is the marriage date?" The host asked.

I looked at her begging her to please stop, with my face balled up, and she did. We danced in the front of the boat. My heart beat real fast while sweating up a pool that Cathy kept patting from my forehead.

We went home to find the boyz up in the house at 1:00 a.m. That caused Cathy to show each and every one of them the ring. "Jean finally told me he love me. So don't you boyz be jealous 'cause I been tired of hearing him tell all of you he got love for you and 'I love you,' and not me. Especially you, Syco."

Syco smirked, "you my sister-in-law. I'm going to be the Best Man when both of you get married."

Cathy went to the room glowing about our night.

Ricardo said, "you just now told her you love her? I tell all my bitches within one hour I love them."

"I'm not hating on that Ricky, but when I got love for some- one, I'm all in for life, good or bad with that person. I'm going in the room to celebrate, so hold the noise down. And you been smoking in here, I can smell it bro."

Crip hugged me saying, "I love that you make them put in time first."

Ricky whispered, "Biya out of gas then." "Goodnight y'all."

When I walked in the room, Cathy took out the white bulb light and put a red one in. I said, "oh, oh, you about to turn into Kitty Kat."

We made love and embraced each other through the night. Every time I told her I love her, Cathy shivered out with butter- flies bursting from her pores with billions of love bumps. She must have came three of four times. In the morning, she got out the shower saying how she love that hook dick, it hit the spot, and how I'm a real Haitian.

I said, "boo, I'm going to take you to school. But hitch a ride back with Walker, he told me he wanted to come by to talk to Crip about something."

She said, "cool. Now, tell me you love me again." "I love you Cathy."

We pulled up to University of Miami's south parking lot, Cathy jumped out. I saw a dude coming from a hallway to the parking lot that I knew. I got out, "Boobie-Boobie, that's you?"

"Jean, what the fuck you doing out here?" "My girl goes to school here."

"Oh yeah, I'm trying to get out the game bro."

"I heard about the work in the Matchbox projects in Carol City." We hugged telling each other, 'you look good since I seen you in the county jail.'

"So, what you studying out here?"

"Accounting. That might take three years to finish. I've been here for six months, but niggas done even came out here to catch me slipping. I'm on point, you feel me?"

"Yeah, yeah. You heard from Bam?"

"Nah. I heard about Gee and Pierre, but what's up with

Ricardo and Syco? You know Syco's my dude when you left the county."

"He told me that."

"Listen, I'm going to Washington D.C. to hear a speech that Louis Farrakhan is having. It's called the Million Man March. You should come with me."

"I've been real bored, that sounds cool. Can the rest of the boyz come?"

"They looking for a million black men, of course. We taking a tour bus there. Take my phone number bro."

I took his number watching nine promotional trucks from House of Fire Records. I told Boobie, "yo, I want to do a record label one day."

"Why you don't holla at Uncle Luke? He always talking like he be with Haitian Posse all day."

We laughed. Getting back in my car, I put the window down saying, "this weekend right, Boobie?"

"Just call me. Yeah, it's this weekend."

Walking in my house, I seen Crip, Ricardo, and Syco, count- ing a mountain of money. I asked if everything was sold.

"Yeah," Syco answered.

The last two weeks we chose to sell all the jewelry, five cars, and the six-bedroom home in Pembroke Pines, so that we could just gather up the money. We all still have money from the last robbery on the port and sold that coke slower for a little more money.

To see Ricardo with a rubber band stopwatch was a major encouragement for all of us to throw everything in till we knew which direction in the game we were heading without Gerald and Pierre. We kept talking to Pastor about looking for a business. We had a total of 1.4 million dollars in cash, plus Pastor was supposed to give us a check for three hundred sixty thousand dollars to put in the bank account. Me and Syco thought he was ducking us because he put everything in storage, and someone came by saying they bought the house. I planned to call Pastor and put that 1.4 million in the stash at the ware- house. We still had about twelve cars and I thought two more should go. The BMW, Ford

Explorer, and I forgot at least two of those four-wheelers.

Lil Bam-Bam said, "I want to get one of those four-wheelers." "Cool, we'll talk," I said. "Let's ride to put this money up. If we could sell clothes, we might have another million."

Syco said, "let everybody else go, I want to talk to you about something real important Jean."

I looked at Ricardo to read if he knew what it was about. He shrugged his shoulders. I said, "oh, I seen Boobie. He going to Washington D.C. to something called the Million Man March that Louis Farrakhan is hosting." Ricardo said, "give me his number to call him. We never been out of town before, you think we should go strapped?"

"Of course, Ricky, but he wanted to talk to you and Syco anyway so call him and set everything up. I'll be here with Syco chilling."

Crip said, "I like the sound of that Washington D.C. trip. They walked out the door with our life savings."

Me and Syco walked back into the room. After I locked the door, I said, "so what's up bro?"

He went under the bed and pulled out a folder with a couple of sheets of paper in it. "Jean, I never usually ask to have a meeting, but I got a plan that I want you to study and explain to the family. Please listen real carefully before we call a meeting with everybody else."

"Go ahead bro. I'm listening."

Spreading four sheets of paper on the bed, Syco continued.

"I've been plotting on how to get Gee and Pete out of Dade County jail. I know the county like the back of my hands. When I used to go to medical and get put on suicide watch, all I did was study the jail inside out. I thought one of these days will come where we had to go in there to get one of the boyz. You listening?"

"Well, look, if we go right here," he pointed to his map of the garage where a bus came every week to transport inmates in and out of the jail. "Four of us can sneak in with the bus with big-boy guns and the grenade launcher might have to be used on this mission right here. Three people stay outside while the four of us is inside. The guard that opens up the door to the jail is going to open the door when we put the gun to the bus driver and his two buddies that be in the front. If he fails to open when you ask him, then I'll shoot one guard in the head. If he force us, the second gets shot. By then the door will open. I'll stay right there with the AR-15 grenade launcher while three of you take a staff member with the key up the elevator to the sixth floor. One person hold the elevator and the two go to the hallway block yelling for Gee and Pierre. We can't tell them to be prepared 'cause they might make the wrong move. When they get to the elevator and come down, I'll back everybody out the jail to the car. You already know I-95 is right there. We home."

Looking deep in Syco's squinted eyes, I asked, "how many times you been to jail?"

"Three times. But I got a lot more studying to do."

"Look, Syco, DON'T go to the jail no more. And I got the plan from here okay? It's possible. But listen carefully, I got it from here! Just stay far away from that jail homeboy, alright?" "Yeah, I know you and Crip going to master the plan, right?" "Yeah man, now let's go get some 305 shirts made to go to D.C."

"How Boobie looking?"

"He done got a little bigger. He goes to the University of Miami."

"Yeah?"

"Yep."

Later that day when Cathy and Walker came over, I told Cathy that I was going to the Million Man March in Washington

D.C. She loved the idea.

"You making some quick choices about changing your ways. Please cleanse yourself baby, because I can't stand to lose you."

"It's going to be a different experience."

"I wish I could go, but I can't because I have to work." Early in the morning, Ricardo, Syco, Crip, Little Bam-Bam,

220

and myself, sat across from Roy's and Williams's conference room. On the table was a whole lot of papers, newspaper arti- cles with Haitian Posse in them, videos and other incriminating things. Looking us in the eyes, William said, "as you know, the other two codefendants pleaded to twenty years on this case. The case with Gerald and Pierre is set for trial in two weeks. Both of them were adamant to us about filing for a Speedy Trial and they'll get their wish within two weeks. Now, before I start, Roy wants to mention something to you."

Roy nodded. "I've been in at least three meetings with the prosecutors, City of Miami Police, and Coast Guard agents."

Ricardo said, "what the City of Miami Police got to do with this?"

"Well listen. At everything I've been to, they asked to speak to Pierre and Gerald for a lower plea about a gun shop robbery they insist the two codefendants know about it. They've been occupied about the gun shop robbery at every meeting. I looked straight at them telling each agency my clients will not sit down with the government under any circumstances and beg for a plea of eight years. They said thirty years is the offer."

"Shit," we all said at the same time.

"But listen, there's more about murders and especially a guy named Duke. Detective Kitchen tells me he has a witness who saw a face. There's also a juror from Jean's murder case who claimed she was approached by a young lady during the trial, which shows their allegations must be weak. I answered by telling them to just let me know if they have a warrant for anyone of my clients."

I said, "what they say?"

"Nothing, because it must be weak, but the government has plenty of money to make people talk and keep investigations running."

William said, "we have to get fully prepared for Pierre's and Gerald's case. I have no witnesses to put on the stand and technicalities is our strongest approach trying to find out why the authorities were there in advance. The guns have the guys' prints on them, so they got found guilty on that, it will be ten years maximum. I've taken the depositions on nine different officers and those boys still want to go to trial. Jean, your mom also wants them to go to trial. I want under no circumstanc- es for anyone of you to be in the courtroom. Let your aunts, uncles, just pack the courtroom with older people for us. Are there any questions?"

Syco jumped in. "You better beat this case!!" I got up putting my hand on his mouth, but he still let out, "there's a grenade with two names on it, motherfuckers."

Crip got up. "Sorry about that, he misses his brothers."

The lawyers, looking helpless, wept out, "we are studying the case, trust me MAN!!"

Pulling Syco by the arm walking to the door, I said, "call me if you change anything on the case." Ricardo stayed with

Crip. I got in the elevator with Syco saying, "my nigga, we can't tell them we going to kill them if they lose the case, but I'm glad you put that bug in them Jews' heads."

While driving in the car, I mentioned to Ricardo and Little Bam-Bam to go take Annie five thousand dollars. "We still going to try to holla at a juror for them boyz. Fuck that shit they talking. I'm going to holla at Biya about paying people to be in the courtroom that stay in the projects and them boyz coming home! I know they coming home!"

Crip said, "I believe that too. But on another note, I just got off the phone with Pastor, and he talking about we owe him money for the warehouse, his house, taxes, and all kinds of bullshit. He said we should let him hold the money to pay off bills for us."

"What? He done lost his mind?! He think we some kids or something?!"

Syco said, "we might have to kidnap dad and put the thir- ty-eight pistol by his asshole."

I said, "I'm going to talk to him about our money, my nigga."

CHAPTER SIXTEEN

We sat for nineteen hours from Miami to Washington D.C. on a tour bus that sat at least ninety-six people. There were some high-ranking civil rights activists on the bus such as Rev. Victor Curry, Rev. Al Sharpton, Rev. Jesse Jackson, and more. It was a ride of powerful black ideology with strong spiritual theology. I sat next to Ricardo with Boobie and Syco sitting in front of us. Crip was ahead of them with eleven young Haitians from the hood that we took with us. We all had 305 on the front of our black shirts and the Haitian flag on the back. Boobie had two homeboys he took with him named Piccolo and E-Fore that we had met at the bus terminal at the Joseph Caleb Center on 54th Street and 27th Avenue, in Liberty City. Eight buses full of black men had been there to take the journey of Unity

of black people.

The one thousand-dollar per head was the best mon- ey I thought Haitian Posse ever spent as a whole. Rev. Al Sharp- ton preached during half of the ride. Other black men stood up to express their minds. Sharpton mentioned that Thurgood Marshall fought for Blacks to be able to attend the same good schools as white kids, which resulted in the victorious case of Brown v. Board of Education. He also reminded us that Abra- ham Lincoln signed the Emancipation Proclamation in 1863 that freed the Blacks from slavery from white slave masters. He yelled out with a passion. "Stop fearing these white people.

The physical pain is over!"

Hearing about how Rosa Parks was arrested for refusing to give up her seat on a public bus to a white man, I scooted up tell- ing Boobie, "I done learned more on this bus ride than I learned at school."

"Yeah, these brothers go deep. I've been around them for five months now."

Pulling up to the Hilton hotel, we all shared prayers and headed to our hotel room to get some sleep. All of us woke up before 11:00 a.m. to get on the bus to the March. When we got to 1600 Pennsylvania Avenue, I got out to glance at the White House. It had a built stage out front where Louis Farrakhan was clearing his throat to address the massive crowd of black people that spread out as far as my eyes can see. Our crew of eighteen from Miami walked quickly to any available spots to hear Farrakhan speak.

He started by saying, "I asked for one million black men, and we got over one million black men in front of the White House. Speaking of White House, it's where everything imposed on my people came from. This White House behind me is where our problems came out of.

These are the people that got money for war but can't feed the poor. The destruction of black civilization that killed some of our powerful black men such as Dr. Martin Luther King Jr., Malcolm X, and dismantled the Black Panthers and plenty other great black philosophers came from this White House behind me that Blacks built.

I've recently been offered one billion dollars from Libyan President Muammar Kaddafi, to help my people; and this White House said I would be considered a terrorist." He looked around, smirking. "Now I ask who's going to label them terrorists for kidnapping our people? Huh? As I stand on this podium to talk to you and over twenty million people watching on TV, I want for you to understand parts of this White House's mental slav- ery. A chief of police and every urban community sits on a podium at times in the morning and looks out at his officers. He says, 'look, we low on budget, so I want you to go out there and give people some traffic tickets, arrest some drug deal- ers, get our unit some guns off the streets.' And where do you think these targets are, who these dictators order to be arrest- ed? South Beach? Beverley Hills? Manhattan? Huh? Or maybe you can't find five grams of crack in whitey neighborhoods. You can't put him in the feds for five years because of the one hundred to one powder to crack ratio. That's the case, right? Oh no, maybe it's those millions of hunters who police never go after. All those guns they have are legal, right? Huh? I want to know why there's two hundred twenty million whites, thir- ty million Blacks, and we sit more of our people in jail? Why are we so targeted? I will tell you it's fear of black unification, of a collectively productive black mind. We must stay united black people. I want you to look at each other and say, 'I AM UNBREAKABLY YOURS.'"

Looking at Boobie, I repeated. "I'm unbreakably yours."

Farrakhan continued, "It's sad to see a black lobbyist called Fed Cure, headed by Congressman Danny Davis from Chicago, can't get one hundred thousand letters to bring to the White House about changing an 85 percent mandatory sentence in the Feds that Ronald Reagan signed in 1988, and let them hear the fight is on. We want 65 percent. But we look breakable in this White House's eyes. Stand together black people. Stand together please black people. It takes a man to teach a man how to be a man."

Through the two-hour speech, my right arm remained on my chin, as I grasped the lessons I was hearing. The speech closed with Farrakhan asking everybody to get each other's numbers to swap out and have dialogues past the two-hour speech.

I told Boobie and his homeboys to let me talk to Haitian Posse for five minutes. Finding a little corner I looked at Lil Bam-Bam, Syco, Crip, Ricardo and the other ten young Haitians and said, "listen, I don't know about none of you right here, but when we get back to Miami, we going to get some money somehow and I'm going straight to Haiti with my portion of it, my brothers."

Ricardo said, "I'm coming with you."

Syco, Lil Bam-Bam, Crip and the younger Haitians all said they were coming with me too.

I said, "look, we got heart and we going to take over Haiti from that brutal administration that's doing nothing for our people. We done seen how America do, so we the new souls that overthrow the French 1804. I'm serious about going to Haiti and changing things. No Pape Joe Avic Calabayo."

The boyz said, "yeah Jean." "Let's do it."

"Haiti here we come!"

When I walked back towards Boobie he said, "you look like you ready

225

to take over Haiti."

You must could read minds, I thought in a fearless eye to eye view of Boobie.

Getting off the bus in Miami, Ricardo said, "I'm going to get some weed at Ruff Neck's spot in Little Haiti. You want me to bring anything to the warehouse?"

Syco went walking with him towards the car. Ricardo con- tinued saying, "Jean call my dad, he called two more times since last night."

"Just tell him I will call him. Me and Crip with the young Haitians all going to be at the warehouse waiting on both of you. Lil Bam-Bam going to give you everybody's order once you get to Ce Ce Bon Restaurant."

Ricky yelled, "alright! I love that look in your eyes Jean, it's the same look you have when we were in Krome Detention Center."

Me and Crip got in my truck while the rest followed us to the warehouse. I turned the volume down on the radio. "We got to hit a major lick Crip, what you think we should go after, an armored truck or boat on Port-of-Miami?"

"We need to study both of them, Jean, and whichever one slipping we hit that bitch."

"Well, early tomorrow morning go get the hotel room for a week, because we cleaning out whoever comes our way!"

Crip said, "what Malando want?"

"I don't know, call him if you want, I'll talk to him on my way to Haiti Bro."

Chilling at the warehouse eating and smoking weed, we sat with Biya and Annie as they told us everything Pierre and Gerald needed for trial next week. I couldn't believe they were worried about the bitches sneaking them some weed in the county jail when trials in five days. The four of us studied the boats on the sea with full alert. During the day we sat to time an armored truck picking up money at the rear door of the Miami Heat basketball arena. The timing seemed to have changed from the last time we watched the bags of money. The days are passing and greeting Gerald and Pierre with a couple of millions, were thoughts of a dream that had to come true. I sat with the binoculars staring out the window at around

11 p.m. Ricardo said, "my niggas go to trial tomorrow. A sweet one need to come through just for them boyz."

Crip said, "Jean, ain't that the same boat parking that we hit the first time?"

Yeah, that's Poravion with a Columbian flag on there.

They back!"

Ricky and Syco, looking over our back said, "that's that bitch."

"That's her all right."

I said, "yeah, we know what they about. Call them boyz at the warehouse and tell them to stay on point."

Watching the boat through the night, me and Crip patiently switched waiting for customs to lift the boat inserted. At 11 o'clock and the morning, customs finally came. Kathy called to say that the trial had started at 8:00 a.m. and my mom, with a courtroom full of people, was there to support Pierre and Gerald. I told Syco to sit down and relax because he kept pacing in the small room, and it was making me dizzy. He sat down and Crip said, "it look like the boat is clear. A couple of Customs Agents done left."

Cathy called crying through the phone, yelling, "Jean, Jean!!"

The boys just looked at me when I answered the phone. Cathy cried out to the worst news since losing my relatives on the Freedom Boat. "Jean, the jury came back with a guilty verdict on all accounts!! They sentenced your brother and Gerald to life with the possibility of parole after twenty-five years."

Shit, Shit, SHIT!!! I can't believe this shit!"

With all the commotion of my mom in the background of Cathy's phone and others crying, Ricky, Syco, and Crip all wanted to know what happened. I just looked at the three of them and said, "life sentences."

They sat down in silence. Crip dialed some numbers on his phone.

Cathy continue yelling, "Jean this is the shit I can't take. They said life sentences. What does that mean?" I said, "Cathy, I'll call you back."

"No Jean! I can't go through with this. It's me or the stupid money you chasing Jean."

I yelled, "can I say a word without you talking for a minute? Where's my mom?"

"She's laying on the bench outside the courtroom crying, you can't hear her?"

"Fuck!!"

"Listen Jean, your brother is twenty-two years old, what do they mean by a 'life sentence?' Are they for real?"

"Look Cathy, I'll talk to you and my mom tonight, okay?" "No, are you dumb or deaf? You can't hear me? No more of that warehouse bullshit with your friends. It's either me or them. I am sitting here coughing up blood Jean."

"What's wrong with you?" "I'm fucking pregnant Jean." "What do you mean pregnant?"

"Yeah I'm pregnant. I've been waiting to tell you, but you been at that stupid warehouse. My dad spent all his money for me to go to college and I fell in love and got pregnant with a gangster."

"I'm sorry Cathy, please calm down and I will be there tonight."

"Why not now Jean? They just gave your brothers a life sentence."

"How many times you going to say a fucking life sen- tence, I get it!"

"Your mom and this other lady are getting treated as we speak, by the paramedics." I could hear Cathy coughing.

"Please, Cathy calm down. I will be there."

Crip said, "I just got off the phone with Pinky and Annie. They going mentally crazy. Biya wanted to talk to you, but I told her you busy. She says she could hear you yelling with Cathy and that the juror thing did not come through." I said, "look, we got to still get this boat."

Syco said, "Jean can we tell everybody the plan for Gee and Pierre now?"

Crip, looking in the binoculars, said, "look at the same little Spanish man. He doing something funny."

Looking also, I said, "fuck, we done miss the target. He unloading coffee boxes and that U-Haul truck." Ricardo said, "I can tell the young niggas to come."

I said, "it's too late man, I can't understand why he did that shit just three hours after Customs left."

Crip said, "but look, they parking the truck across the street and the Spanish man driving it."

I said, "yeah, he done jumped out and going back up the ramp. Call Lil Bam-Bam them, in fact, Crip and Syco go to the warehouse and make sure they all come correct. Pick us up on your way back from the warehouse."

They left quickly. Me and Ricardo stayed just watching for about twenty-five minutes. I said, Ricky tear up your jeans and T-shirt some and walk by the U-Haul truck to see if it's the same type package like the first one. Don't open your mouth so nobody won't see your gold teeth. And leave the Mac-10."

He left. Minutes later, I watched Ricky on the dock check- ing something. He was parked in the parking lot for a little while. I call Little Bam-Bam's car. "You talked to Crip?"

He said, "yeah. He told me to park in the parking lot behind him."

"Perfect. Stay on Crip's move. I'm going to get in the car with you and chill."

I saw Ricardo look in the truck twice. He called to tell me that it was the same package."

"Okay," I said. "I'm going to get dropped off to you with two goons. Go walk to the corner café and order a soup." I called Crip saying, "look, I'm going on the dot with Ricky. We going to pull a gun on the little Spanish motherfucker and take the truck. You and Little Bam-Bam stay on our tail. Once we get the truck just make sure you get over the drawbridge."

"Alright Jean."

Getting in the car with Little Bam-Bam and two others, I said, "drop me off to the dock. Little Fabin, Little Jawara, give me those two handguns. Take this Mack-10 and if you see anything funny call me to back out, okay?"

"Yeah Jean."

I got out by the take-out-only café and walked up to order a soup. Waiting on Ricky to walk back towards the café. I got a pack of Newport cigarettes and opened it up, putting one in my mouth. Ricky walked up saying, "hey, let me get a cigarette?" "No problem. It's a nice time to go fishing. The sea is flat out there." Walking away with the hot nasty soup, I whispered,

"you see anything funny?" I blew the hot soup.

"Nah, no signs of police or Custom Agents. Let's go between those two cars and pass me the gun."

Doing that, I put my back to Ricky while he took a piss between the cars, cuffing the gun on him. We walked down the half-mile dock twice. I said, "what's taking these moth- erfuckers so long to come down the ramp?"

Little Bam-Bam's truck came up the corner of the block for the second time around in our walking site. I could see Crip parked in a sweet parking spot right next to the U-Haul truck with the dope in it.

The third cigarette started to get me a little dizzy. If I had to put another one in my mouth, I made up my mind that I will not light it up. I called Crip, "if you get a little too far from the truck and homeboy come down the ramp, tell Syco and Lil Riff to get out and get Homeboy." "All right, we on point."

Walking back towards the truck, I told Ricky, "it's starting to look suspicious. If we got to walk back one more time."

The little Spanish man came speed-walking down the ramp with a folder in his hand. We peeped the target and timed our walk while coming to a stop talking to each other. He got sev- en steps closer to the truck and I ran to grab him. Digging in his pocket with Ricardo's going on him, I tossed Ricky the keys. I then put the little Spanish man in the middle of the truck seat. "Stop looking at me, motherfucker."

Ricky pulled off. I saw Crip on our tail turning the corner going over the drawbridge. As soon as Ricky made a right, I told the little motherfucker to stop looking at me, and he kept on saying something in Spanish. "Chico, what he saying?"

"He saying 'please let me go, please don't kill me?'"

I saw little Bam-Bam catch up and told him to slow down while I threw the little Spanish motherfucker out. Making the next right we drove staring at the rear-view mirror. Little Bam-Bam called saying there were two police cars behind me. I said, "I see them fam, just stay calm for now."

Writing five minutes down a straightaway road. The police had made a right into a Dunkin' Donuts parking lot. Pulling up to the warehouse Crip rolled up next to us to hit the garage button on his keys. We rolled to the left inside the garage wait- ing for the door to go back down. I opened my door pumping my fist saying, yes!!!'"

Little Bam-Bam clipped the lock in the back of the truck and the door slid up and KILOOOS looked at us viciously. Crip, hopping fast with his bad leg, said, "that's them bitches my nig- ga!" While pulling his knife to check a couple of them. I grabbed two starting to check them and Crip said, "this one right here not no dope."

I said, "these two not no dope either."

Ricardo said, "these three I checked ain't no dope either. It tastes like baking soda."

Little Bam-Bam said, "what the fuck is this thing in here?

It look like a computer."

Crip looked, grabbing it out of Lil Bam-Bam's hand. "This one of those navigation systems, I think. It looks like a GPS system."

BOOOOM!!!

An explosion pushed the whole garage door, sending it flying off and on top of five cars. Shots rang out after the explosion, tapping the cars next to me.

Tap. Tap. Tap. Tap.

I dropped, seeing three black trucks with masked men out- side of them shooting M-16s and AK-47s. Little Jawara and Young Yoshi each had Carbon 15s shooting in viewing of me. Little Bam-Bam raised up jumping on the hood of Crip's BMW shooting the hundred-round Calico screaming, "I was built for this pusssieesss."

Boom. Boom. Boom. Boom.

Four suicidal masked gunmen with hair hanging from the back of their mask holding street sweepers ran inside the garage and was getting hit with blows of Ricardo's .223 hundred-rounder.

Baum.

Baum. Baum. Baum.

Seeing two masked men drop, my Glock shots did nothing towards the rapid shots coming from inside and outside.

Riff-raffing around for a rifle with some thump, Little Steve and Little Riff's mouths were wide open showing their mouth full of gold teeth shooting the Mini-14's 72-round clip.

Blacka. Blacka. Blacka. Blacka. Blacka.

I looked over my left and Little Fabine to see his head split wide open. His Chopper fallen from his hands and blood was pouring down the front of his body from his head wound.

Crawling to grab Fabine's Chopper, a voice came from the back of the warehouse matching my eye view of someone running towards the middle of the garage doorway.

Syco shouted this, "HAITIAN POSSE MOTHERFUCK- ERS!!!" Letting out the grenade in the AR-15 Grenade Launcher. BOOM!!! A huge explosion outside as he stood in the middle doorway following up with hundred-round drum shots. He stood there eating the bullets that were hitting him from the outside.

I yelled, "NOOOOO!!!!! SYCO!!! NOOOOOO!!!"

Steady letting loose wildly right to left, then left to right, he dropped dead on the ground. Outside, the black trucks hur- riedly screeched off. Running outside with the AK-47 to let off some shots. The first thing I saw was one of the trucks which had flipped over. About eight people were dead outside of it.

I went to Syco and rested his head on my lap closing his eyes. I started crying heavily. "No, no, no." I looked around and saw nothing but bodies. "Ricardo get up. Little Riff get up. Little Steve get up!"

Crip came out from behind Pierre's convertible Chevy. "Jean, what the fuck?"

"It look like everybody dead! Get up Ricky!! Get up Ricky!" Crip walked off and came back with a five-gallon gas tank.

"Jean get the fuck up. Go get the Ford Temp and the money." "What the fuck you doing?" I watched him pour gas all over

Little Sawar, Little Fabine, and Young Yoshi.

"Get the fuck up, Yo!!!" He went over to put some gas on Ricardo.

I put Syco down and rushed to pick up Ricky. Crip said, "look Jean, I'm not going on death row or under some jail. I'm going to shoot you if I have to and put you out your misery. And I'll shoot at the cops as they get here before we leave."

"How the fuck can you do this to our family man? This Ricky!! That's the next generation of Haitian Posse."

233

He pushed me off Ricardo and I let him, cry with slobber coming down my nose. I yelled, "NOOO!!. This is our family!" "I'm going to kill the motherfuckers," pouring gas on Syco,

he yelled, "get the fucking money. We don't even know who the enemy is, Yo! Now get yourself together man!"

When I came back with the money, Crip told me to take off the bloody clothes I had on. He had put two sets in the Ford Tempo.

We got in the car and drove off. I said, "turn back Crip, let me pull the mask off one of those motherfuckers face."

"It's too late. Don't you hear those police sirens?"

As we got on I-95 north, I hit the dashboard four times saying, "Fuck! Fuck! Fuck! Fuck!"

"I know, I know." Crip started crying and put his hand on my back.

I just let it all out, venting. "AAAAHHHH!! I love you Syco, I love you Ricardo. Dammnn take me back, I want to die with them."

After two hours on I-95, I asked Crip where the fuck we were going. My phone rang. It was Pastor calling.

Crip said, "don't answer. Don't answer no one. We dead also to everybody. That warehouse should be burnt down with nothing but ashes in there."

The phone rang again. "It's Mr. Malando, shit."

It rang again. Crip said, "Who is that? Cathy? Let me get that phone Jean."

I passed the phone to him. Crip put the window down throw- ing it in the grass with no battery in it. I asked, "where we going man?"

"I don't know, New York, Cuba, Venezuela, Haiti. Just the fuck out of the United States."

Made in the USA
Middletown, DE
11 December 2021

54025130R00144